AF564692

BIODIVERSITY OF AQUATIC ECOSYSTEM
SIGNIFICANCE, THREATS AND CONSERVATION

BIODIVERSITY OF AQUATIC ECOSYSTEM

SIGNIFICANCE, THREATS AND CONSERVATION

Edited by

Dr. Pawan Kumar 'Bharti'

Environmental Scientist
Centre for Agro-Rural Technologies (CART-India)
20, Jamaalpur Maan, Raja Ka Tajpur, Bijnore (UP) - 246 735 (India)

&

Prof. H.A.H. Kaoud

Professor
Department of Animal, Poultry
Aquaculture & Environmental Pollution
Faculty of Veterinary Medicine
Cairo University, Cairo, Egypt

Associate Editors

Dr. Avnish Chauhan

Department of Applied Science
College of Engineering
Teerthanker Mahaveer University
Moradabad (UP) - 244 001 (India)

&

Dr. Pawan Kumar

J.M. Environet Pvt. Ltd.
Gurgaon (Haryana) (India)

DISCOVERY PUBLISHING HOUSE PVT. LTD.
NEW DELHI-110 002

Published by:
Tilak Wasan

DISCOVERY PUBLISHING HOUSE PVT. LTD.
4383/4B, Ansari Road, Darya Ganj
New Delhi-110 002 (India)
Phone : +91-11-23279245, 43596064-65
Fax : +91-11-23253475
E-mail : discoverypublishinghouse@gmail.com
sales@discoverypublishinggroup.com
parul.wasan@gmail.com
web : www.discoverypublishinggroup.com

***First Edition:* 2013**

ISBN: 978-93-5056-297-0

Biodiversity of Aquatic Ecosystem
Significance, Threats and Conservation

Printed at:
Aditi Fine Art Press
Delhi

Preface

Aquatic species are at a higher risk of extinction than mammals and birds. Human activities are causing species to disappear at an alarming rate. Losses of this magnitude impact the entire ecosystem, depriving valuable resources used to provide food, medicines, and industrial materials to human beings. Declining biodiversity worldwide is a major and ongoing environmental dilemma. Although aquatic biodiversity has been declining continually, species extinction rates have gone from about one species per year over the past 600 million years to hundreds of species per year in recent times. Runoff from agricultural and urban areas, the invasion of exotic species, and the creation of dams and water diversion have been identified as the greatest challenges to freshwater environments.

Aquatic biodiversity can be defined as the variety of life and the ecosystems that make up the freshwater, tidal, and marine regions of the world and their interactions. Overexploitation of aquatic organisms for various purposes is the greatest threat to marine environments, thus the need for sustainable exploitation has been identified by the Environmental Defense Fund as the key priority in preserving marine biodiversity. Other threats to aquatic biodiversity include urban development and resource-based industries, such as mining and forestry that destroy or reduce natural habitats. Beside these, air and water pollution, sedimentation and erosion, and climate change also pose threats to biodiversity of aquatic ecosystems.

This book provides comprehensive coverage of the fundamental principles and current practices and trends in the field of aquatic ecosystem, biodiversity, significance, conservation and environmental threats.

This book updates the subject matter, illustrations and problems to incorporate new concepts and issues related to aquatic biodiversity, aquatic ecosystem, conservation and management, aquaculture, fisheries and environmental pollution.

Particularly thanks are due to all contributors from Egypt, Nigeria, India; and publisher also for their contribution and assistance.

I hope this book will be of benefit to researcher / academia who is working in the field of environment, ecology, freshwater ecology, aquatic ecosystem, environmental threats, fisheries and aquaculture.

Dr. Pawan Kumar 'Bharti'

E-mail: gurupawanbharti@rediffmail.com

Contents

List of Contributors

Anis Siddique, Department of Zoology, Govt. Holkar Science College Indore (MP) (India).

Arun Kumar Roy Mahato Gujarat Institute of Desert Ecology, Post Box No. 83, Mundra Road, Bhuj, Kachchh - 370001, (Gujarat) (India).

Akriti Gupta, M-Phil Scholar, Ranchi University, Ranchi (Jharkhand) 834 001 (India).

A.K. Upadhyay, Professor and Head, Department of Fish Processing Technology, College of Fisheries, G.B. Pant University of Agriculture and Technology, Pantnagar, (Uttarakhand) (India).

A.K. Prusty, Project Directorate for Farming System Research (PDFSR), (Meerut) (Uttar Pradesh) 250 110 (India).

A.K. Sahoo, Central Inland Fisheries Research Institute (Indian Council of Agricultural Research), Barrackpore, Kolkata, (West Bengal) 700 120 (India).

A.M. Reddy, Department of Fish Processing Technology, College of Fisheries, Mangalore, 575 001 – (India)

A.P. Sharma, Central Inland Fisheries Research Institute (Indian Council of Agricultural Research), Barrackpore, Kolkata, (West Bengal) 700 120 (India).

B.C. Joshi, Assistant Professor, Department of Science, Surajmal Agrawal Kanya Mahavidyalaya, Kichha, Kumaun University, Nainital, (Uttarakhand) (India).

B.K. Behera, Central Inland Fisheries Research Institute, Barrackpore, Kolkata 700 120 (India).

D.K. Meena, Central Inland Fisheries Research Institute (Indian Council of Agricultural Research), Barrackpore, Kolkata, (West Bengal) 700 120 (India).

E.D. Oruonye, Department of Geography, Taraba State University, PMB 1167, Jalingo, Nigeria.

G.G. Phadke, Department of Fish Processing Technology, College of Fisheries, Mangalore, 575 001 (India).

H.A. Kaoud, Department of Veterinary Hygiene and Environmental Pollution, Faculty of Veterinary Medicine, Cairo University, Egypt.

Imtiyaz Tali, Department of Zoology, Govt Holkar Science College Indore (MP) (India).

I.P, Udo-James, Department of Geography and Regional Planning, Delta State University, PMB 1, Abraka, Nigeria.

Keerti Meena, Veterinary officer Dausa, Rajasthan -303315 (India).

K.K. Sharma Research Associate (RA) in VPKAS, Almora, (Uttrakhand) 263 601 (India).

L.K. Mudgal, Department of Zoology, Mata Jijabai Govt P. G. Girls College Motitabela Indore (MP) (India).

Manjulata Bisht, Retired Professor, Department of Zoology, DSB Campus, Kumaun University, Nainital, (India).

Nikunj B. Gajera, Gujarat Institute of Desert Ecology, Post Box No. 83, Mundra Road, Bhuj, Kachchh - 370 001, (Gujarat) (India).

N. Saharan, Division of Aquaculture, Central Institute of Fisheries Education, Versova, Mumbai-61 (India).

Shailendra Sharma, Department of Biotechnology and Life Science, Adarsh Institute of Management and Science, Dhamnod, Devi Ahilya University, Indore (M.P.), (India).

S.K. Gupta, Directorate of Coldwater Fisheries Research, Chhirapani Fish Farm, Champawat - 262 523 (Uttrakhand) (India).

S.V.K. Reddy, Department of Fish Processing Technology, College of Fisheries, Mangalore - 575 001 (India).

Utpal Bhaumik, Central Inland Fisheries Research Institute (Indian Council of Agricultural Research), Barrackpore, Kolkata 700 120 (West Bengal) (India).

V.N. Ojeh, Department of Geography and Regional Planning, Delta State University, PMB 1, Abraka, Nigeria.

V. Vijaykumar, Gujarat Institute of Desert Ecology, Post Box No. 83, Mundra Road, Bhuj, Kachchh - 370 001 (Gujarat) (India).

Zahoor Pir, Department of Zoology, Mata Jijabai Govt P.G. Girls College Motitabela Indore (MP) (India).

CHAPTER – 1

Effects of Aquatic Pollution on Fish and Fisheries

H.A. Kaoud, ***Egypt***

ABSTRACT

However, the effects of pollution are dangerous especially for all the living inhabitants of the seas and oceans. These consequences are diverse. Primary critical violations in the functioning of living organisms under the influence of pollutants occur at the level of biological effects: after changing the chemical composition of the cells are broken processes of respiration, growth and reproduction of organisms, may mutate and carcinogenesis; violated the motion and orientation in the marine environment. Morphological changes are often manifested in the form of various pathologies of internal organs: changes in size, development of abnormal forms. Particularly often, these phenomena are recorded in case of chronic pollution.

All this affects the state of individual populations, their relationships. Thus, there are environmental consequences of pollution. An important indicator of disturbances of ecosystems is a change in the number of higher taxa - fish. Changes significantly the photosynthetic action in general. Increases the biomass of microorganisms, phytoplankton and zooplankton. This is characteristic of the eutrophication of marine waters; they were especially significant in the inland seas, seas closed. In the Caspian Sea, Black Sea, Baltic Sea over the past 10-20 years, microbial biomass increased almost 10 times. In the Sea of Japan scourge became "red tides", a consequence of eutrophication, in which rapidly developing microscopic algae, and then disappears oxygen in the water, killing aquatic animals and formed a huge mass of decaying residues of toxic, not only sea but also the atmosphere.

Pollution of the oceans leads to a gradual reduction of primary biological production. Scientists estimate that it declined to the present time to 10 per cent. Accordingly, the annual growth rate is reduced and other sea creatures.

ITRODUCTION

Pollution is the introduction of contaminants into an environment that causes instability, disorder, harm or discomfort to the ecosystem i.e. physical systems or living organisms. Pollution can take the form of chemical substances, or energy, such as noise, heat, or light. Pollutants, the elements of pollution, can be foreign substances or energies, or naturally occurring; when naturally occurring, they are considered contaminants when they exceed natural levels. The most important types of environmental pollution are: *Water pollution, Air pollution and Soil pollution* (Fig.1.1).

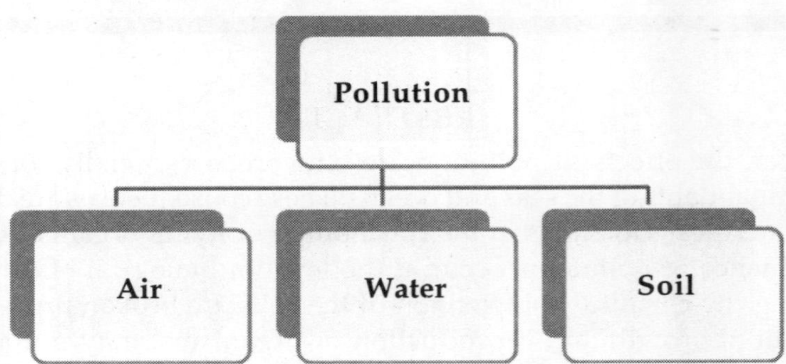

Fig. 1.1: The most Important Types of Environmental Pollution are: Water Pollution, Air Pollution and Soil Pollution

Forms of Pollution

Chemical pollution is not the only form of pollution. There are several forms of pollution (Fig. 1.2):

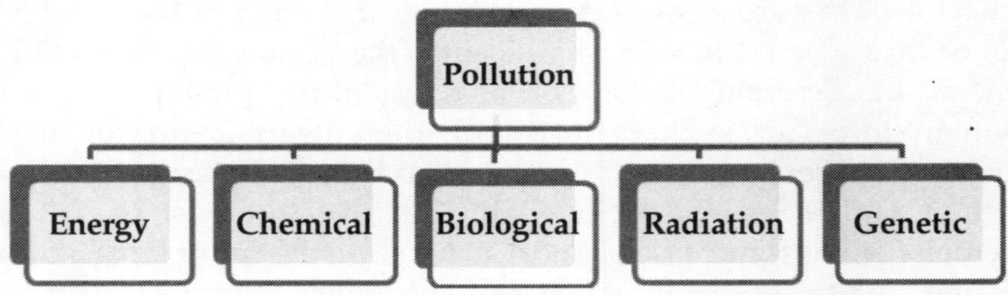

Fig. 1.2: There are Several Forms of Pollution

1. Chemical pollution.
2. Physical pollution.

Noise is an example simply adding water to a river at a different temperature to the ambient can affect life in the river. This is a form of thermal pollution, which a toxic chemical caused the massive fish kill in the photo. But the fish were not killed by a chemical spill—they died because of thermal pollution. When the temperature of a body of water, such as a lake or stream, increases, can result. Thermal pollution can occur when power plants and other industries use water in their cooling systems and then discharge the warm water into a lake or river. Thermal pollution can cause large fish kills if the discharged water is too warm for the fish to survive. But most thermal pollution is more subtle. If the temperature of a body of water rises even a few degrees, the amount of oxygen the water can hold decreases significantly. As oxygen levels drop, aquatic organisms may suffocate and die. If the flow of warm water into a lake or stream is constant, it may cause the total disruption of an aquatic ecosystem.

3. Biological:
   (a) Waterborne diseases caused by polluted drinking water:
   - Typhoid
   - Amoebiasis
   - Giardiasis
   - Ascariasis
   - Hookworm

   (b) Waterborne diseases caused by polluted beach water:
   - Rashes, ear ache, pink eye
   - Respiratory infections
   - Hepatitis, encephalitis, gastroenteritis, diarrhoea, vomiting, and stomach aches

   (c) Conditions related to water polluted by chemicals (such as pesticides, hydrocarbons, persistent organic pollutants, heavy metals etc):
   - Cancer, incl. prostate cancer and non-Hodgkin's lymphoma
   - Hormonal problems that can disrupt reproductive and developmental processes
   - Damage to the nervous system
   - Liver and kidney damage
   - Damage to the DNA
   - Exposure to mercury (heavy metal):
   - *In the womb:* may cause neurological problems including slower reflexes, learning deficits, delayed or incomplete mental development, autism and brain damage.

- *In adults:* Parkinson's disease, multiple sclerosis, Alzheimer's disease, heart disease, and even death.

(d) Other effects:

- Water pollution may also result from interactions between water and contaminated soil, as well as from deposition of air contaminants (such as acid rain).
- Damage to people may be caused by fish foods coming from polluted water (a well known example is high mercury levels in fish).
- Damage to people may be caused by vegetable crops grown/ washed with polluted water.

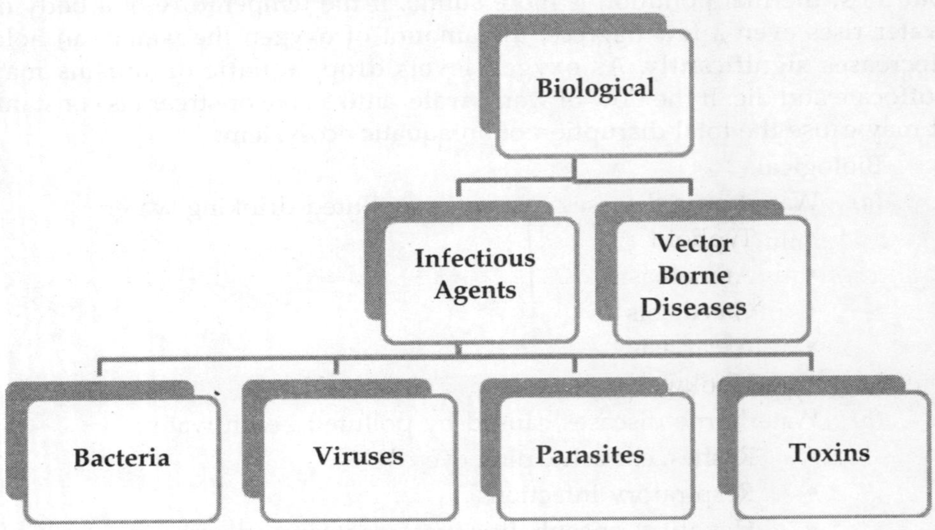

Fig. 1.3: The Biological form of Pollution

Pollution is, however, often associated with the introduction of chemical compounds into the environment. Popular opinion usually sees these as unnatural (and therefore harmful.) substances: Perhaps one of the best known current examples is the concern over the emission of chlorofluorocarbons (CFCs). These have been used in aerosol sprays and oilier applications and are linked with the depletion of ozone in the atmosphere.

Contamination: implies that the chemical present at a higher concentration than would occur normally, but does not necessarily cause any harmful effects to the target organisms. The effects of a pollutant on the target organism may be either acute or chronic. Acute effects occur rapidly, and are often fatal and rarely reversible; however chronic impacts of pollution occur after long exposure to low concentration of the pollutant.

Water pollution, pollution can be defined as anything humans do to cause harmful effects to our bodies of water. This can include pollution of rivers, lakes, oceans, and ground water pollution. The causes of pollution in the water are virtually endless. Manufacturing plants are major causes of water pollution, using bodies of fresh water to carry away waste that can contain phosphates, nitrates, lead, mercury, PCBs, Dioxins and other harmful and toxic substances.

Pollution is often broadly classified according to its source of emission into point source pollution and non point source pollution.

Point source pollution is pollution with a clearly identifiable point of discharge; for example the outflow from Waste water treatment plant or smoke-stack Non-point pollution is pollution without an obvious single point of discharge. The implications for control are quite different. Control of non-point pollution is difficult because of the large areas involved and having to deal with multiple sources. Emissions of pollutants are either caused naturally or by human activity *Natural-made emission* of pollutants by volcanoes or swamps may caused considerable effects 'to the local environment.

Anthropogenic or (homogenic) emission is used to indicate human induced pollution of the environment. At the community or ecosystem level, pollution might cause several effects including toxic effects to man and animals, the loss of some living species with possibly gain in others and a reduction in species diversity. The generalized pathway of a pollutant from the source of emission to the target organism. There are three important rate processes in the pathway of a pollutant:

1. The rate of emission of the pollutant from the source of pollution. This rate determines the concentration of the pollutant at the point of emission and the quantity of pollutant emitted over time.
2. The rate of transport of the pollutant through the ecosystem. This rate depends on three important factors:
   (a) The diffusion rate of the pollutant.
   (b) Several environmental factors.
   (c) The properties of transport within the organism.
3. The rate of removal or accumulation of the pollutant in the pathway and this rate will determine the concentration of the pollutant at the target organism as well as the quantity of the pollutant that reaching the target organism.

Water pollution is the introduction of chemical, physical, or biological agents into water that degrades water quality and adversely affects the organisms that depend on the water. Almost all of the ways that we use water contribute to water pollution. However, the two underlying causes of water pollution are industrialization and rapid human population growth. In the last 30 years, developed countries have made great strides in cleaning up many polluted water supplies. Despite this progress, some water is still dangerously polluted in the United States and in other countries. In developing parts of the world, water pollution is a big problem. Industry is usually not the major cause of water pollution in developing countries. Often, the only water available for drinking in these countries is polluted with sewage and agricultural runoff, which can spread waterborne diseases. To prevent water pollution, people must understand where pollutants come from.

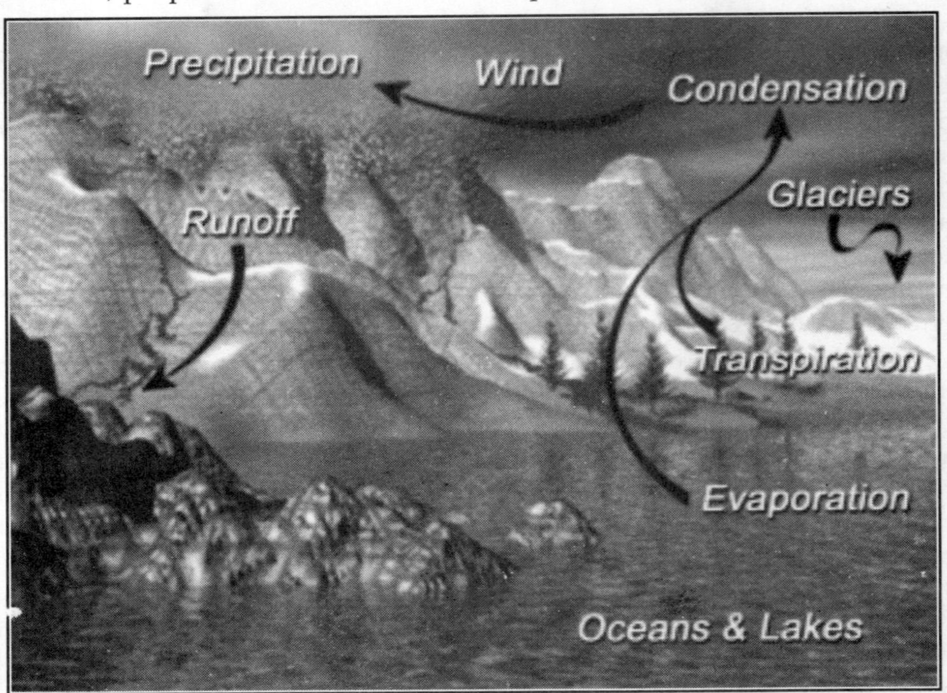

Fig. 1.4: In the Hydrologic Cycle, Individual Water Molecules Travel Between the Oceans, Water Vapour in the Atmosphere, Water and Ice on the Land, and Underground Water

WATER POLLUTION AND ECOSYSTEMS

Water pollution can cause immediate damage to an ecosystem. For example, toxic chemicals spilled directly into a river can kill nearly all living things for miles downstream. But the effects of water pollution can be even more far reaching. Many pollutants accumulate in the environment because they do not decompose quickly. As the pollutant levels increase, they can threaten an entire ecosystem.

Consider a river ecosystem. Soil tainted with pesticides washes into the river and settles to the river bottom. Some of the pesticides enter the bodies of tiny, bottom-dwelling organisms, such as insect larvae and crustaceans. A hundred of these organisms are eaten by one small fish. A hundred of these small fish are eaten by one big fish. A predatory bird, such as an eagle, eats 10 big fish. Each organism stores the pesticide in its tissues, so at each step along the food chain, the amount of the pesticide passed on to the next organism increases. This accumulation of pollutants at successive levels of the food chain is called Biomagnifications, which is illustrated in fig 1.5, has alarming consequences for organisms at the top of the food chain. Biomagnifications is one reason why many regions limit the amount of fish that people can eat from certain bodies of water.

Table 1.1: One Estimate of Global Water Distribution

	Volume (1000 km³)	Per cent of Total Water	Per cent of Fresh Water
Oceans, Seas, & Bays	1,338,000	96.5	–
Ice caps, Glaciers and Permanent Snow	24,064	1.74	68.7
Groundwater	23,400	1,7	–
Fresh	(10,530)	(0.76)	30.1
Saline	(12,870)	(0.94)	–
Soil Moisture	16.5	0.001	0,05
Ground Ice and Permafrost	300	0.022	0,86
Lakes	176.4	0.013	–
Fresh	(91.0)	(0,007)	0.26
Saline	(85.4)	(0.006)	–
Atmosphere	12.9	0.001	0.04
Swamp Water	11.47	0.0008	0.03
Rivers	2.12	0.0002	0.006
Biological Water	1.12	0.0001	0.003
Total	**1,385,984**	**100.0**	**100.0**

Source: Gleick, P.H., 1996: Water resources. In Encyclopedia of Climate and Weather, ed. by S. H. Schneider, Oxford University Press, New York, Vol. 2, pp. 817-823.

Aquatic Pollution

Aquatic systems are considered as suitable sites for disposal of and recycling the sewage andtoxic wastes and drain off the excess to the sea. However, the increasing pollutant load and theover exploitation of the water resources for potable supplies, irrigation, industries and thermalpower plants to meet the requirements of the ever-increasing population, significantly reducestheir assimilative capacity. Thus, the dual stress exerted on the watercourses is ultimately facedby the biological communities inhabiting them. Of this fish is the most important aquatic community concerning the man.

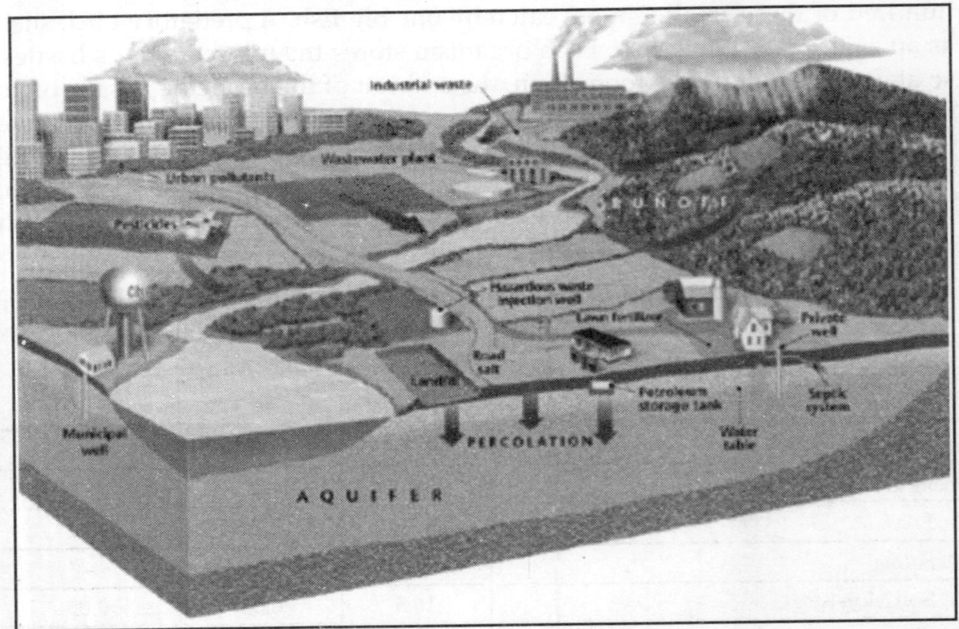

Fig. 1.5: Environmental Pollution

Sources of Water Pollution

To understand the causes, effect and control of pollution, the sources of pollution should be clearly classified. The sources of water pollution with reference to fisheries can be classified into following:

- Domestic sewage
- Soil erosion and sedimentation
- Industrial organic and inorganic wastes
- Agricultural wastes
- Oil and oil dispersants
- Radioactive wastes
- Waste heat
- Solid wastes
- Acid rain

There are two main sources of water pollution; point sources and non-point sources. Point sources include factories, wastewater treatment facilities, septic systems, and other sources that are clearly discharging pollutants into water sources. Non-point sources are more difficult to identify, because they cannot be traced back to a particular location. Non-point sources include runoff including sediment, fertilizer, chemicals and animal wastes from farms, fields, construction sites and mines. Landfills can also be a non-point source of pollution, if substances leach from the landfill into water supplies.

The United States Environmental Protection Agency (EPA) divides water pollution into the following categories:

1. Biodegradable waste consists mainly of human and animal waste. When biodegradable waste enters a water supply, the waste provides an energy source (organic carbon) for bacteria. Organic carbon is converted to carbon dioxide and water, which can cause atmospheric pollution and acid rain; this form of pollution is far more widespread and problematic than other forms of pollutants, such as radioactive waste. If there is a large supply of organic matter in the water, oxygen-consuming (aerobic) bacteria multiply quickly, consume all available oxygen, and kill all aquatic life.
2. Plant nutrients, such as phosphates and nitrates, enter the water through sewage, and livestock and fertilizer runoff. Phosphates and nitrates are also found in industrial wastes. Though these chemicals are natural, 80 per cent of nitrates and 75 per cent of phosphates in water are human-added. When there is too much nitrogen or phosphorus in a water supply (0.3 parts per million for nitrogen and 0.01 parts per million for phosphorus), algae begin to develop. When algae blooms, the water can turn green and cloudy, feel slimy, and smell bad. Weeds start to grow and bacteria spread. Decomposing plants use up the oxygen in the water, disrupting the aquatic life, reducing biodiversity, and even killing aquatic life. This process, called eutrophication, is a natural process, but generally occurs over thousands of years. Eutrophication allows a lake to age and become more nutrient-rich; without nutrient pollution, this may take 10,000 years, but pollution can make the process occur 100 to 1,000 times faster.
3. Heat can be a source of pollution in water. As the water temperature increases, the amount of dissolved oxygen decreases. Thermal pollution can be natural, in the case of hot springs and shallow ponds in the summertime, or human-made, through the discharge of water that has been used to cool power plants or other industrial equipment. Fish and plants require certain temperatures and oxygen levels to survive, so thermal pollution often reduces the aquatic life diversity in the water.
4. Sediment is one of the most common sources of water pollution. Sediment consists of mineral or organic solid matter that is washed or blown from land into water sources. Sediment pollution is difficult to identify, because it comes from non-point sources, such as construction, agricultural and livestock operations, logging, flooding, and city runoff. Each year, water sources in the United States are polluted by over one billion tones of sediment! Sediment can cause large problems, as it can clog municipal water systems, smother aquatic life, and cause water to become increasingly turbid. And, turbid water can cause thermal pollution, because cloudy water absorbs more solar radiation.

5. Hazardous and toxic chemicals are usually human-made materials that are not used or disposed of properly. Point sources of chemical pollution include industrial discharges and oil spills. The oil pollution fact sheet includes more detailed information about oil spills, as well as other sources of oil pollution. Non-point sources of chemical pollution include runoff from paved roads and pesticide runoff. Many people think industries produce the greatest amount of chemical pollution. But domestic and personal use of chemicals can significantly contribute to chemical pollution. Household cleaners, dyes, paints and solvents are also toxic, and can accumulate when poured down drains or flushed down the toilet. In fact, one drop of used motor oil can pollute 25 liters of water! And, people who use pesticides on their gardens and lawns tend to use ten times more pesticide per acre than a farmer would!

Fig. 1.6: The Oil Pollution Fact Sheet Includes more Detailed Information about Oil Spills, as well as Other Sources of Oil Pollution

6. Radioactive pollutants include wastewater discharges from factories, hospitals and uranium mines. These pollutants can also come from natural isotopes, such as radon. Radioactive pollutants can be dangerous, and it takes many years until radioactive substances are no longer considered dangerous.
7. Pharmaceuticals and personal care products (often abbreviated PCPs), including medications, lotions and soap, are being found in increasing concentrations in lakes and rivers. Scientists have discovered that many PCPs act as hormone disrupters, which means that the synthetic hormones in the products interfere with the natural hormones in animals,

especially fish that live in the water. There has not been enough research to determine the effects that PCPs can have on humans, but there is evidence to suggest that these chemicals may be partially responsible for an increase in cancer and birth defects.

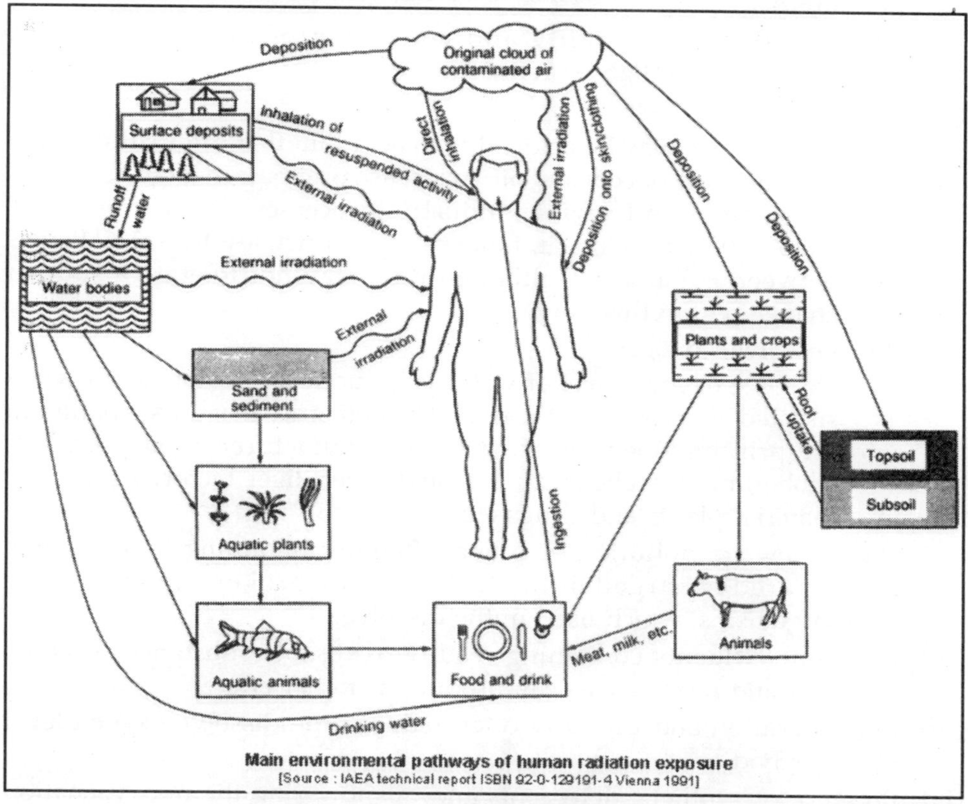

Main environmental pathways of human radiation exposure
[Source : IAEA technical report ISBN 92-0-129191-4 Vienna 1991]

Fig. 1.7: Radioactive Pollutants

Changes in the physico-chemical parameters of water due to pollution:

A. Physical parameters

(a) Temperature:

Temperature of water may increase due to thermal pollution when water is used to cool power stations and due to waste heat from industries.

(b) Turbidity and colour:

Turbidity of water may increase due to soil erosion or heavy algal bloom due to high level of organic and inorganic nutrients from sewage water arigricultural waste. Turbidity, dye and pigment pollutants affect the general color of water.

(*c*) Depth and flow:
Flow and depth of the water body may be reduced due to heavy siltationof sediments coming from land erosion.

(*d*) Light:
Due to high turbidity and coloration of the water bodies, penetration of light is reduced.

B. Chemical parameters:

(*a*) pH of water may be acidic due to acid rain that originates largely from burning of coal and oil. Acids also originate in large quantities from mines and various industrialprocesses (waste from DDT factory, battery, vinegar, tanneries). Fish ùsually live at pHlevels between 6.0 and 9.0, although they may not tolerate a sudden change within this range.

(*b*) Dissolved oxygen:
Dissolve oxygen level of water is reduced to greater extent when situated on the bank of the river. The industries that causes pollution are printing, electroplating,soap manufacturer, food products, rubber, plastic, chemical, petroleum, fertilizer factories,synthetic material plants and drugs etc.

(*i*) Heavy sewage pollution or other effluents containing high organic matter aredischarged into it. These are broken down by the microorganisms, which used upthe dissolved O_2.

(*ii*) Inorganic effluents containing readily oxidisable substances such as sulphites and ferrous salts can produce a similar effect.

(*iii*) Eutrophication and turbidity often reduced the dissolve oxygen level of water bodies.

(*iv*) Presence of synthetic detergents and oils lowering the re-oxygenation rate of water.

(*v*) Discharge of cooling water from industries also reduced the dissolve oxygen levelof water bodies.

(*c*) CO_2: Eutrophication and organic pollutants responsible for depletion of dissolve oxygenincrease the CO_2 level in water bodies, due to decomposition of undecomposed orpartially decomposed organic matter.

(*d*) Alkalinity: Wastes associated with tanning, wool scouring, the mercerizing of cotton andthe manufacture of certain chemicals (in chloro-alkali industries) may contain causticsoda (NaOH), sodium carbonate or lime. Such alkaline effluents may have a pH of 12-14and lethal to all types of stream life, including bacteria.

(*e*) Salinity: Excessive amount of salts brought by sewage; and effluents from chloro-alkali industries increase the chloride level thereby salinity of water, which is responsible forincrease in the osmotic pressure. Salinity also reduces dissolve oxygen level.

(*f*) Dissolved solids:

1. Nitrates and phosphates: Water polluted by agricultural wastes, soil erosion andorganic pollutants (sewage & biodegradable synthetic detergents) are rich in nitrates and phosphates.
2. Heavy metals: Hg, Zn, Ni, Cd, Pb, Mn, Cu, Fe, Cr, As, Se etc. are present in natural water in very trace amount that's why they are called trace elements. However, inpolluted waters their concentrations are increased in many folds. They come from mining, refining, paper and pulp industries (Cr), mercury electric appliance industries,vinyl chloride synthesis, caustic soda industries using mercury cell, organo-mercuric fungicides industries, lead processing industries, storage batteries, water pipes (Pb), industrial discharges, metal or plastic pipes (Cd), metal processing and dye industries,mines, drainage (Zn), trade wastes from pickling and anodizing, leather, dye-manufacturing, explosives, ceramics. Heavy metals are non-biodegradable, watersoluble, persistent and strongly bonded to polypeptides and proteins.

EFFECTS ON FISH AND FISHERIES ON ECOLOGY

Eutrophication: Pollution due to domestic sewage increases the organic load and pollution due to agricultural waste (residual fertilizers) and soil erosion containing nutrients such as nitrates; phosphates, potassium etc. fertilize the water and increase the rate of productivity of the aquatic ecosystem. This results in higher growth of phytoplankton. Water becomes turbid due to excessive growth of phytoplankton and soil eroded particles. Excessive amount of nutrients change the algal community from one of great diversity of species to one of a few; the species which are eliminated are commonly those which form the food of the herbivorous animals which in turn feed the fisheries resources of the area. The species, which grow in abundance, are generally the blue-green algae or other species, which are mostly unsuitable or less valuable as food for fishes and grazing animals. The changes in the plant population thus indirectly cause changes throughout the entire ecosystem, even in organisms,which are not directly effected by the pollution. Aquatic lives face severe oxygen shortage due to: *(i)* Bacterial Decomposition of untreated sewage into their inorganic components assimilates dissolve oxygen from the water in the process; *(ii)* High turbidity restricts the penetration of sunlight in deeper layers and benthic plants could not photosynthesize; *(iii)* When algal bloom die, they sink to the deeper waters and in the process of decomposition, allthe oxygen can be consumed.

This leads to anaerobic decomposition and generation of toxic substances like hydrogensulphide, ammonia, mercaptans and organic amines. At times when dissolved oxygen in water is at it's lowest and these substances at their peak values the water smells bad and become unsuitable. The whole process is referred to as 'eutrophication', as a result of which there is excessive growth of phytoplankton due to nutrient enrichment, increase in turbidity and death of benthic plants, depletion of dissolved oxygen and consequent suffocation of fish and mollusks that in habit deeper waters. The species able to survive are usually less valuable as fisheries resources from an economic point of view. Among the species to disappear from over enriched lakes or estuaries are the trout and salmon, and the survivors are the pollution tolerant cyprinids.

Accelerated aging of lakes and ponds: Sewage pollution even at in small quantities may change the character of an aquatic environment over a period of years. Thus, with the gradual process of aging, deep, clear oligotropic lakes may be sedimented; becoming mesotrophic, then becomes eutrophic andeventually turning into bog.

BIOLOGICAL EFFECTS ON FISH

Pollutants might effect a given population without being lethal to adult organisms in many ways:

1. *Migration:* Mechanism used for orientation and navigation by migrating organisms is not well known, but in some cases chemo toxicants clearly plays an important role. Sub-lethal concentration of pollutants may interfere with the normal migration pattern of organisms thereby change the composition of population or species diversity. Salmon, trout and many other anadromous fishes have been excluded from their home streams by pollution, though it is not known whether the reason is that a chemical cue has been masked or because the general chemical environment of pollution is offensive to the fish. On the other hand, heavy siltation and flow of heated coolant water may block migratory channels and long distance migratory fishes during some phases of their life history may be adversely affected by highly localized pollution of river.
2. *Incidence of diseases:* A long-term exposure of sub lethal concentration of pollutants may make an organism more susceptible to a disease. It is possible that some organic pollutants will provide an environment suitable for the development of disease producing bacterial and viruses. In such case, even though the pollutant is not directly toxic to the adult organism it could still have a profound effect on the population of the species over a longer period.
3. *Behaviour:* Much of the day-to-day behaviour of a species may also be mediated by means of chemo toxic responses. The finding and capture

of food and the search for a mate during thebreeding season are included in this category of activity, and again any pollutant interfering with the chemo receptors of the organism would interfere with the behavioural patterns essential to asurvival of the population.

4. *Physiological Processes:* Pollutant may interfere with various physiological processes without necessarily causing death, which may interfere in the survival of a species. DDT depresses photosynthesis inplanktonic algae, but only at concentrations greater than its solubility in water. Respiration might also be adversely affected, as could various other enzymatic processes. The toxic substances and suspended sediments when injure the mucous membrane of the gills effects the respiration. Heavy metals particularly mercury inhibit the activities of digestive enzymes but it has most damaging effect on the nervous system.
5. *Life cycle:* The larval forms of many species are much was sensitive to pollution than the adults. In many aquatic species millions of eggs are produced and fertilized but only two of the larval produced need to grow to maturity and breed in order to maintain the standing stock of thespecies. For these species, the pre-adult mortalities rate is enormous even under the best of natural conditions. An additional stress on the developing organisms might cause failure of enough individual to survive and maintain the population of the species. Interrupting any stage of the life cycle can be as disastrous for the population as death of the adults from acute toxicity of the environment. Example. Silt sedimentation, eutrophication and increased pollution level had affected the standing fish stock in many Indian rivers by spectacular mass mortalities.
6. *Nutrition and food chain:* Pollutants may interfere with the nutrition of organisms by affecting their ability to findpray, by interfering with digestion or assimilation of food, by contaminating the pray species so that it is not accepted by the predator. On the other hand, if predator species is eliminated by pollution the pray species may have an improved chance of survival. An example of the latter effect was shown in the Kelp resurgence after the oil spill in Tampico Bay, California (North,1967). The oil kills the sea urchins, which used young, newly developing kelp as food and the kelp beds developed luxurious growth within a few months. Heavy metals and halogenated hydrocarbons e.g. DDT, BHC, Endosulfan etc. are particularly harmful because they tend to bio-accumulate. These chemicals are easily adsorbed into the body but excreted very slowly resulting in bioaccumulation, which may further enhance in the food chain. Organisms at the bottom of the food chain absorb the chemicals from the water and accumulate it in the tissues. Animals atthe second trophic level, such as fish, feeding on these organisms receive a higher dose, and further accumulation takes place

in their tissues and so on, up the food chain. Thus, organisms atthe top of the food chain receive the chemical at a much higher level than present in the water.This concentration of the toxic chemicals through the food chain is called 'bio-magnification'. This is further complicated by the 'synergistic effects' i.e. two or more chemicals acting together to produce a much more pronounced effect, than the sum of the total of the effects of the two acting separately.

7. *Genetic effects:* Many pollutants produce genetic effects, which can have long-range significance for the survival of species. Radioactive contamination can cause mutations directly by the action of radiation on the genetic material. Oil and other organic pollutants may include both mutagenic and carcinogenic compounds. A large majority of these mutations is detrimental to the survival of the young and many are lethal.

Effects of pollution on eggs, spawn, fry on breeding grounds and feeding grounds.

Effects on Fish Eggs; Spawn and Fry

Fish eggs are much more resistant than the adult fish. Toxicity thresholds for lead, zincand nickel to be about 20, 40 and 2000 ppm respectively, values for higher than those found for about animal. Eggs would develop normally between pH 6 to 9. In water more acid than pH 4.0, the eggs displayed exosmosis and collapsed, in water more alkaline than pH 9.0 there was endosmosis, the eggs swelled and yolk became white. The critical oxygen tensions are about 40mm Hg for newly fertilized eggs and rises, as the embryo develops, to about 100 mg Hg (about 60% saturation) at the time of hatching. Trout and Salmon lay their eggs in gravel, through which water must percolate while the eggs batch and the fry live on the food from the egg yolk. Then the gravel must allow the fry to emerge. A suitable area must not accumulate silt and sand during the gravel life and it must not freeze or shift with floods. Oxygen shortage due to pollution in the water flowing through the gravel, an insufficient rate of water flow due to deposition of silt in the spawning beds, or a combination of both these adverse factors will hold up the development of fish eggs, delay hatching and proves fatal to the embryos.

Survival of larval fish fry and fingerlings:

(a) *Food acquisition:* Larval fish is able to feed only on the tiniest of zooplankton and phytoplankton, thus early growth and survival of fish depends upon the densities of small cladocerans and rotifers and phytoplankton. Aquatic pollution is toxic to these plankton and pose threat to survival of fishfry.

(b) *Predation:* Survival of larval fish is probably influenced more by predation than by feeding. These very small fish are vulnerable to virtually every other predator. Not only visual feeding fish but also other predators such as predaceous copepods may have considerable influence on larval fish densities. Protective cover, such as aquatic macrophytes must be especially critical in minimizing fish predation on small fish. Any factor(s), such as turbidity, wave action, siltation that would reduce vegetative cover, could also minimize larval fish survivorship. Reducing or lowering the water level (due to siltation) below the vegetative zone would seem to be especially disastrous to larval fish. Structural complexity, especially aquatic vegetation, while providing refuge for larval and fingerlings fish, may reduce the ability of piscivorous fish to feed on small fish.Fry and fingerlings are more susceptible to pollution than adult fish. Resistance to pollution: Egg> Adult>Larvae.

Destruction of Breeding and Spawning Grounds

For any nest, building fish or any fish in which the eggs attach to a particular substrate the nature of the substrate is important in successful spawning. Aquatic vegetation often provides the very substrate within which or on which eggs are laid and may protect eggs from wave actionand erosion. Gravel bed is good for spawning. The role of nearby structure (gravel) of aquatic vegetation is less clear, but it doubtless makes nest defense from predator more effective. High level of turbidity caused by pollution often precludes the development of substantial littoral zone vegetation. With increase of water level and flow rate of water, spawning success was found toincrease.

A lowered level of dissolved oxygen due to the presence of organic pollution, which initself is not toxic to may significantly reduce the chances of salmon reaching the spawning grounds because of fatigue and reduction of swimming velocity. Base metals in rivers have been shown to cause Atlantic Salmon to return to sea without spawning, resulting in over all reduce reproduction. Soil particles due to land erosion carried out run-off water and suspended matter presentin sewage and trade wastes gets deposited on the river bed or behind the weirs and cause siltingof the bed. Siltation in river and reservoirs diminishes the: *(i)* quantum of water flow; *(ii)* flow rate of water; and *(iii)* water level, thereby reducing the spawning success. Heavy siltation also destroy the nesting materials (e.g. Aquatic vegetation) for fishes and cover the gravel structureby silt deposits thereby natural spawning of fish is prevented due to lack of suitable spawning area and increases egg mortality. This can be serious in respect of major carps, trouts, salmonids and other fishes requires special environment for breeding. Either fish failing to reach their spawning or feeding areas, because they avoid polluted waters or perhaps because pollutants interfere with their chemical sense and they are not able torecognize their home waters.

Effect on Feeds and Feeding Grounds of Fishes

Turbidity: Silts and clay greatly reduce the euphotic zone in rivers and reservoirs.Turbidity severely restricts the zone within the water body where visually feeding fish can efficiently find and attack their pray. Turbidity also reduces fish vision within the euphotic zone.

Siltation: Heavy silt deposits smoothers benthic vegetation and invertebrate checking itsgrowth. This reduces the production of benthic vegetation. Salmonoids in streams need places to feed and hide from predators. The feeding places are usually in or below the gravel riffles that produces aquatic food organisms. This feeding place is destroyed by siltation. Larval fish is able to feed only on the tiniest of zooplankton and phytoplankton, thus early growth and survival of fish depends upon the densities of small cladocerans and rotifers and phytoplankton. Aquatic pollution is toxic to these plankton and pose threat to survival of fishfry.

Eutrophication: Excessive amount of nutrients changes the algal community from one of great diversity of species to one of a few; the species, which are eliminated commonly those, which from the food of the herbivorous animals which in turn feed the fisheries resources of the area. The species, which grow in abundance, are generally the blue-green algae and other species,which are mostly unsuitable as feed for fishes.

Heat discharge: Because of this macro algae and sea grass disappear resulting decline of fish product due to lack of shelter for juvenile stages of commercial species of food organisms and reduced food for associated herbivores.

Effects on Fishing and Fishery Products

Fishing: Fishing gear and operations may be adversely affected by various kinds of pollutants. Over fertilization may cause fouling and clogging of nets, traps and other fishing gears by masses of macro algae or other plants and animals drifting in the water or using the materials as substratum. In the areas of oil exploitation nets are frequently clogged by crude oil and lumps of oily tar and catches have had to be discarded because of tainting. The numerous objects caught inthe bottom trawls (from plastic containers to explosives) often interfere with fishing operations. Wrecked cars and other junk have hampered fishing particularly in the North sea and the Balticby mechanical damage to nets and boats, and good fishing areas have been closed because of the danger from dumped military waste such as explosives, cyanide compounds, biological and chemical warfare agents and radio active wastes.

Fishery products: A common reason for the discarding of catches and the discontinuance of fishing in certain areas is the tainting of the fish by unpleasant ordours and tastes caused by petroleum derivatives, even at concentrations significantly below lethal levels. Waste from refineries and discharges of petroleum from ships are causing increasing damage to fishing in this respect. 0.01-0.02 ppm concentration is sufficient to cause bad taste in rainbow trout, Japanese mackerel and some other species. Mullet, which is rich in body fat, is likely to acquire taint more readily than other fish species in the same environment.

Colouring: Colouring has a similar effect to tainting on the fish's marketability that is a fish product with a modified colour is practically worthless. The "green Oyster" of Japan and Portugal, coloured by incorporated copper and zinc and "red herring" of Canada due to internal bleeding by elemental phosphorous are examples. There is evidence that pollution can cause morphological changes, teratogenic effects, skin ulcerations and other lesions, as well as various other diseases especially fungal in fish and shellfish. This has generally been associated with water is chronically contaminated by waste from industry or municipal sewage and sludge. In some countries fisheries product are eaten rawproviding opportunities for human infection by pathogenic such as viruses, bacteria, and nematodes. Bacterial contamination from domestic sewage is a particular problem to the shellfish (e.g. oysters, mussels, cockles etc.) may be marketed, however, after appropriate treatment (sterilization, relaying or purification) which, when properly carried out, results inproducts safe for human consumption. Swordfish fishery has suffered economically because of rather high contamination of mercury found in this fish (M.R.L. for Hg 0.05 mg/kg body weight). In some cases, it has been observed that "blooms" of toxic species of plankton were related to the disposal of nutrients into the water, as by sewage pollution. The danger to consumers is evident and mass mortalities of fish and other organisms are frequent consequence.This has led to the temporary closure of certain fishing areas or to the prohibition of the sale of the product.

Ciguatera Toxins and Paralytic Shellfish Poisoning

Ciguatera toxins and paralytic shellfish poisoning are naturally occurring toxins. Ciguatera is the most common non-bacterial food poisoning disease associated with the consumption of fish primarily in tropical regions of the world, including Caribbean, Atlantic, Indian and Pacific Ocean regions and Middle Eastern and Australian areas. Ciguatera isconsidered a world health problem. Studies have shown that more than 20 toxins are responsible for ciguatera phenomenon. The primary toxin, ciguatera toxin, has been isolated from large carnivores, and in smaller amounts, in herbivores. This is due to the greater lipid solubility of ciguatera. Considerable circumstantial evidence has linked Gamberdicus toxicus and other dinoflagellates to the group of ciguatera toxins. Paralytic shellfish poisoning may occur because of ingestion by certain species of bivalves (e.g. mussels, calms, oysters) of planktonic poisonous dinoflagellates such as Gonyauflux. Murate et al. (1990) reported the structures of ciguatoxin from the morey eel (Gymnothorax javanicus) and has not yet been conclusively demonstrated that the toxin produced by the dinoflagellate is either identical to, or is a precursor to, ciguatoxin(s) accumulating in fish. However, research workers have suggested recently that there lease of inorganic substances because of mining activities into the water of tropical regions ininsular areas triggers off naturally occurring biotoxicity cycles such as "Ciguatera" and other fishpoisoning. This makes the normally valuable food resource dangerous for human consumption and thereby instances of human death caused by such poisoning.

CONTROL OF WATER POLLUTION

In discussing the reduction of pollution, it has to be emphasized that the pollutants should whenever possible be removed at the source, where they are most concentrated. After they are released to the water and diluted, removal becomes much more difficult and may even be impossible. Some of the methods of water pollution control are discussed below:

1. *Dilution:* Dilution seems to be the most attractive method of waste disposal. Diluting the polluted water mass to such an extent that the harmful effect of the pollutant is made ineffective. However, the disposal programme must be in coordination with a programme of environmental management to guarantee adequate supplies of fresh water for the dilution process.
2. *Efficient use* (*Reuse*): One of the most important conservation activities is the use of freshwater in such a way that we get the very most for our efforts, without depleting it. Efforts should also be directed to increase the usability of low grade or polluted water. Treatment of domestic sewage for industrial cooling is a good example of efficient use. Water reuse has aspecial significance in mining and similar industries where the resources are scarce.
3. *Alternative use:* Where the waste material recovery is not economical, its alternative use should be examined e.g. pulp, which cannot be easily recovered, is being trapped at the outfall area of sulphite waste and is being used for the manufacture of cardboards. The uses of heated water for fish culture in many European countries and in North America have encouraging results. In the temperate region, many species of fish and shellfish grow during only a brief part of the year because the water is too cold for growth during the winter. In U.K. water from power plants has been used for the growing of Plaice and Sole in tanks and ponds and it has been demonstrated that these fish can be brought to marketable size about two years earlier than if leftin their natural conditions. If the discharge of warm water in sea is closely regulated the warmer water, being less dense than the receiving water, would entrain and carry the nutrient-rich watersto the surface and increase the fertility of the area.

4. *Recovery of by-products:* Recovery of by-products such as sodium hydroxide from sulphite waste, calcium oxide from sulphite waste, oil from hydrogenated vegetable oil and soap, mercury from chloro-alkali industry effluents and so on should be practiced.
5. *Appropriate technology:* We should develop, import and adopt only appropriate technology, which is pollution free. As an example, the mercury cell in the chloro-alkali industry should be replaced by diaphragm cell to avoid mercury pollution in the cell room itself and through effluents in water bodies. Use of natural gas instead of coal as fuel along with pollution control measures by industries and automobiles, will reduce the production of gases causing acid rain.
6. *Waste treatment/Purification:* There are many processes available for treatment and purification of waste beforedisposal:
   (a) *Chemical treatment:* Chemical treatment has long been used for industrial waste and for treatment of water for human consumption. Recently it has come into use also for treatment of domestic sewage in order to remove phosphates, heavy metals and other pollutants. For industrial wastewater treatment, this treatment is desired if the colour of effluent is too intense. Normally colour removal is carried away by adsorption on clays and activated carbon, coagulation with lime, aluminum sulphite etc. but treatment costs are high and not suitable for removing organic matter.

   (b) *Biological treatment:* In biological treatment optimum conditions are provided for natural self-purification in lagoon with the help of trickling filters, activated sledge or waste stabilizing ponds. Use of treated or partially treated sewage for fish culture is a traditional method of 11 biological treatment of organic waste, in which organic matter is mineralized, nutrient content considerably reduced and producing over one ton of fish per hectare per year without additional feeding. Under Indian conditions, water hyacinth (Eichhornia crassipes) can be used for purifying municipal and industrial wastes on a large scale. Researches have shown that water hyacinth grown in one-hectare water spread area can absorb the nitrogen and phosphorus wastes of over 600 persons. It also accumulates high rate of heavy metals and phenolic compounds from industrial effluents along with minerals.

   (c) *Biochemical treatment:* It is considered better than chemical treatment because it not only removes colour, but also help in BOD reduction and removal or organic matters. Biochemical oxidation is in fact a unit operation that conveys water-soluble organic compounds and eachcapable of converting 30-70 per cent of soluble convertible carbonaceous materials having high BOD to insoluble carbonaceous material, CO_2, water and energy.

(d) *Accelerated bio-chemical process (ABC):* It is recommended for high BOD removal upto 90 per cent suspended solids and phosphorus removal as well as reduction in aeration time to asmuch as 30-45 minutes against 3-4 hours via conventional bio-chemical process and 20-30 per cent lower construction costs. The process involves a two-stage biochemical system. The first stage isaerobic biological treatment, which receives raw effluents, deaerates, and converts the soluble and colloidal organic solids into a particulate insoluble form. It consists of a reaction vessel and aseparator. The influent residence time is 30-60 minutes; separator is a sedimentation vessel. Thesecond stage has a flocculator, clariflocculator aerator and a settler in sequence.

7. *Trapping:* Control of pollution from agricultural drainage and land erosion by conventional methods of treatment is not possible. In addition, the drainage from the agricultural land cannot be checked. Therefore, the best way to check the agro chemicals and soil particles from entering the water courses is to trap them on their land route. This can be achieved by adopting the following practices:
   (a) Provision of optimum soil cover (vegetation, crop residue) to dissipate raindrop impact and reduce runoff velocity.
   (b) Provision for optimum soil infiltration and flow path to minimize erosion through soild etachment and transport, and reduce runoff volume through enhanced filtration.
   (c) Minimization of soil solution concentration of pesticides, plant nutrients and other chemicals at the soil surface or within the root zone during periods of high runoff, thereby minimizing the movement of such substances in runoff and percolate.
   (d) Judicious application of pesticides and fertilizer to crops so that a potential pollutant isless available for detachment and transport.
   (e) To replace use of chemical fertilizers and pesticides by biofertilizers and botanical & bio-pesticides.

8. Water pollution control legislations:
   (a) Water (prevention and control of pollution) Act-1974, first legislation towardspollution controls.
   (b) The water (prevention and control of pollution) Cess Act, 1977.
   (c) The Environment (protection) Act, 1986.
   (d) Ganga Action plan (1985).

The central Ganga Authority was constituted in Feb. 1985 to evolves and oversee the implementation of long term Ganga Actionplan for cleaning the river Ganga.

Conclusion

The ultimate solution to pollution - The quatrain-

"The solution To pollution Is prevention Not dilution" exposes a dilemma, which can be correlated, at least in part, by improved manufacturing processes.

PRESENT STATUS OF RIVERS AND RESERVOIR POLLUTION IN INDIA

All the major 14 rivers and 55 minor rivers in the country are polluted in most of the stretches asper the Global Environmental Monitoring System (GEMS) and Monitoring of National Aquatic Resource System (MNARS) survey. According to the assessment made, water pollution is 90 per cent by volume due to domestic and household activities, while 10 per cent is contributed by the industries,of which 70 per cent is contributed by large and medium industries and 30 per cent by small-scale industries (Khoshoo, 1984). Domestic sewage of above 8500 mld (million liters/day) from different cities find their way into rivers, lakes, sea and land. It was estimated that as per 1985 price Index, Rs. 10,000 crores are required for sewage collection and treatment.

Present Status of Ganga River Pollution

Ganga and its various tributaries constitute the largest river system in India. Many major and minor tributaries join the river in its entire course. During the recent years the water quality and quantity of the mighty river Ganga have gone down considerably due to increased deforestation in its catchments areas, rapid development of various industries on the river banks, developmentof irrigation projects, many fold increase in the discharge of domestic, industrial and agricultural waste into the system and river modifications along with population explosions. Along the course from Gangotri to Sagar, there are 29 major cities, more than 70 towns and thousands of villages along with 132 large industries units (86 in U.P., 3 in Bihar and 43 in W.B.). Both the banks of entire river course are thickly populated and industrialized and contribution of these two sources to the BOD load is given in Table 1.2.

Table 1.2: BOD Load (Khoshoo, 1986)

States	Total BOD Load Tones/day %	Contribution from Domestic Source %	Contribution from Industrial Source
U.P.	1089	34.1	65.9
W.B.	379	70.2	29.8
Bihar	107	52.5	47.5

Causes and Magnitude of Pollution at Different Places

River Yamuna (Delhi-Agra)

Out of the total quantity of water supplied in Delhi 20 per cent covers consumptive use, the remaining 80 per cent flows back into the river. River Yamuna at Delhi is daily contaminated by about 320000 kilo tones of nearly untreated city sewage in its 24 KM stretch.About 17 openings discharge waste in the Yamuna. The Najafgarh drain contains high quantityof DDT and chloral hydrate in its 15000 m^3/day of industrial effluents. Out of these 6000 kg/day of fixed dissolved solids, 3000 kg/day of heavy metals, 300 kg/day ink and dye, 3800 kg/day organics, 1800 kg/day oil and grease, 1000 kg/day acids, 700 kg/day alkali and 200 kg/day detergents. It also receives large volume of extremely hot water from the power generator plants.

Fig. 1.8: Industrial Pollution

Groundwater Pollution

Pollutants usually enter groundwater when polluted surface water percolates down from the Earth's surface. Any pollution of the surface water in an area can affect the groundwater. Pesticides, herbicides, chemical fertilizers, and petroleum products are common groundwater pollutants. Leaking underground storage tanks are another major source of groundwater pollution. It is estimated that there are millions of underground storage tanks in the United States. Most of the tanks—located beneath gas stations, farms, and homes—hold petroleum products, such as gasoline and heating fuel. As underground storage tanks age, they may develop leaks, which allow pollutants to seep into the groundwater.

Pollution is widely recognized as one of the most serious challenge to the sustainable management of groundwater resources. The significance of pollution for groundwater resources is increased by the long time scale at which processes affecting groundwater function. It is important to appreciate the differences between surface water and groundwater systems. In the former, the water is typically being replenished, at least in the case of rivers, within time-scales of weeks or at most months. Replenishment times for groundwater systems are very much longer. This is because water usually takes many years to move through the soil and unsaturated zone of the aquifer. Once there, it can take a further period of many tens or hundreds of years to flow into a supply borehole." In some of the deeper aquifers, groundwater is likely to be thousands of years old. In addition to the relatively slow movement of water in many aquifers, rocks and soil absorb and otherwise attenuate the presence of pollutants. Not all aquifers are equally vulnerable to pollution. Those where fractures or cavities permit rapid flow tend to be more vulnerable than those where water flows slowly through porous media and more opportunities exist for attenuation of pollutants. However, vulnerability to pollution has an inverse relationship to the difficulty of remediation. Once polluted, slow movement of groundwater through a porous aquifer generally makes cleanup difficult, expensive, and in some cases impossible.

Beyond the inherent vulnerability of aquifers to contamination, much depends on the nature of pollutant sources. Contaminant behaviour varies greatly with respect to the specific transport properties in each aquifer system. In addition, the range of contaminant types is increasing as new products appear in effluent disposal and land application. Three main sources of groundwater pollution are: agricultural, urban and industrial.

Agricultural Pollution

In many developing countries, agricultural chemical use has been low in comparison to levels in industrialized countries. This may no longer be the case, particularly in countries such as India and China where irrigation is extensive. Concerns over groundwater pollution from agricultural chemicals were raised as a major issue in India more than two decades ago but few data were available. At that time, the level of agricultural chemical use was very low. However, by 1991, fertilizer use per hectare of agricultural land was 60 per cent higher than in the United States of America. At present, no agency in India has a systematic programme for monitoring potential non-point sources of pollution. However, fragmentary data indicating the potential extent of agricultural pollution problems are available.

For example, maps prepared by the Central Ground Water Board (CGWB) show nitrate concentrations in Gujarat exceeding 45 mg/liter (the WHO's recommended maximum for drinking-water) in more than 370 sample sites scattered across the state. How much of this pollution is related to agricultural pollution and how much to domestic or other sources is unknown. Aside from non-point-source considerations, it is important to recognize that nitrate and other nutrient pollution in groundwater is often related to agricultural practices other than the use of chemical fertilizers. Any location where animal wastes are concentrated, such as feed lots or poultry farms, can release high levels of nutrients into groundwater. In addition to nutrients, pesticides and herbicides are other major sources of groundwater pollution related to agriculture. In some circumstances, soils can absorb or immobilize a large fraction of such agricultural chemicals. However, many pesticides and herbicides break down slowly under aquifer conditions or can transform into more toxic compounds. As a result, they can persist over long time periods.

In any case, groundwater pollution data are generally scarce and chemical analysis of water samples needs to be specific to detect their presence. The dispersed nature of sources of pollutants is a core challenge facing both monitoring and control of groundwater pollution related to agriculture. Unlike industry or municipal sewage systems, agricultural pollutants are dispersed over large land areas. While return flows in drainage canals can be monitored, it is difficult to determine the extent of direct seepage of pollutants through soils and into the groundwater until contaminant concentrations in groundwater become significant.

Urban Groundwater Pollution

The additional recharge in urban areas is derived principally from leaking sewers and other wastewater sources. Broken sewers in the United States of America are estimated to lose 950 Mm^3 of wastewater each year. Much of this represents polluted recharge to groundwater. Direct leakage of wastewater to groundwater in developing countries is probably much higher. In many cities, a large portion of the wastewater generated is discharged directly into unlined canals. Where sewer systems exist, leakage levels are almost certainly much higher than in the United States of America because of lack of resources for maintenance, variability in construction materials and absence of adequate treatment facilities. Furthermore, in many urban and peri-urban areas, pit latrines and soak pits are used to dispose of domestic wastewater.

These are often relatively deep (more than 3 m) and discharge wastes below the soil and weathered zone layers that have the greatest capacity to filter, absorb and otherwise attenuate pollutant concentrations. The impact of urban wastewater discharges on groundwater is well illustrated by the cases of Santa Cruz, Bolivia, and Hat Yai, Thailand. In both these cities, direct discharge of untreated wastewater has led to substantial increases in pollutants (NO_3^-, NH_4^+, Cl^-, faecal coliforms, and dissolved organic carbon) in the shallow aquifers. The quality of deeper groundwater is still good but pollution fronts are moving downward in response to extraction from deeper levels for drinking-water supply and other uses. This situation is typical of many cities, particularly in rapidly urbanizing sections of the developing world.

Water supply officials tend to recognize the potential impact of waste discharge on chemical contamination of groundwater by nitrates and other compounds. However, it is often assumed that the filtering action of aquifers and relatively long residence times underground are sufficient to remove pathogens except where open or poorly sealed wells are contaminated directly by surface water inflows. This perception is inaccurate. "Bacteria can survive up to 50 days or more in subsurface environments and viruses for far longer." Overall, the pollution of shallow aquifers under cities represents a major threat to the sustainability of drinking-water supplies in many urban areas throughout the world. This threat is particularly high where regional hydrogeological conditionspermit rapid flow of contaminated water into aquifers and the wells tapping them.

For example, aquifers in karstic carbonate rocks or fracture zones are far more susceptible to contamination than aquifers where groundwater flows through porous media such as soil or sandstone. The threat is also particularly high where large portions of the urban population both dispose of untreated wastes directly through soakaways and latrine pits and also depend on shallow wells for drinking-water supply.

Industrial Pollutants

Public attention with regard to groundwater pollution often focuses on 'hot spots' where industrial activities have polluted large areas. Sites of this type often receive national attention. Jetpur, a textile town in Gujarat, India, where more than 1 200 small industrial units drain effluents containing cadmium, zinc, mercury, chromium and other pollutants into small rivers and thence into groundwater, is a prime example. Governmental monitoring and cleanup activities also tend to focus on high-profile sites. The 'superfund' sites in the United States of America and the activities of the state and central pollution control boards in India are typical of many governmental initiatives, particularly during early phases, when the significance of groundwater pollution is only beginning to be recognized. In India, the Central Pollution Control Board has a programme to monitor groundwater quality in 22 critically polluted sites. However, there is no baseline monitoring of potential industrial pollutants except within these hot spots.

The hot-spot focus of public attention and many government initiatives tends to downplay the importance of dispersed sources of industrial pollutants such as trace metals and organic solvents. Because of their low solubility, many such pollutants have extremely long residence times in aquifers. Because they do not dissolve rapidly, they can remain indefinitely as a concentrated source of pollution within an aquifer. In some cases, gradual volatilization of organic solvents in aquifers can become an air-quality hazard. Dispersed sources of industrial pollutants are much harder to identify, monitor and control than the effluent from specific factories or industrial areas. As such, these dispersed sources may well represent a greater threat to groundwater resources than concentrated industrial effluent flows. Data on groundwater pollution in developing countries are generally unavailable. This is particularly the case for pollution related to disperse sources such as mining activities, underground storage tanks and direct discharge of effluent to water bodies and watercourses.

However, with increases in transportation needs and industrial activities, the number of sites where pollution is occurring is increasing rapidly.

Implications of Groundwater Pollution

The full impacts of groundwater pollution on health, agriculture and the environment have not been assessed comprehensively. In the case of health impacts, the contribution made by contaminated groundwater to the global incidence of waterborne disease cannot be assessed easily; for many countries the incidence of waterborne disease is not known accurately and the data for groundwater usage are not available. Where public health statistics are available, the data are insufficient to determine the source of the water involved in the transmission of the disease." However, in comparison with other topics such as the environment, collection of public health data is widespread and relatively well established.

The difficulty of assessing the impact of groundwater changes on health (where at least some data are available) gives an indication of the magnitude of the challenge in assessing impacts on other values. Lack of information on the health and other costs associated with groundwater pollution and quality declines may lead to questions regarding the importance of these problems. While the dangers of pathogenic organisms are recognized, officials in developing-country situations often emphasize informally the lack of evidence that diseases, such as methoglobanemia, or responses to toxic substances are occurring in any but the most polluted areas. Based on this perception, they often advocate relaxation of standards. Part of this response may be due to the widespread incidence of many other health and disease problems, making diagnosis difficult. Part may also be because of priorities. Pollution control and aquifer remediation are expensive.

Ocean Pollution

Marine ecosystems, including oceans, estuaries, salt marshes, sea grass beds, coral reefs, kelp beds, and mangrove forests.

Coastal and estuarine ecosystems have been, and still are, heavily influenced by the human species through pollution and habitat loss throughout the world. This coastal pollution and its impacts have resulted in a number of environmental issues including the enrichment of enclosed waters with organic matter leading to eutrophication, pollution by chemicals such as oil, and sedimentation due to land-based activities or sea level rise due to the global change. Over 80 per cent of all marine pollution originates from land-based sources which are primarily industrial, agricultural and urban. Pollution accompanies most kinds of human activities, including offshore oil and gas production and marine oil transportation.

Types of Ocean Pollution:

1. Red tides
   - Storms bring nutrient-rich runoff to the oceans
   - These nutrients cause a bloom in phytoplankton in the oceans

A

B

Fig. 1.9: (A): Trash Pollutants; (B) Oil Spills Pollution

2. Trash

The most obvious type of pollution is physical. Physical pollution includes all of the solid, liquid, and dissolved materials that harm marine organisms or alter marine ecosystems. All of the substances that people use on land, release into the air, or take out onto the water can eventually be washed, precipitated, or spilled into the oceans. The most widespread and dangerous of these are trash, toxins, and oil.

Trash is deliberately dumped into the sea as well as blown or washed in from land. Some of this material quickly sinks to the bottom or breaks down rapidly. But much of it, particularly plastics, can drift through the ocean for miles and for years. Trash kills in many ways—animals that get tangled in trash, or lost fishing gear, are maimed, drowned, or strangled. Those that swallow debris choke or starve. Material that settles to the seafloor crushes and smothers bottom dwellers.

3. Oil

Oil spills have occurred in most of the shipping lanes in the world (as of 1985) Large effects on sea surface critters.

4. Sewer waste/runoff

Many countries of the world (inc. U.S.) dump their waste into ocean results in diseases, abnormalities in organisms.

Toxic materials – chemicals and heavy metals – attack organisms from the inside, causing disease, genetic mutations, birth defects, reproductive difficulties, behavioural changes, and death. Toxins flow into the ocean mainly from the runoff and discharge of industrial, agricultural, and human wastes into rivers that then empty into the sea. Many of the most dangerous toxins settle to the seafloor and then are taken in by organisms that live or feed on bottom sediments. Because these compounds aren't digested, they accumulate within animals that ingest them, and become more and more concentrated as they pass along the food chain. This process, called biomagnifications, means that higher-level predators—fish, birds, and marine mammals—are most severely affected.

Many toxins, like mercury, dioxins, PCBs, and radioactive isotopes, are clearly hazardous. But even otherwise beneficial compounds can act as dangerous pollutants at high enough levels. Nutrients such as phosphorus, nitrogen, and ammonia disrupt the balance of ecosystems when they are flushed from lawns and gardens and farms into the sea. The resultant bloom and then decay of algae and other plants can use up all the oxygen in shallow or slowly circulating waters and lead to the formation of "dead zones."

Oil spills combine the worst effects of trash and toxins. Some plants and animals smother quickly when coated with oil. Birds and marine mammals die of exposure when sodden feathers and fur lose their insulating abilities. Fish, reptiles and mammals erupt in skin and eye lesions and can develop serious infections and blindness. Animals that swallow or inhale oil can suffer organ damage, develop crippling and fatal diseases, and experience reproductive failure.

Nearly 1 billion gallons of oil are released into the oceans each year. Large spills from oil tankers are spectacular and garner much attention, but are responsible for only 5 per cent of all oil pollution. By far the largest source is motor oil. More than half of the oil that contaminates the sea each year is dumped a few quarts at a time into drains or dripped slowly onto roads and parking lots and then washed into sewers, rivers and finally the sea.

Effects of Aquatic Pollution on Fish and Fisheries

In recent years, the problem of marine environmental pollution with heavy metals (e.g. cadmium, lead, chromium, copper and zinc) has begun to raise a public attention especially in coastal areas. Dumping wastes into marine environments contribute to the larger problem of aquatic pollution, which can seriously damage the marine environment and cause health hazards to people in some areas.

Although several adverse health effects of heavy metals have been known for a long time, the exposure to these elements continues; moreover, it is even increasing in some parts of world, in particular in the less developed countries, though emissions have declined in most developed countries over the last 100 years (Jarup, 2003). Owing to their toxicity persistence and tendency to accumulate in water and sediment, heavy metals and metalloids, when occurring in higher concentrations, become severe poisons for all living organisms (Has-Schon et al., 2006).

Increased concentrations of metals; mainly mercury, cadmium and lead; have been observed in freshwater fish in open waters. This is important because the water metal concentration correlates positively with concentrations in fish tissue (Svobodova et al., 1996). The level of heavymetal bioaccumulation in fish tissues is influenced by biotic and abiotic factors, such as fish biological habitat, chemical form of metal in the water, water temperature and pH value, dissolved oxygen concentration,water transparency, aswell as by fish age, gender, body mass, and physiologic conditions (Has-Schon et al., 2006). After the catastrophe in Minamata, Japan, caused by fish consumption containing methyl mercury, the study of the effects of heavy metals present in fresh fish heavy metals in fresh fish as part of human diet is of particular interest.

Mercury

Mercury (Hg) is one of the most toxic heavy metals in our environment including the lithosphere, hydrosphere, atmosphere and biosphere (Fig. 1.11). A series of complex chemical transformations allows the three-oxidation states of Hg cycle in the environment (Barbosa et al., 2001).

Heavy Metals

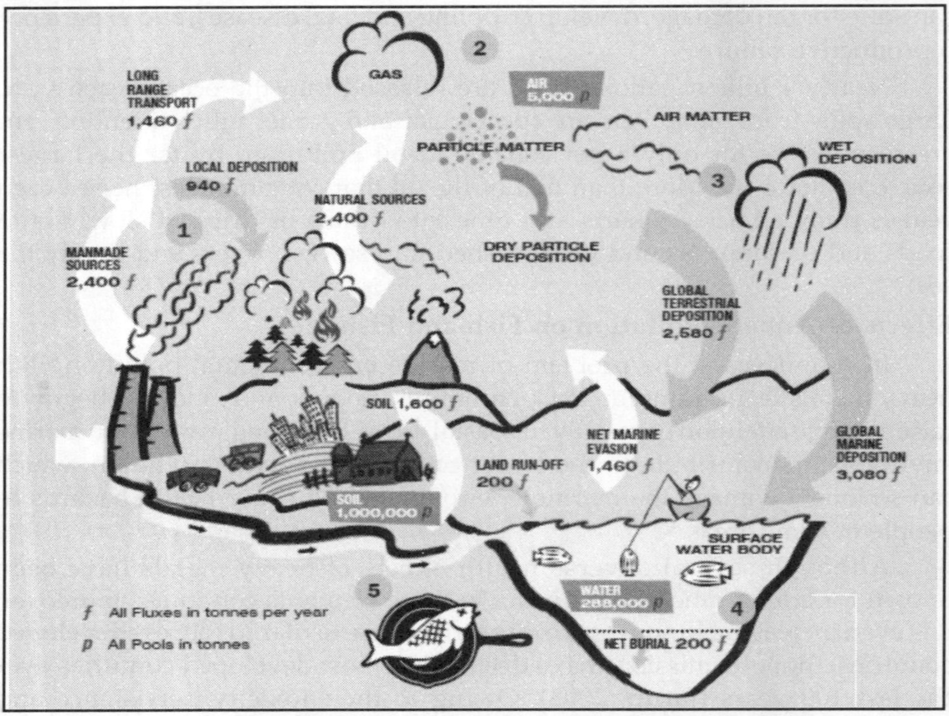

Fig. 1.10: The Sources of Heavy Metal Pollution

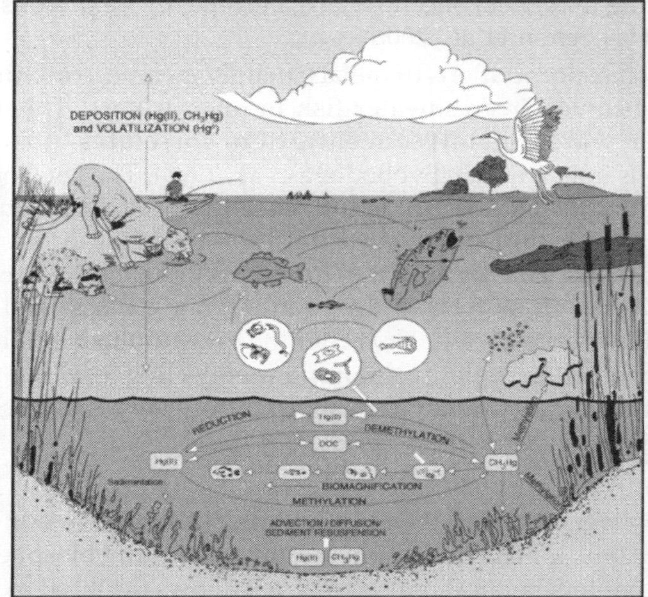

Fig. 1.11: Sources, Cycle and Impacts of Mercury Pollution

Natural and anthropogenic and re-emitted sources are the three major sources of Hg emissions, whereas the most important anthropogenic sources of Hg pollution in the environment are urban discharges, agricultural materials, mining and combustion and industrial discharges (Jackson, 1997; Zhang and Wong, 2007). The contamination chain of Hg follows, closely, the cyclic order: industry, atmosphere, soil,water, phytoplankton, zooplankton, fish and human (Kadar et al., 2000). The general population is most commonly exposed tomercury primarily fromtwo sources: *(i)* eating fish and marine mammals (e.g., whales, seals) that may contain somemethylmercury in their tissues or *(ii)* from the release of elemental mercury from the dental amalgam because it may dissolve in saliva and be ingested (Sallsten et al., 1996; ATSDR, 2003c); relative contribution of mercury fromthese twomain sources will vary considerably for different individuals (ATSDR, 2003c).

Cadmium

Cadmium is an industrial and environmental pollutant that affects adversely a number of organs in humans. Cadmium is a metal from group II B that has an atomic weight of 112.41; the ionic form of cadmium (Cd_2^+) is usually combinedwith ionic forms of oxygen (cadmium oxide, CdO_2), chlorine (cadmium chloride, $CdCl_2$), or sulfur (cadmium sulfate, $CdSO_4$). There are estimates that 30,000 tons of cadmium are released into the environment each year, with an estimated 4000-13,000 tons coming from human activities (ATSDR, 2003b). Natural aswell as anthropogenic sources of cadmium, whichinclude industrial emissions and the application of fertilizer and sewage sludge to farm land, increased cadmium environmental levels (ATSDR, 2003b). It has been established that, although cadmium occurs in the aquatic organism and marine environment only in trace concentrations, the salinity can affect the speciation of this metal, and bioaccumulation is affected both by temperature and salinity (Ray, 1986).

Lead

Lead (Pb) is one of the most ubiquitous and usefulmetals known to humans and it is detectable in practically all phases of the inert environment and in all biological systems. Environmental levels of lead have increased more than 1000-fold over the past three centuries as a result of human activity; the greatest increase occurred between the years 1950 and 2000 (ATSDR, 2005). Lead is a naturally occurring element; it is a member of Group 14 (IVA) of the periodic table, has an atomic weight of 207.2 and exists in three states: Pb (0), the metal; Pb (II); and Pb (IV). Lead is a blush-gray heavy metal and it is usually found combined with two or more other elements to form lead compounds (ATSDR, 2005). Lead reaches the aquatic system because of superficial soil erosion and atmospheric deposition. The concentration of lead in deep oceanwaters is about0.01–0.02_g/l, but in surface ocean waters is about 0.3_g/l (Sepe et al., 2003).

Arsenic

Arsenic, a naturally occurring element, is a worldwide contaminant that is found in rock, soil, water, air and food. Arsenic has a complex chemical structure and can be found in elemental, trivalent (+3 arsenite), and pentavalent (+5 arsenate) inorganic forms and trivalent and pentavalent organic forms. Organic arsenic is formed when arsenic ions are combined with carbon and hydrogen. Inorganic arsenic is present in groundwater, which is used for drinking in several countries all over the world; whereas organic arsenic compounds are primarily found in fish and shellfish (ATSDR, 2003a). Inorganic arsenic, the form found in soil and water, is classified by the Environmental Protection Agency (EPA) as a Group A human carcinogen (EPA, 1999; ATSDR, 2003a). High doses of organic arsenic can produce the same toxicological effects as a lower dose of inorganic arsenic (ATSDR, 2003a). Inorganic arsenic is released into the environment from a number of anthropogenic sources, which include geothermal discharges, industrial products and wastes, copper and lead smelters, and glass manufactures that add arsenic to raw materials (Goyer and Clarsksom, 2001). The use of arsenic compounds as herbicides, pesticides, and fungicides are other sources of environmental arsenic contamination.

Heavy metal pollution of the marine environment has long been recognized as a serious environmental concern. The presence of some heavy metals in aquatic environments and their accumulations in fish and in the other organisms has been investigated during recent years (Barbosa, Gutierrez-Galindo, & Flores-Munoz, 2000; Bassi & Sharma, 1993; Bei *et al.*, 1992; Freedman, 1989; Wolfe, 1974). Heavy metals are present in the aquatic environment where they bio accumulate along the food chain. Accumulation occurs in the tissues of aquatic animals and may become toxic for fish and also for people when it reaches a substantially high level. An early example of an environmental problem due to heavy metal occurred, starting in 1952, in the vicinity of the Japanese fishing harbor of Minimata. A hitherto unknown disease (Minimata disease) arose and grew rapidly into a real epidemic and was shown to be due to organomercury compounds (Vandecasteele & Block, 1991). Especially, since well-known instances where fishermen from Minimata Bay and villagers from Jintsu River died or became paralyzed from mercury and cadmium poisoning, respectively. For this reason, determination of chemical quality of aquatic organisms, particularly the contents of heavy metals is extremely important for human health (Cid *et al.*, 2001; Ravera, 1979; Dural *et al.*, 2007).

Contamination of marine sediments poses a potential threat to marine resources and human health, e.g. through consumption of seafood. Marine sediments are exposed to a wide range of potential contamination by chemicals that tend to sorb to fine-grained particles, such as heavy metals. Metal particles frequently bind with the sediments and do not easily dissolve or migrate with water.

Fishes are often at the top of the aquatic food chain and may concentrate large amounts of some metals from the water (Mansour & Sidky, 2002). Furthermore, fish is one of the most indicative factors in freshwater systems, for the estimation of trace metals pollution and risk potential of human consumption (Barak & Mason, 1990; Papagiannis *et al.*, 2004).

Shellfish, especially oyster and mussel, are used as biomonitor organisms worldwide because of their ubiquity, sessile way of life, filtering mode of feeding, and relatively long biological half-life of metals in their body (Cooper *et al.*, 1982; Presley *et al.*, 1990; Schuhmacher and Domingo, 1996; Cantillo, 1997, 1998; Reinfelder *et al.*, 1997; Beliaeff *et al.*, 1998; O'Connor, 1998; Geffard *et al.*, 2002; de Astudillo *et al.*, 2005; Saha *et al.*, 2006). Due to the well developed detoxification mechanisms these organisms tolerate much higher metal concentrations than the other living species, therefore in natural conditions a number of pathological effects of metals in these organisms is relatively small (Avery *et al.*, 1996; Rainbow, 1996; Geret *et al.*, 2002). Shellfish may contain higher level of these heavy metals than that found in the water and sediment in which they grow to a level that constitutes a public health hazard (Depierre and Ernster, 1987, De Gieter et al., 2002). Also, moullscus (bivalves) are frequently consumed raw or lightly cooked in addition to shellfish are consumed as a whole including all organs rather than just the muscle tissue as in case offish (Saleh, 2004).

Manufactured PCBs are mixtures of forms (congeners) of the PCB molecule that differ in their chlorine content. Different mixtures can take on forms ranging from oily liquids to waxy solids. Although their chemical properties vary widely, different mixtures have many common PCB congeners. Because of their flame retardant properties, chemical stability, and insulating properties, commercial PCB mixtures were used in many industrial applications. These chemical properties, however, also contribute to the persistence of PCBs after they are released into the environment In the environment, PCBs also occur as mixtures of congeners, but their composition differs from the commercial mixtures. This is because after release into the environment, the composition of PCB mixtures changes over time, through partitioning, chemical transformation and preferential bioaccumulation of certain congeners. Some PCB congeners can accumulate selectively in living organisms. PCBs are widespread in the environment because of past contaminations, and humans are exposed through multiple pathways: ambient air, drinking water, and diet. Consumption of contaminated fish was considered to be the dominant source of PCB exposure. Exposure through the food chain is associated with higher risks than other exposures. Specifically, preferential bioaccumulation through the food chain tends to concentrate certain highly chlorinated congeners which are often among the most toxic and persistent.

Dioxins are environmental pollutants. They have the dubious distinction of belonging to the "dirty dozen" - a group of dangerous chemicals known as persistent organic pollutants. Dioxins are of concern because of their highly toxic potential. Experiments have shown they affect a number of organs and systems. Once dioxins have entered the body, they endure a long time because of their chemical stability and their ability to be absorbed by fat tissue, where they are then stored in the body. Their half-life in the body is estimated to be seven to eleven years. In the environment, dioxins tend to accumulate in the food chain. The higher in the animal food chain one goes, the higher is the concentration of dioxins. The chemical name for dioxin is: 2, 3, 7, 8-tetrachlorodibenzo para dioxin (TCDD). The name 'dioxins' is often used for the family of structurally and chemically related polychlorinated dibenzo para dioxins (PCDDs) and polychlorinated dibenzofurans (PCDFs). Certain dioxin-like polychlorinated biphenyls (PCBs) with similar toxic properties are also included under the term "dioxins". Some 419 types of dioxin-related compounds have been identified but only about 30 of these are considered to have significant toxicity, with TC. Although formation of dioxins is local, environmental distribution is global. Dioxins are found throughout the world in practically all media. The highest levels of these compounds are found in some soils, sediments and food, especially dairy products, meat, fish and shellfish. Very low levels are found in plants, water and air. DD being the most toxic.

Persistent Organic Pollutants (POPs) Organochlorine pesticides (OCPs) are capable of persisting in the environment, transporting between phase media and accumulating to high levels, implying that they could pose a risk of causing adverse effects to human health and the environment. Consequently, most OCPs are designated as persistent organic pollutants (POPs) and even as endocrine disrupting chemicals (EDCs). POPs, including aldrin, chlordane, chlordecone, DDT, dieldrin, endrin, heptachlor, hexachlorobenzene, α/β-hexachlorocyclohexanes, lindane, mirex, pentachlorobenzene, and toxaphene.

CONCLUSION

Pollution prevention includes all measures and methods that aim to reduce and eliminate different forms of pollution that occur on our planet.

Preventing air pollution and water pollution as the two most important forms of pollution would require less fossil fuels burning, reduced industrial activity and use of clean technologies in correlation with adequate legislation all across the globe.

The global transition to renewable energy sources would greatly contribute to reduction and elimination of different pollutants from our environment because many common air and water pollutants have their origin in fossil fuel burning.

The lack of adequate education in many poor countries around the globe is making pollution prevention efforts much harder.

Even educated people need to develop so called „environmental conscience" because there are many people in developed countries who care very little for our environment and pollution issues.

The best examples of countries where pollution prevention efforts failed totally are China and India. The levels of air pollution in many Chinese cities are out of the control while in India there are many rivers experiencing extreme water pollution, even the holy river Ganges.

In United States there are also several cities where pollution prevention efforts have so far proved to be inadequate. For instance, the city of Los Angeles belongs to the areas with the most polluted air in the world.

Many countries have started introducing different educational programmes in order to explain to the people the seriousness of pollution issue on global level. In spite of these praiseworthy efforts pollution is still running out of control in many parts of the world. However there are many people who still believe that combating this problem through the education is the only solution.

The successful pollution prevention is a key to our future wellbeing. Each and every one of us can contribute to global pollution prevention by for instance stop littering and teach others to appreciate more our environment instead of taking it for granted.

REFERENCES

Agency for Toxic Substance and Disease Registry.(2003a). Toxicological Profile for Arsenic U.S. Department of Health and Humans Services, Public Health Service, Centres for Diseases Control, Atlanta, GA.

Agency for Toxic Substance and Disease Registry.(2003b). Toxicological Profile for Cadmium, U.S. Department of Health and Humans Services, Public Health Service, Centres for Diseases Control, Atlanta, GA.

Agency for Toxic Substance and Disease Registry (2005). Toxicological Profile for Lead, U.S. Department of Health and Humans Services, Public Health Service, Centres for Diseases Control, Atlanta, GA.

Agency for Toxic Substance and Disease Registry (2003c). Toxicological Profile for Mercury U.S. Department of Health and Humans Services, Public Health Service, Centres for Diseases Control, Atlanta, GA.

Avery, E.L.; Dunstan, R.H. and Nell, J.A. (1996). The Detection of Pollutant Impact in Marine Environments: Condition Index, Oxidative DNA Damage, and Their Associations with Metal Bioaccumulation in the Sydney Rock Oyster *Saccostrea commercialis*. Archives of Environmental Contamination and Toxicology, 31: 192-198.

Barak, N.A. E. and Mason, C.F. (1990). Mercury, Cadmium and Lead Concentrations in Five Species of Freshwater Fish from Eastern England. Science of the Total Environment, 92: 257-263.

Barbosa, A.M.; Gutierrez-Galindo, E. A. and Flores-Munoz, G. (2000). *Mytilus californianus* as an Indicator of Heavy Metals on the Northwest Coast of Baja California, Mexico. Marine Environmental Research, 49: 23-144.

Barbosa, A.C., Jardim, W., Dorea, J.G., Fosberg, B., Souza, J.(2001). Air Mercury Speciation as a Functioning of Gender, Age, and Body Mass Index in Habitants of the Negro River Basin, Amazon. Brazil. Arch. Environ. Contamin. Toxicol. 40, 439-444.

Bassi, R. and Sharma, S.S. (1993). Changes in Proline Content Accompanying the Uptake of Zinc and Copper by *Lemna minor*. Annals of Botany, 72: 151-154.

Bei, F.; Catsiki, V.A. and Papathanassiou, E. (1992). Copper and Cadmium Levels in Fish from the Greek Waters (Aegean and Ionian seas). Rapports de la Commission International pour la Merthe Caudal Peduncle and Méditerraneée, 33:167.

Beliaeff, B.; O'Connor, T.P. and Claisse, D. (1998). Comparison of Chemical Concentrations in Mussels from the United States and France. Environmental Monitoring and Assessment, 49: 87-95.

Cantillo, A.Y. (1997). World Mussel Watch Database. NOAA Tech. Memo. NOS ORCA 109. NOAA/NOS/ORCA, Silver Spring, MD, 197 pp.

Cantillo, A.Y. (1998). Comparison of Results of Mussel Watch Programmes of the United States and France with Worldwide Mussel Watch Studies. Marine Pollution Bulletin, 36: 712-717.

Castro-González, M.I. and Méndez-Armenta, M. (2008). Heavy Metals: Implications Associated to Fish Consumption. Environmental Toxicology and Pharmacology, 26: 263-271.

Cid, B.P.; Boia, C.; Pombo, L. and Rebelo, E. (2001). Determination of Trace Metals in Fish Species of the Ria de Aveiro (Portugal) by Electrothermal Atomic Absorption Spectrometry. Food Chemistry, 75: 93-100.

Cooper, R.J.; Langlois, D. and Olley, J. (1982). Heavy Metals in Tasmanian Shellfish. Journal of Applied Toxicology, 2: 99-109.

de Astudillo, L.R.; Yen, I.C. and Berkele, I. (2005). Heavy Metals in Sediments, Mussels and Oysters from Trinidad and Venezuela. Revista de Biologia Tropical, 53: 41-53.

Dural, M.; Ziya Lugal Göksu, M. and Özak, A.A. (2007). Investigation of Heavy Metal Levels in Economically Important Fish Species Captured from the Tuzla Lagoon. Food Chemistry, 102: 415-421.

Freedman, B. (1989). Environmental Ecology. The Impacts of Pollution and Other Stresses on Ecosystem Structure and Function. London: Academic Press.

Geffard, A.; Amiard, J.C. and Amiard-Triquet, C. (2002). Use of Metallothionein in Gills from Oysters (*Crassostrea gigas*) as a Biomarker: Seasonal and Intersite Fluctuations. Biomarkers, 7: 123-137.

Geret, F.; Jouan, A.; Turpin, V.; Bebianno, M.J. and Cosson, R.P. (2002). Influence of Metal Exposure on Metallothionein Synthesis and Lipid Peroxidation in Two Bivalve Mollusks: the Oyster (*Crassostrea gigas*) and the Mussel (*Mytilus edulis*). Aquatic Living Resources, 15: 61-66.

Goyer, R.A., Clarsksom, W.T.(2001). Toxic Effects of Metals. In: Klaassen, C.D. (Ed.), Casarett and Doull's Toxicology. The Basic Science of Poisons. McGraw-Hill, New York, pp. 811-867.

Has-Schon, E., Bogut, I., Strelec, I.(2006). Heavy Metal Profile in Five Fish Species included in Human Diet, Domiciled in the End Flow of River Neretva (Croatia). Arch. Environ. Contam. Toxicol. 50, 545-551.

Jackson, T.A.(1997). Long-range Atmospheric Transport of Mercury to Ecosystems, and the Importance of Anthropogenic Emissions—A Critical Review and Evaluation of the Published Evidence. Environ. Rev. 5, 99-120.

Jarup, L.(2003). Hazards of Heavy Metal Contamination. Brit. Med. Bull. 68, 167-182.

Jarvinen, R., Knekt, P., Rissanen, H., Reunanen, A. (2006). Intake of Fish and Long-chain $n^{-}3$ Fatty Cids and the Risk of Cornary Herat Mortality in Men and Women. Br. J. Nutr. 95, 229-824.

Jarvinen, A.W. and Ankley, G.T. (1999). Linkage of Effects to Tissue Residues: Development of a Comprehensive Database for Aquatic Organisms Exposed to Inorganic and Organic Chemicals. SETAC Press. Pensacola, Florida, pp.: 1-358.

Kadar, I., Koncz, J., Fekete, S., (2000). Experimental Study of Cd, Hg, Mo, Pb and Se Movement in Soil-plant-animal Systems. In: Kniva, International Conference Proceedings, Patija, Croatia, pp. 72-76.

Kingsford, M.J. and Gray, C.A. (1996). Influence of Pollutants and Oceanography on Abundance and Deformities of Wild Fish Larvae. Detecting Ecological Impacts: Concepts and Applications in Coastal Habitats. Academic Press, San Diego, California.

Mansour, S.A. and Sidky, M. M. (2002). Ecotoxicological Studies: 3. Heavy Metals Contaminating Water and Fish from Fayoum Governorate, Egypt. Food Chemistry, 78: 15-22.

O'Connor, T.P. (1998). Mussel Watch Results from 1986 to 1996. Marine Pollution Bulletin, 37: 14-19.

Papagiannis, I.; Kagalou, I.; Leonardos, J.; Petridis, D. and Kalfakakou, V. (2004). Copper and Zinc in Four Freshwater Fish Species from Lake Pamvotis (Greece). Environ. Int., 30: 357-362.

Presley, B.J.; Taylor, R.J. and Boothe, P.N. (1990). Trace Metals in Gulf of Mexico Oysters. The Science of the Total Environment, 97/98: 551-593.

Rainbow, P.S. (1996). Heavy Metals in Aquatic Invertebrates. In: Beyer, W.N.; Heinz, G.H. and Redmon-Norwood, A.W. (eds.): Environmental Contaminants in Wildlife. Lewis Publishers, pp.: 405-419.

Rao, L.M. and Padmaja, G. (2000). Bioaccumulation of Heavy Metals in *M. cyprinoids* from the Harbor Waters of Visakhapatnam. Bulletin of Pure and Applied Science, 19(2): 77-85.

Ravera, O. (1979). Biological Aspects of Freshwater Pollution. New York: Pergamon press, pp.: 129-165.

Ray, S.(1986). Bioaccumulation of Cadmium in Marine Organisms. Experientia 50(Suppl.), 65-75.

Reinfelder, R.; Wang, W.X.; Luoma, S.N. and Fisher, N.S. (1997). Assimilation Efficiencies and Turnover Rates of Trace Elements in Marine Bivalves: A Comparison of Oysters, Clams and Mussels. Marine Biology, 129: 443-452.

Saha, M.; Sarkar, S.K. and Bhattacharya, B. (2006). Interspecific Variation in Heavy Metal Body Concentrations in Biota of Sunderban Mangrove Wetland, Northeast India. Environment International, 32: 203-207.

Saleh, E.A. (2004). Monitoring of Some Heavy Metals in Shellfish. Alex. J. Vet. Science, 21(1): 314-324.

Sallsten, G., Thoren, J., Barregard, L., Schutz, A., Skarping, G.(1996). Long-term use Nicotine Chewing Gum and Mercury Exposure from Dental Amalgam Fillings. J.Dent. Res. 75, 594-598.

Schuhmacher, M. and Domingo, J.L. (1996). Concentrations of Selected Elements in Oysters (*Crassostrea angulata*) from the Spanish Coast. Bulletin of Environmental Contamination and Toxicology, 56: 106-113.

Sepe, A.; Ciaralli, L.; Ciprotti, M.; Giordano, R.; Fumari, E. and Costantini, S. (2003). Determination of Cadmium, Chromium, Lead and Vanadium in Six Fish Species from the Adriatic Sea. Food Addit. Contam., 20: 543-552.

Svobodova, Z., Beklova, M., Machala, M., Drabeck, P., Dvorakova, D., Kolarova, J., Mar¡salek, B., Modra, H.(1996). Evaluation of the Effect of Chemical Substances, Preparation, Wastes and Waste Waters to Organisms in the Aquatic Environment. Bull. VURH Vodnany 32, 76-96.

Vandecasteele, C. and Block, C. B. (1991). Modern Methods for Trace Element Determination. New York: John Wiley & Sons Inc., pp.: 259.

Wolfe, D. A. (1974). Pollution and Physiology of Marine Organisms. London: Academic Press, pp.: 492.

CHAPTER – 2

Conservation and Management of Coral Reef Ecosystem in India

G.G. Phadke, *India*; D.K. Meena, *India*; A.K. Sahoo, *India*
B.K. Behera, *India*; S.V.K. Reddy, *India*; A.M. Reddy, *India*

ABSTRACT

Coral reefs are among the world's richest ecosystems, second only to tropical rain forests in plant and animal diversity. The major reef formations in India are restricted to the Gulf of Mannar, Palk bay, Gulf of Kutch, Andaman and Nicobar Islands and the Lakshadweep islands. While the Lakshadweep reefs are atolls, the others are all fringing reefs. Patchy coral is present in the inter-tidal areas of the central west coast of the country. Coral reefs in India are being damaged and destroyed at an increasing rate. They face serious problems of stress from anthropogenic pressures and interference. However we cannot be precise about how much and where, because of special difficulties of monitoring underwater.

The Reef condition is generally poor and declining in near shore waters and areas of high population density. Relatively pristine reefs are located around uninhabited islands or barrier type reefs located away from population centers. Sedimentation, dredging and coral mining are damaging near shore reefs, while the use of explosives and bottom nets in fishing are damaging offshore reefs in specific sites. Although institutions and laws are sufficient in theory to manage and protect the reefs in India, authorities in the field have taken little effective action in implementing these laws.

Key words: Atolls, Coral, Coelenterata, Anthozoa, SCUBA diving, Zooxanthellae.

INTRODUCTION

Corals themselves are tiny animals which belong to the group cnidaria (the "c" is silent). Comprising over 6,000 known species, anthozoans also include sea fans, sea pansies and anemones. Stony corals (scleractinians) make up the largest order of anthozoans, and are the group primarily responsible for laying the foundations of, and building up, reef structures. For the most part, scleractinians are colonial organisms composed of hundreds to hundreds of thousands of individuals, called polyps. Other cnidarians include hydras, jellyfish, and sea anemones. Corals are sessile animals, meaning they are not mobile but stay fixed in one place. They feed by reaching out with tentacles to catch prey such as small fish and planktonic animals. Coral reefs provide habitats for a large variety of organisms. These organisms rely on corals as a source of food and shelter.

Besides the corals themselves and their symbiotic algae, other creatures that call coral reefs home include various sponges; molluscs such as sea slugs, nudibranchs, oysters, and clams; crustaceans like crabs and shrimp; many kinds of sea worms; echinoderms like star fish and sea urchins; other cnidarians such as jellyfish and sea anemones; various types of fungi; sea turtles; and many species of fish. Coral Reefs are shallow water tropical marine ecosystems characterized by remarkably high biomass production and a rich faunal and floral biodiversity. The structure of a reef is formed by calcareous skeleton which houses the coral, a type of soft bodied radially symmetrically marine invertebrate belonging to phylum Coelenterata.

Coral reef system as also the ecosystem of the tropical rain forest, are the most matured marine ecosystems of our planet. The coral reefs characterize an ecosystem of high biological diversity, having the greatest number of species of any marine ecosystem. Livelihood of many millions of people is dependent on this unique ecosystem as a considerable proportion of their food and earning from the productivity of coral reef. Coral reefs are considered as one of the most important critical resources for various ecological, environmental and socio-economic reasons. They play an important role in global biochemical processes and in the reproduction of food resources in the tropical regions. The people living along the coast obtain a considerable proportion of their food and earnings from the productivity of coral reefs.

Coral reefs act as a barrier against wave action along coastal areas thus preventing coastal erosion. In addition, coral reefs protect mangroves and sea grass beds in certain areas, which are the breeding and nursing grounds of various economically important fauna. Coral reefs are also important breeding, spawning, nesting, and feeding areas for many economically important varieties of fishes and other marine organisms.

CORAL REEFS IN INDIA

Corals belong to the phylum Anthozoa and they are objects of beauty and utility. The hermatypic corals with their symbiotic zoothanllae build the mighty reefs beneath the waves that are exposed only at low tides. Corals are exclusively marine and taxonomically belong to the order scleratinia. They are both solitary and colonial, the solitary forms are called ahermatypes and they do not have symbionts. Reef building corals grow actively in the photic zone of the ocean. Coral reefs are found in the tropical waters as a belt around the globe. Coral reefs are distributed in the world in some restricted places only. These are not found everywhere in the world, even these are not found anywhere and everywhere in the India. The coral reefs of the Indian Ocean have been built up during the tertiary and quaternary periods. The coral reef ecosystems are restricted in the main seven regions in India:

1. Coral reef ecosystem in Kerala coast.
2. Coral reef ecosystem in Goa coast.
3. Coral reef ecosystem in Gulf of Kutch.
4. Coral reef ecosystem in Lakshadweep Islands.
5. Coral reef ecosystem in Gulf of Mannar.
6. Coral reef ecosystem in Palk Bay.
7. Coral reef ecosystem in Andaman and Nicobar Islands.

Among the coral reefs of India, fringing reefs are found in the Gulf of Mannar and Palk bay, Platform reefs are found along the Gulf of Kutch, Atoll reefs are found in the Lakshadweep archipelago, Patchy reefs are found near Ratnagiri and Malwan coasts, Fringing and barrier reefs both are found in Andaman and Nicobar islands. Remote sensing technology shows the extent of reef flat in Gujarat coast as 148.4 sq km, that of Tamil Nadu coast as 64.9 sq km, Lakshadweep 140.1 sq km and that of Andaman and Nicobar Islands as 813.2 sq km. In addition to that coraj knolls and lagoon reefs also form roughly 50 sq. km of reef formations.

BIODIVERSITY OF CORAL REEFS IN INDIA IN BRIEF

India has a coast line of nearly 8000 km but the reef formation is restricted to four major centres, viz. Gulf of kutchh. Gulf of Mannar, Lakshadweep and Andaman and Nicobar Islands. Lakshadweep is exclusively atolls but others have fringing reefs or patch reefs. Barrier reefs are found in Andamans. Additionally the Malvan area and Kanyakumari district of Tamil nadu have patchy reefs. The vast stretch of Bay of Bengal except for Andaman and Nicobar Islands is devoid of any coral formation. Estimation of reef flats of Indian reefs by remote sensing has shown that the extent of the area in Gulf of Kutchh is 148.4 km^2 that of Tamil Nadu coast as 64.9 km^2. Lakshadweep 140.1 km^2 and that of Andaman and Nicobar Islands 813.2 km^2. Additionally knolls and lagoon reefs from roughly 50 km^2.

The composition of coral reef is really interesting rather unique, and it includes near about 185 species of benthic algae, 15 species of sea grass, 15 species of sea weeds, 110 species of poriferas, 6 species of crustaceans, 105 species of echinoderms, 599 species of bony fishes, and additionally, different species of crabs, bivalves, gastropods, cephalopods, in Indian coral reef ecosystems. Coral reefs are hard limestone structures built up by the cementing process and depositional activities of the class Anthozoa, scyphozoan, and Hydrozoa, and also the calcifying algae. In some areas of coral reef in India, rich algal diversity is seen such as *Sargassum*, *Ulva*, *Cladophora* etc.

A rich biodiversity of 70 species of sponges, 27 species of prawns, 200 species of molluscs, 3 species of marine mammals has also been recorded. Both stony and soft corals are present in the sub-tidal regions of the reefs. The genera of stony corals found in the Indian reefs are *Favia, Favites, Goniopora, Montipora, Sinularia* etc. The genera of soft corals found are *Nephthya, Dendronephthya* etc. The different Indian coral reefs contain about 23 species of ammonifying bacteria, 15 species of nitrifying bacteria, 3 species of nitrogen fixing bacteria, 23 species of phosphate producing bacteria etc. About 50 species of diatoms out of 55 species of phytoplankton were found in the Gulf of Mannar and other different reefs of India. In Lakshadweep islands about 20 groups of Polychaete worms, and different types of Nematodes were found.

CONDITIONS NECESSARY FOR THE CORAL REEF FORMATION

Coral animals are well adaptive in warm, shallow, well illuminated and well oxygenated aquatic bodies. These conditions are found in tropical and subtropical seas. Thus the reef building corals remain quite restricted in their distribution.

Coral reefs extend over an area of 68 million square miles in tropical and subtropical seas. They are best developed where the mean annual temperature of the water lies within the range of 23°C to 25°C, they do not develop to any significant extent in the regions where temperature fall below 18°C. Ample amount of oxygen supply is very important. Another important factor for coral reef formation is the intensity of surface illumination of radiant energy.

Types of coral reefs mainly found in India

1. **Fringing reefs:** This type of reef lies much closer to the shore of mainland; this may be either an island or a stretch of continental coast line. But in either case the intervening water constitute only a narrow channel i.e. Lagoon. These types of reefs have an edge, the reef front, where the most effective coral growth occurs.
2. **Barrier reefs:** There are also reefs similar to fringing reefs but are separated from the mainland by a narrow strip of sea perhaps upto 1000 ft. deep, which is not much less than greater depth obtained by the lagoons. The greater barrier reef in Australia is the best known example outside the India.

3. **Atolls:** These are mainly oceanic and without association with land. They consist of low reef rising no more than 30 ft. above the sea level and enclosing a central area of water called lagoon.
4. **Platform reefs:** These are flat reefs without lagoon. They rest on the shallower part of the continental shelves, they may appear between the coast and the barrier reefs or they may be associated with atolls.

SOCIAL AND ECONOMIC VALUE OF CORAL REEFS

Coral reefs rank as the most biologically productive and diverse of all natural ecosystems . Reefs are equivalent to tropical rain forests for their rich biological diversity. A large number of reef building and reef dwelling organisms live on reefs that are objects of beauty. The value of coral reefs to mankind are both extractive and non-extractive. The non-extractive uses of the tropical reefs centres around recreation, tourism, scientific research, shoreline protection and SCUBA diving. The extractive uses are very many, only if judiciously exploited. Coral reefs are huge mounts of Calcium carbonate which forms the raw material for many lime based industries, such as lime, cement, calcium carbide. They are also used as building blocks in many parts of the Indo-Pacific. The fin fish fauna of reefs is extremely rich and varied.

The estimated fish production from the global reef environs varies from 6 to 9 million tonnes per equivalent to about 10 per cent of the marine fish exploited annually. The potential fish yield from the reefs of India is provisionally estimated to the tune of 0.18-0.27 × 10* tonnes yr.' The diversity of fish fauna on the reefs varies in space and time. The total number of species of fishes from Lakshadweep reefs and surroundings is bout 600. Approximately 600 species of fishes are known from Andaman and Nicobar waters . The shellfish resources of the reef is constituted by at-least four species of lobsters and many species of crabs. The common species of lobster on the reef flats of Lakshadweep is *Pamilirus versicolar*.

Among the crabs, *Scylla serrata, Portuniis pelagicus, P. sangtiinolentiis* and *Otarribdes* spp. are commercially caught from reef environs. The moUuscan resources of our reefs are rich and varied. *Trochus niloticus* and *Turbo mawtoratiis* are costly gastropods of commercial value from Andaman reefs. Many species of cowries are fished from our reefs. The giant clam *Tridacna* is fairly common in Andaman and Nicobar and Lakshadweep. There exists potential scope of this mollusc in reef mariculture. *Octopus* and cuttle fishes are also fished from the reefs. There exists vast resources of reef fishes that are of ornamental value on reefs.

The surgeon fishes, parrot fishes, damsel fishes, the soldier fishes and cardinal fishes are of great demand as aquarium samples and there is vast scope of their live export. The reef associated fishes of the group clupids and apogonids form the live-bait along with pomacentrids both in Lakshadweep and Andaman Nicorbar Islands. A large resource *Spratelloides delicatiiliis* was located by the scientist of CMFRI in the marine park of Wandoor . especially along the near shore waters fringed by mangroves. The traditional pole and line fishery for tunas in Lakshadweep solely depends on tlie availability of these fishes on the coral reefs on Lakshadweep.

The echinoderm resources of the reef environs is of significant economic value. The holothurians that irxhabit the lagoon and reefs are processed as *beche-de-mer.* Fishery for them exists in S.E. India and Lakshadweep. The benthic algae of the reefs are rich and varied. Atleast 180 species divided among 99 genera of benthic algae are reported from the southeast coast of . Altogether, 62 genera and 114 species of seaweeds are recorded from the 12 islands from Lakshadweep, of which 18 genera and 43 species belong to chlorophyceae, 14 species divided among 11 genera belong to phaeopaycea and 54 species of 30 genera are of rhodophycea. The total number of sea grass species was estimated to. In addition to these the reefs harbour a rich marine biological diversity of sponges, coelenterates, worms, molluscs, echinoderms etc. that are of great pharmacological value. The biodiversity of reefs associated flora and fauna of Andaman and Nicobar Islands still remains to be studied.

DEGRADATION OF CORAL REEFS

The degradation of coral reefs is severe due to the human stress and also by natural agents. The coral mining for lime, sand mining, pollution, sedimentation, fisheries, population pressure, commercial shell collection and industrial development has led to the increase in coral reef degradation in India.

Coral reef ecosystems are very sensitive to external impacts both natural and manmade, which violate their homeostasis. The majority of damage to coral reefs around the world has been through direct anthropogenic stress. 57 per cent of the world's coral reefs are potentially threatened by human activity such as coastal development, destructive fishing, over exploitation, marine pollution, runoff from deforestation and toxic discharge from industrial and agricultural chemicals. As a result of the increasing human population along the coastal area, anthropogenic impacts on the coastal zone have become severe over the past few decades.

1. Anthropogenic Stresses

Increase in human population and economic activities in the area have increased the pressure on the adjacent reefs. The major causes of coral reef degradation includes; over fishing and destructive fishing practices, sea weed collection, commercial shell collection, coral mining, poor land use practices, coastal urban development, harbour and dredging activities, industrial development and pollution. Corals and coral reefs all over the tropical waters are under stress due to various anthropogenic and natural interventions.

OVER FISHING AND DESTRUCTIVE FISHING PRACTICES

Fishery is the primary economic activity of the people of the coast. However practices such as use of explosives to capture fish, diving for collecting holothurians, anchoring of vessels on reef areas, dredging and trawling are destructive in nature and cause direct damage to the corals and indirectly affect their growth by increasing turbidity and suspended sediment in the coastal waters and reducing the clarity of seawater and increasing sediment loads on reefs. Unfortunately, some current fishing practices are destructive and unsustainable. These include cyanide fishing, overfishing and blast fishing.

Although cyanide fishing supplies live reef fish for the tropical aquarium market, most fish caught using this method are sold in restaurants, primarily in Asia, where live fish are prized for their freshness. To catch fish with cyanide, fishers dive down to the reef and squirt cyanide in coral crevices and on the fast-moving fish, to stun the fish making them easy to catch. Although some large tropical fish can metabolize cyanide, smaller fish and other marine animals, such as coral polyps, are poisoned by the chemical cloud produced during this process.

Overfishing is another leading cause for coral reef degradation. Often, too many fish are taken from one reef to sustain a population in that area. Poor fishing practices, such as banging on the reef with sticks (muro-ami), destroy coral formations that normally function as fish habitat. In some instances, people fish with explosives (blast fishing), which blast apart the surrounding coral.

SEAWEED COLLECTION

Seaweeds form one of the most important marine living resources. Because of their commercial value, the seaweeds are harvested by fishermen for agar industry. Over exploitation of seaweeds in localized areas may lead to coastal erosion and removal of the coral reefs.

COMMERCIAL SHELL COLLECTION

Commercial shell collection is another human activity which causes coral reef degradation to some extent. Increased human activities increases turbidity in coastal water leading to the death of coral.

CORAL MINING

Coral mining activity is one of the major human activities which have caused extensive degradation of reefs through coastal erosion and sedimentation in a number of countries all over the world. Coral reefs are used on a large scale as raw material by the lime industries. Mining also destroys coral. Sometimes coral pieces are removed for use as bricks or road-fill. Or, sand and limestone from coral reefs are made into cement for new buildings. But corals aren't only removed from their habitat for construction;

they are also sold as souvenirs. Coral curios and jewelery are often sold to tourists and exporters in the markets of developing countries. The use of explosives for reef mining pose serious problems to the coastal and marine ecosystems like erosion and sedimentation, coral reef degradation and reduction of marine faunal population.

POOR LAND USE PRACTICES

Another cause for the damage of coral reefs is poor land use practices, such as agricultural activities, changing land use practices and deforestation etc, which increases land derived sediment flowing onto coral reef. The poor agricultural practices increase the agriculture waste like pesticides and fertilizers, which are dumped into the coastal water through surface runoff during rainy season and through rivers. This encourages rapid algal growth, which chokes coral polyps and cut off the supply of light and oxygen.

COASTAL URBAN DEVELOPMENT

Increasing urban population along the coastal area has lead to pollution due to sewage discharge into the coastal waters. Discharge of sewage is responsible also for the loss of coral reefs in large quantities. As a result of this rapid urbanization there is an increase in the amount of discharge of sewage waste into coastal waters, which cause the death of corals.

HARBOUR AND DREDGING ACTIVITIES

Dredging and other harbour related activities like anchoring and ship grounding have increased sedimentation in the coastal waters and caused the degradation of coral reefs. Dredging and other harbour related activities like anchoring and ship grounding have increased sedimentation in the coastal waters and caused the degradation of coral reefs. In the study area the New Tuticorin harbour has been constructed at the upstream side of the Tuticorin group of island. This harbour has a breakwater, which has changed the current flow pattern and sediment movement along the Tuticorin coast and islands. The periodic dredging operations at the entrance of the harbour and anchoring of ships have increased the amount of silt plume, which in turn has increased water turbidity, and lowered the light intensity, leading to coral death. This problem has been extensively observed in Tuticorin group of islands.

INDUSTRIAL DEVELOPMENT AND POLLUTION

Industrial development and their waste discharge into coastal water affect the coral reefs. The industrial development has led to marine pollution and coral reef degradation. Industrial development and their waste discharge into coastal water affect the coral reefs. The coast of Gulf of Mannar is experiencing an accelerated growth in the rate of industrialization, since the New Tuticorin port became operational. The industrial development has led to marine pollution and coral reef degradation. The dumping of fly ash slurry into Karapad Bay by the Thermal power station resulted not only in filling up of an extensive portion of the bay, but also letting out of ash directly in to the sea causing extensive damage to the coral reef. Effluents discharged from industries contain mercury, sodium carbonate, ammonium chloride and sodium bicarbonate etc. which are harmful to the coral reefs and the environment.

OCEAN ACIDIFICATION

"Since the beginning of the Industrial Revolution, the release of carbon dioxide (CO_2) from human activities has resulted in atmospheric CO_2 concentrations that have increased from approximately 280 to 385 parts per million (ppm). The atmospheric concentration of CO_2 is now higher than experienced on Earth for at least the last 800,000 years and probably over 20 million years, and is expected to continue to rise at an increasing rate, leading to significant temperature increases in the atmosphere and oceans in the coming decades.

"The oceans have absorbed approximately 525 billion tons of carbon dioxide from the atmosphere, or about one third of the anthropogenic carbon emissions released. This absorption has benefited humankind by significantly reducing the greenhouse gas levels in the atmosphere and minimizing some of the impacts of global warming. However, the ocean's uptake of carbon dioxide is having negative impacts on the chemistry and biology of the oceans. Hydrographic surveys and modeling studies have revealed that the chemical changes in seawater resulting from the absorption of carbon dioxide are lowering seawater pH.

The pH of ocean surface waters has already decreased by about 0.1 units from an average of about 8.21 to 8.10 since the beginning of the Industrial Revolution. Estimates of future atmospheric and oceanic carbon dioxide concentrations, based on the Intergovernmental Panel on Climate Change (IPCC) CO_2 emission scenarios and coupled ocean-atmosphere models, suggest that by the middle of this century atmospheric carbon dioxide levels could reach more than 500 ppm, and near the end of the century they could be over 800 ppm. This would result in an additional surface water pH decrease of approximately 0.3 pH units by 2100.

"When CO_2 reacts with seawater, the reduction in seawater pH also reduces the availability of carbonate ions, which play an important role in shell formation for a number of marine organisms such as corals, marine plankton, and shellfish. This phenomenon, which is commonly called "ocean acidification," could have profound impacts on some of the most fundamental biological and geochemical processes of the sea in coming decades. Some of the smaller calcifying organisms are important food sources for higher marine organisms. Declining coral reefs due to increases in temperature and decreases in carbonate ion would have negative impacts on tourism and fisheries. Abundance of commercially important shellfish species may also decline and negative impacts on finfish may occur. This rapidly emerging scientific issue and possible ecological impacts have raised serious concerns across the scientific and fisheries resource management communities." (Quoted from NOAA's Pacific Marine Environmental Laboratory Carbon Dioxide Programme)

OCEAN WARMING AND CORAL BLEACHING

Global warming is caused by the accumulation of carbon dioxide and other heat-trapping gasses in the atmosphere. These gases act as a blanket, preventing the heat of the sun to escape through our atmosphere. This is primarily due to fossil fuel burning and deforestation and many scientists believe that this is causing sea surface temperatures to rise. Ocean warming is extremely dangerous to coral organisms, which are very sensitive to changes in temperature.

Increased water temperatures, which may be linked to global warming, can cause mass coral bleaching. This occurs when coral polyps, stressed by heat or ultraviolet radiation, expel the algae that live within them. These algae, called zooxanthellae (zo-zan-THEL-ee) normally provide the coral with up to 80 per cent of its energy, making zooxanthellae essential for coral survival. The algae are also normally responsible for the colour of coral, so when they are expelled, the coral appears white or "bleached." There is a chance that bleached coral can recover if conditions return to normal quickly enough. However, in the face of other human-induced pressures, corals have become vulnerable. In many cases, bleached coral colonies die.

CARBON DIOXIDE

In the past few decades, the amount of carbon dioxide in the air has increased by one-third. This is harmful to corals because increased amounts of carbon dioxide are dissolving into the water, which appears to be dissolving the skeletons of corals. As a result, coral in waters with large amounts of carbon dioxide form weaker skeletons, making them more vulnerable to damage from waves, careless tourists, and destructive fishers.

WATER POLLUTION

Scientists have identified pollution as one of the leading causes of coral reef degradation. This threat comes from a variety of sources. For example, oil, gas and pesticide contamination poisons coral and marine life. Reefs are harmed when human, animal waste and/or fertilizer is dumped into the ocean or when river systems carry these pollutants to reef waters. These pollutants increase the level of nitrogen around coral reefs, causing an overgrowth of algae, which smothers reefs by cutting off their sunlight. Trash also kills coral reef animals. Floating trash can cover reefs, blocking off sunlight that polyps need to survive. Turtles often mistake plastic bags for jellyfish and eat them. Plastic blocks the turtle's digestive tract, causing them to starve to death. Lost or discarded fishing nets - called "ghost nets" - can snag on reefs and strangle thousands of fish, sea turtles and marine mammals.

SEDIMENTATION

Construction along coasts, inshore construction, mining, logging and farming along coastal rivers can all lead to erosion. As a result, particles end up in the ocean and cover coral reefs. This 'smothers' coral and deprives it of the light it needs to survive. Mangrove trees and seagrasses, which normally act as filters for sediment, are also being rapidly destroyed. This has led to an increase in the amount of sediment reaching coral reefs. Mangrove forests are often cut for firewood or removed to create open beaches. They are also destroyed by prawn harvesters to open up areas to create artificial prawn farms.

COASTAL DEVELOPMENT

Coastal populations have risen, increasing the pressures on coastal resources. This has led to a multitude of problems for coral reefs. In many areas, developers have constructed piers and other structures directly on top of coral reefs. At one time, big cities such as Hong Kong, Singapore, Manila and Honolulu had thriving coral reefs. Long ago, these reefs were destroyed by human pressures. Now, reefs growing near other coastal communities are experiencing the same coral degradation.

CARELESS TOURISM

Tourist resorts that empty their sewage directly into the water surrounding coral reefs contribute to coral reef degradation. Wastes kept in poorly maintained septic tanks can also leak into surrounding ground water, eventually seeping out to the reefs. Careless boating, diving, snorkeling and fishing can also damage coral reefs. Whenever people grab, kick, walk on, or stir up sediment in the reefs, they contribute to coral reef destruction. Corals are also harmed or killed when people drop anchors on them or when people collect coral.

OZONE DEPLETION

The destruction of the ozone layer, which accompanies global warming, is caused by the presence of chlorofluorocarbons (CFCs) and other chemicals in the atmosphere. This presence causes the depletion of protective ozone in the atmosphere and increases the intensity and nature of ultraviolet radiation that reaches the earth's surface. Although corals have a natural sunscreen to protect themselves from the tropical sun, most scientists believe that increased levels of ultraviolet radiation damage coral in shallow areas.

2. Natural Stress

Natural problems are those that are not caused by man, but occur naturally over the long history. Natural problems such as storms, waves, sea level variation, fresh water runoff, volcanic activity etc cause the degradation of coral reefs. Corals and coral reefs all over the tropical waters are under stress due to various anthropogenic and natural interventions. The interference of these factors on Indian reefs has been reported by several workers (Wells, 1988, Pillai, 1996; Venkataraman, 2002, Wilkimson, 2000, Patterson, *et.al*, 2007). The major natural causes for the destruction of corals include siltation, cyclone, local tectonic upheavals, tsunami, pests and predators and EI Nino.

During 1988 a notable rise in surface water temperature was observed and large scale mortality to corals was reported as a result of 1997/98 El Nino southern oscillation. Venkateraman (2000) reports that this has affected reefs in Gulf of Mannar and many species of corals were bleached. However subsequent studies by Patterson (loc. cit.) show that the southern part of Gulf of Manner has densely populated reefs and there is no sign of impact of El Nino event.

CORAL DISEASES

Corals are also affected by various fungal and bacterial diseases. In Gulf of manner and Lakshadweep three types of disease have been recorded in the recent past, viz. white band diseases, black band disease and bacterial/ fungal infection. The exact cause of this being studied by various institution. Venkataraman (2000) states that it is stress related. Silt and sedimentation cause asfixia on polyps and corals die. Sea erosion, dredging the reef environs, deforestation and construction activities stir up silt and sediment. Pests and predators also cause death of corals. Among the predators the echinoderm *acanthaster planci* is the most disastrous. This is reported from Lakshadweep and Andamans. The population of the starfish in Lakshadweep is normal and is doing little harm. There was a great increase of the starfish in Andamans but the damage was minimum. The star fish feed on coral polyps leaving the skeleton white.

Bio-closion is the reef go hand in hand with reef building molluscs, polychaetes and echiuroid are the major bioeroding agents on a reef. Blasting of the reef is a human activity that cause destruction to reefs. In the post independent years introduction of mechanized fishing crafts resulted in the blasting of the reefs to deepen the boat channel in Lakshadweep. Quarring of corals for various industrial purposes and construction work in Gulf of Mannar resulted in the total lose of fringing reefs in some islands. Dredging the lagoon for navigational purposes degraded the atoll reefs of Lakshadweep. Only in some part of Nicobor Islands and Andamans undisturbed reefs remain.

Coral bleaching is the whitening or paling of coral tissues due to the loss of microscopic symbiotic algae (zooxanthellae) and/or reduction of their photosynthetic pigment concentrations. The zooxanthellae live in the tissues of the host coral and provide it with most of its colour and energy. Bleaching occurs as a result of various harsh environmental conditions including high sea temperatures, abnormal salinity, and bacteriological or viral infection. In most reported incidences high sea temperature (1-20C above normal maximum) appears to be the main stress. Low wind speed may also be important, as this apparently favours localized heating and a greater penetration of solar (UV) radiation.

Prolonged bleaching conditions (for over c. 10 weeks) eventually kill coral polyps and ultimately the colony, but in many cases colonies recover after a certain time. Even though there is no 'cure' for bleaching, MPAs can play an important role in mitigation and aiding recovery, helping to maintain sources of coral larvae that can repopulate damaged areas and using zoning schemes to ensure full protection for corals that consistently resist bleaching and resilient reefs that recover quickly. Determining the start of a bleaching event is important but not always easy.

CONSERVATION AND MANAGEMENT MEASURES

It is necessary to create awareness among the coastal communities in the study area, in order to protect and conserve the coral reefs through effective involvement of educational institutions and NGOs. Stringent measures need to be under taken with immediate effect to ban coral mining and to take into task those involved in or those who encourage the exploitation of corals for any purpose. Patrolling the coast to check coral mining should be carried out. Law should be enacted to regulate and stop trawl boat operation in the zone earmarked for non-mechanized boat. The Department of Forest and the Department of Fisheries should take steps to stop anchoring of vessels on coral reefs, pair trawling and dynamite fishing. Indiscriminate picking of budding seaweeds needs to be banned. Commercial shell collection should be controlled and closely monitored.

Marine Resources Management Centers should be established to improve the skills of fishermen communities in areas other than coral mining, which in turn will lead to efficient management of coral reefs. Initiatives to train the coastal fishermen in mechanized boat operation, shell collection, seaweed collection and conservation of coral reefs need to be taken up so that they could find alternate sources of livelihood. Deforestation along the coast and islands of Gulf of Mannar should be banned. The Forest Department should take up afforestation along the coast and islands of Gulf of Mannar to protect soil erosion. Discharging of untreated sewage and urban wastes into the coastal waters should be totally banned. Dumping of any kind of material that would affect the coral reef ecosystem should be banned.

Systematic efforts related to conservation and management been initiated by India way back in 1986. To achieve this goal, the Ministry of Environment and Forests (MoEF) launched a Scheme in 1986. On the recommendations of the National Committee on Mangrove and Coral Reefs all the four major coral reefs in the country have been identified for intensive conservation and management. Major activities include conservation, protection, eco-development and awareness amongst the communities.

Our reefs are under severe pressure from many reasons. This valuable natural gift is almost irreparably exploited. Coral reefs and corals protect the coast from wave action. The value of reefs is both extractive and non extractive. The extractive values include many food organisms including fishes, molluscs and crustaceans. Pearl oysters are normally found in the reef environs. Corals are traditionally used for medicine. The reef associated organisms provide raw material for many life saving drugs and reefs are potential areas for pharmacological research. The genetic structure of reef corals is little investigated and it is of great value in the determination of species. They have decorative value. They provide raw material for lime, cement and calcium carbonate since the skeleton of corals contain 98.5 per cent pure calcium carbonate. They are building blocks for houses in atolls and coastal areas.

The non-extractive use of coral reefs is chiefly tourism. They are excellent sites for scientific research. Tourists are mainly attracted to the reef for skin and SCUBA diving and sport fishing. Though, the tourism is yet to fully develop. Due to the above mentioned value of the reefs they have to be protected and conserved for the future generation. Development and conservation rarely go hand in hand. Hence we have to utilise reefs on a sustainable level and as such management strategies have to be taken up.

Steps to Take to Substantially Improve Coral Reef Management

Step	Description	Agents[a]
1.	Decide reefs are wanted; recognize their value	Local communities, NGOs, economists
2.	Adopt the precautionary principle when making management decisions	Managers, governments, local communities
3.	Reduce over-exploitation of reef resources	Managers, local communities, NGOs, governments
4.	Use our existing science to manage more effectively	Managers, local and international science community, NGOs
5.	Do new science needed to advance management	Managers, scientists, NGOs, local communities
6.	Recognize and take advantage of synergy among impacts and among management actions	Managers, local communities, scientists, NGOs, governments

[a] Agents are listed in declining order of importance for taking the particular step.

Source: P.F. Sale (2008), Marine Pollution Bulletin, 56: 805-809.

ACTION TAKEN FOR CONSERVATION OF REEFS IN INDIA

Need for conservation of coral reefs is evident from the value of this marine benthic, tropical community. Though reefs were present and mankind utilized their resources from time immemorial a greater awareness for the conservation and protection emerged only in the later half of the last century. Early workers in the 19th century did not much argue for protection to reefs, for reefs survived in healthy condition. But indiscriminate exploitation and unhealthy interference on reefs by man made them threatened ecosystem and ecologists and naturalists started pointed out to the necessity for reef conservation.

India had the privilege to hoist the first International symposium on corals under the auspices of the Marine Biological association of India in January 1969 where in reef scientists from 11 countries participated. An international committee for the conduct of further symposia in every four years was also constituted. And to date 10 symposia were conducted in various tropical countries. However, our involvement in the series of meetings later was virtually nil. Realising the needs for the protection of this valuable marine resource the Government of India has taken steps to conserve and manage the reefs from early 1986. A national committee on corals and mangrove was constituted by the Ministry of Environment and forests and expert scientists, administrative staff and state govt. officials were incorporated. The mandate of this committee was to advise the govt. on strategies of protection and conservation of the reefs, in addition to eco-development and awareness creation on island population and coastal dwelling people on the need for conservation.

A research committee was also constituted with a view to recommending need based research projects to scientific institutions and non-governmental agencies. State level steering committees were also constituted to oversee the progress of implementation of management action plans. Thrust areas were identified. Marine parks and biosphere reserves were established. The Gulf of Kutchh Marine Park, in Gujarat, Mahatma Ghandi Marine Park in Wandoor S. Andamans, Gulf of Mannar Biosphere and Jhansi Rani Marine Park in Andaman and Nicobar were established. Nodal institutions in these areas were indentified to carry out research and monitoring. Research projects were funded. Non-governmental organisations of repute were encouraged to pursue research and to ensure awareness creation on the protection of reefs.

- The Government of India is committed to conservation and management of coral reefs. Ministry of Environment & Forests has been identified as the nodal agency for conservation and management of coral reefs as per the Allocation of Business Rules.
- The Environmental Action Plan has accorded priority to coral reef conservation by encouraging investigations to evaluate the ecological importance, biotic potential and conservation value of coral reefs.

- The National Committee on Wetlands, Mangroves and Coral Reefs was constituted in 1986 so as to advise the Government on policy issues related to conservation and management of these fragile ecosystems.
- On the recommendations of the National Committee following Coral Reef areas in the country which have been identified for intensive conservation and management includes: Andaman and Nicobar Islands, Lakshadweep Islands, Gulf of Mannar and Gulf of Kutch
- State level Steering Committees have been constituted so as to prepare the Management Action Plans (MAPs) on these coral reef areas.
- Under the Scheme on Conservation and Management of Mangroves and Coral Reefs financial assistance is extended to the State Governments/UTs for implementation of these Management Action Plans. The scheme is being continued during the 9th Five Year Plan.
- On the recommendations of the National Committee on Mangroves and Coral Reefs, the Ministry has established Indian Coral Reef Monitoring Network (ICRMN). The important activities cover monitoring status of health of coral reefs, training and capacity building and strengthening of institutions for effective management of Coral Reefs and Database Management on Coral Reefs in the country.
- Environmental Information Centre on Mangroves, Coral Reefs, Estuaries and Lagoons has been established by the Ministry under the ENVIS Programme at Centre of Advanced Study (CAS) in Marine Biology, Annamalai University, Parangipettai. The Centre has brought out comprehensive documentation including Status Report and Bibliography on Indian Coral Reefs in India.
    1. Ministry has established a Database Network on Coral Reefs in India and launched a Web Site of Indian Coral Reef Monitoring Network (ICRMN).
    2. The existing Centre of Zoological Survey of India at Port Blair in Andaman and Nicobar Islands is designated as the National Coral Reef Research Centre.
    3. Ministry has also been promoting research activities related to Coral Reefs under the Scheme on Conservation and Management of Mangroves and Coral Reefs. Thrust areas for research on coral reefs have been identified. Based on the priorities, the Research Sub-Committee has recommended research projects on Gulf of Mannar with specific reference to status of health of coral reefs, damage caused due to bleaching and the taxonomy of corals.

INTERNATIONAL INITIATIVES RELATED TO CONSERVATION AND MANAGEMENT OF CORAL REEFS IN INDIA

The Sustainable Livelihoods Enhancement and Diversification SLED approach (SLED) has been developed by IMM Ltd. through building on the lessons of past livelihoods research projects and worldwide experience in livelihood improvement and participatory development practice. It aims to provide a set of guidance for development and conservation practitioners whose task it is to assist people to enhance and diversify their livelihoods. Under the Coral Reefs and Livelihoods Initiative (CORALI) this approach has been field tested and further developed, in very different circumstances and institutional settings, in six sites across South Asia and Indonesia.

The sites and the partner organisations include: Aceh (Weh Island), Indonesia: Wildlife Conservation Society (WCS) and Yayasan PUGAR (Centre for People's Movement and Advocacy); Andaman Islands, India: Andaman and Nicobar Environment Team (ANET); Karen Youth Association; Baa Atoll, Maldives: Foundation of Eydhafushi Youth Linkage (FEYLI); Atoll Ecosystem-Based Conservation Project (AEC); Bar Reef, Sri Lanka: Coastal Resource Management Project (CRMP); Community Help Foundation (CHF); Gulf of Mannar, India: Peoples' Action for Development (PAD); Lakshadweep Islands, India: Centre for Action Research on Environment, Science and Society (CARESS)

- Ministry is represented on Global Coral Reef Monitoring Network (GCRMN) of UNESCO/IOC and coordinating with GCRMN, South Asia in organizing various activities on training and capacity building related to Biophysical Monitoring, Socio Economic Studies and Database Management related to Indian Coral Reefs. Monitoring Action Plans developed by GCRMN on all the identified Coral Reef areas in the country have been integrated with the Indian Coral Reef Monitoring Network (ICRMN). Financial assistance is extended to the respective State Governments for implementation of these action plans.
- Ministry has also been identified as the National Focal Point of International Coral Reef Initiative (ICRI) and is represented on the ICRI Planning and Coordination Committee (CPC) and participated in the meetings held at Gaudeloupe (France) and Bali (Indonesia) held in October, 1999 and October, 2000 respectively.
- A delegation of scientists actively involved in the research activities related to Coral Reefs in India lead by representative of the Ministry has participated in the 9th International Coral Reef Symposium held at Bali during October, 2000. Contributions by this delegation covered Status of Coral Reefs in South East Asia, Status of Coral Reefs in India, as well as Status of all the identified 4 Coral Reef areas in the country. Accordingly, 60-85 per cent of the Indian Coral Reefs reported to have been damaged due to recent event of bleaching in 1998.
- Efforts to regenerate/rehabilitate these Coral Reefs are being planned through National/International Cooperation.

- Under the UNDP/GEF PDF B Grant a project on Gulf of Mannar Biosphere Reserves has already been completed and another project on Management of Coral Reefs in Andaman and Nicobar Islands is under implementation.
- A proposal on Coral Reef Degradation in Indian Ocean (CORDIO) proposed to be executed by National Institute of Oceanography (NIO), Goa has been under consideration of the Ministry. This covers monitoring health of Coral Reefs in all the identified Coral Reef areas in the country.
- A proposal on India-Australia Training and Capacity Building (IATCB) on Coral Reefs in India under the Australian Aid (Aus-Aid) has been under active consideration. This proposal has already been cleared by Department of Economic Affairs (DEA) and has been pending on Australian side due to sanctions.

LEGISLATIONS RELATED TO CORAL REEF CONSERVATION

The Govt. of India has promulgated various legislation covering coral reef conservation. The wild life protection act 1972 provides protection to certain marine species. Efforts are being made to bring corals under this act. The Government of India issued a Coastal Regulation Zone notification in 1991 and amendments in subsequent years. The collection of corals either dead or live is strictly prohibited except for scientific research by identified institutions. All scleractinians and gorgonids are brought under wild Life Protection Act. 1972 from July 2001.

Thought India gave a fillip to reef research by organizing the first International symposium on coral reefs, in 1969, subsequent involvement of our country in furthering research in this field is limited. However, to supplement national efforts related to conservation and management of coral reefs and associated living resources the Ministry and environment and Forests, Government of India has been collaborating through some international initiatives in this country. Under the UNDP/GEF programme studies have been undertaken in Gulf of Mannar through MS Swaminathan Research Foundation. Another project in Andaman and Nicobar Islands has been completed.

The ultimate aim of these studies is to evolve a viable Management action plan on Indian coral reefs. The management of coral reefs is currently vested with the forest officials. Marine biodiversity management and eco-development needs trained personals other than forest officials. With the collaboration of Australia India has trained three scientists in Australia on coral taxonomy with a view to capacity building to strengthen reef research the Ministry of Environment has initiated action for the establishment of a National Institute of Coral Reef research at Port Blair. This is currently associated with the Zoological Survey of India and a small laboratory with limited staff is established.Policy issues related to protection of Coral Reefs in India include:

- Environment (Protection) Act, 1986 prohibits the use of corals and sands from the beaches and coastal water for construction and other purposes.
- Conservation of Coral Reefs has been included in the National Conservation Strategy and Policy Statement on Environment and Development and the Environmental Action Plan (1993) prepared by the Ministry.
- The Coastal Regulation Zone (CRZ) Notification (1991) issued by Government of India under the Dredging and underwater blasting in and around coral formations is also prohibited.
- Collection and destruction of corals in Andaman and Nicobar Islands is banned under the Andaman and Nicobar Islands Fisheries Regulation read with the Andaman and Nicobar Islands Shell Fishing Rules, 1978.

Coral Reefs in Gulf of Mannar (Tamil Nadu) and Andaman and Nicobar Islands have been declared as Biosphere Reserves and financial assistance is extended to the respective State Governments for conservation of these areas under the Biosphere Reserve Programme of the Ministry.

It is necessary to create awareness among the coastal communities in order to protect and conserve the coral reefs through effective involvement of educational institutions and NGOs. Stringent measures need to be under taken with immediate effect to ban coral mining and to take into task those involved in or those who encourage the exploitation of corals for any purpose. Patrolling the coast to check coral mining should be carried out. Law should be enacted to regulate and stop trawl boat operation in the zone earmarked for non-mechanized boat. The Department of Forest and the Department of Fisheries should take steps to stop anchoring of vessels on coral reefs, pair trawling and dynamite fishing. Indiscriminate picking of budding seaweeds needs to be banned. Commercial shell collection should be controlled and closely monitored.

Marine Resources Management Centers should be established to improve the skills of fishermen communities in areas other than coral mining, which in turn will lead to efficient management of coral reefs. Initiatives to train the coastal fishermen in mechanized boat operation, shell collection, seaweed collection and conservation of coral reefs need to be taken up so that they could find alternate sources of livelihood. Deforestation along the coast and islands should be banned. The Forest Department should take up afforestation along the coast and islands to protect soil erosion. Discharging of untreated sewage and urban wastes into the coastal waters should be totally banned. Dumping of any kind of material that would affect the coral reef ecosystem should also be banned. Measures such as these will not only protect this sensitive ecosystem but also ensure its growth and proliferation.

CONCLUSION

Our failing management of coral reefs is costly. The ecosystem goods and services provided by them are needed more than ever by our growing coastal populations, while our growing impacts make reefs ever less able to provide them. Still there are several reasons for optimism. First, we largely have the knowledge, the laws, and the administrative structures to undertake an immediate and substantive improvement in reef management. Second, we now understand reasonably well how people operate in groups to build consensus, and we have the capacity to bring about change in attitudes, and then in actions that will improve reef management.

Working locally to build ownership, while building collaborations regionally i.e. Maritime universities and research institutes should be encouraged to take up further reef research for which infrastructure is to be developed, Pharmacological research of marine organisms may be taken up on a priority ground, Eco tourism and eco development should receive attention and continuous monitoring of the reefs may be made to assess various impacts thus to implement remedial measures to ensure appropriate scaling of management actions will be key to success. Above all, we have good evidence that human attitudes can change remarkably rapidly, and galvanize action. We saw this again more recently as An Inconvenient Truth captured people's minds and hearts, and climate change became seen as truly important, no matter what the heads of nations sometimes claimed.

Coral reefs are fragile, living ecosystems increasingly being threatened and damaged by pollution, disease and habitat destruction. EPA has several activities involving the protection of coral reefs. Further education of the coral reef biological indicators is important to bring additional awareness to these very unique ecosystems. It is distinctly possible to create a revolution in thinking about the management of coral reefs, one that will preserve these ecosystems and the value they represent into the future.

REFERENCES

Arjan Rajasuriya., Maizan Hassan Maniku., Subramanian B.R. and Jason Rubene (1999). Coral Reef Ecosystems in South Asia. In: Coral Reef Degradation in the Indian Ocean', Status Reports and Project Presentations, (ed), Olof Linden and Niki Sporrong, pp. 11-24.

E.V. Muley, K. Venkataraman, J.R.B. Alfred and M.V.M. Wafar (2000) Status of Coral Reefs of India In: Proceedings 9th International Coral Reef Symposium, Bali, Indonesia 23-27 October 2000, Vol. 2. p. 1-7.

George Rany Mary and Sandhya Sukumaran. 2007. A Systematic Appraisal of Head Corals (Family Acroporidae) from the Gulf of Mannar Biosphere South-east India. *Bull.cent mar. fish Res. Inst* 50: 118.

http://en.wikipedia.org/wiki/Gulf_of_Mannar_Marine_National_Park

http://www.associatedcontent.com/article/462332/the_coral_reef_ecosystem_and_biodiversity.html http://www.gisdevelopment.net/application/nrm/coastal/mnm/nrmmm008.htm 26/08/2010

http://www.iucn.org/about/work/programmes/marine/marine_our_work/climate_change/publications.cfm

Patterson J K Edward 2007. Coral reefs of Gulf of Mannar Southeastern India, Distribution Diversity and Status, CORDIO *Suganthi devadason Res. Inst.m* pp. 113.

Pillai C S G. 1996. Coral Reefs of India: Their Conservation and Management. In: *Marine Biodiversity Conservation and Management* (Ed. Menon N G and Pillai C S G). CMFRI pp. 16-31.

Pillai C.S.G. 2002. *Biodiversity of Reef Building Corals of India*. Dept. of Biotechnolgoy. Govt. of India (Under publication).

Pillai C.S.G. (1975), 'An Assessment of the Effect of Environmental and Human Interference on Coral Reefs of Palk Bay and Gulf of Mannar Along the Indian Coast', Seafood Export Journal, Vol. 7, pp. 1-13.

Pillay C S G and M I Patil. 1988 Seleaesimain Corals from Gulf of Cutch. *J.Mar.Biol.Ass. India* 30: 54-74.

Pillay C S G. 1983 The Coral Environs of Andaman and Nicobar Islands with a Checklist of Species. *Bull.Cent.Mar. Fish.Res. Inst* 34: 33-43.

Pillay C S G. 1986 Recent Corals from the South-east Coast of India. In: P.S.B.R.James (ed.) *Recent Advances in Marine Biology. Today and Tomorrow* Printers and Publishers, New Delhi; 107-201.

Sale, P.F. 2008. Management of Coral Reefs: Where we have gone Wrong and what we can do about it. *Marine Poll. Bull.* 56: 805-809.

Venkitaraman *et al.* 2002. *Hand Book on Hard Corals*. ZSI. Calcutta. pp. 266.

Wilkinson Clive. 2002. Status of coral reefs of the world GCRMN. *Aust. Inst Mar. Sci* pp. 363.

CHAPTER – 3

Effects of Oil Spill on Water Quality and Fish Production in Otu- Jeremi and Environs Delta State, Nigeria

V.N. Ojeh, *Nigeria*; I.P, Udo-James, *Nigeria*; E.D, Oruonye, *Nigeria*

ABSTRACT

The effects of oil spill on water quality and fish production in Otu-Jeremi and its environs was examined. Water samples from rivers where oil spillages were recorded over time (Otu-Jeremi and Eyara Rivers) and rivers where no spill has occurred (Okwagbe River) used as control site. Additional data was collected via the questionnaires and oral interview. The water quality data were obtained from the laboratory analyses of the collected water samples. These were obtained with the aid of fifteen sterilized 2- litre plastic cans. The water sample parameters analysed include pH, Electrical conductivity (EC), total dissolved solids (TDS), total suspended solids (TSS), turbidity, biological oxygen demand (BOD), chemical oxygen demand (COD), Salinity, total hydrocarbon content (THC) and heavy metals (Cu, Ze, Cr, Fe and Pb). Results were compared with DPR standard for water quality. Each river was stratified into five sampling points and a total number of fifteen samples were collected from the three rivers in the study area. The result from the analyses showed that the water parameters from Okwagbe River fell within the DPR standard.

This indicates that the rivers were polluted and poses great danger to fish production and as such food security for sustainable development is not guaranteed. This study revealed a significant variation in the total number of fishes harvested before and after oil spillage in the communities. This was ascertained with paired 't' test statistics. Which shows that the calculated't' of (3.377) was greater than the critical 't' of (2.353) at $P<0.05$. This study recommends that oil companies operating in the area should strictly follow safe measures of operations in-order to prevent oil spill occurrence which militates against fish production.

Keywords: Oil Spill, Water Quality, Fish Production, Otu-Jeremi, Delta State.

INTRODUCTION

In the last fifty- five years, Nigeria has experienced increased activities in the areas of oil exploration and exploitation, refining and products marketing operations. While these activities have generated immense financial benefits for the country, they have also created serious health and environmental problems to host communities. Oil industry operations have introduced pollutants as liquid discharges and oil spills into the environment. The effects of oil spill on the environment have been very glaring in terms of its negative impacts on the region. Eteng (2007), stated that oil exploration and exploitation, have over the years influenced the social- physical environment of the Niger Delta region. Oil producing communities have been threatened by massive oil spill thus affecting the peasant economy and the entire livelihood system of the people.

There is no doubt that the Nigeria oil industries have affected the country in a variety of ways and at the same time it has fashioned a remarkable economic landscape for the country. However on the negative side, oil spill resulting from petroleum exploration and exploitation has led to environmental pollution with adverse effects on fish production, especially in the study area. This according to Ikporukpo, (1998) has a far reaching effect on the environment. The toxicity of the oil adversely affects the soil, plants and water resources. According to Ekekwe (2010), oil spill in rural communities in the Niger Delta area has led to the destruction of farmlands, vegetation and pollution of streams.

In June 2005, an oil spill occurred in the Otu-Jeremi community in Ughelli Local Government Area of Delta State, Nigeria. With an estimated spill of 30,000 barrels of crude oil was released into the environment as a result of valve failure, the area affected by the spill was seasonally flooded, and contained numerous fish traps, creeks and lakes which serve as a source of drinking and washing water for the community, the spill contaminated the water, and destroyed fishes, crabs, molluses, periwinkles and other aquatic lives in the river (The Nigeria Tribune, 2005).

Also in March 2008, another oil spill was reported in Eyara, Ughelli North Local Government Area of Delta State, Nigeria where an estimated crude oil of 26, 600 barrels spilled into the environment covering over eight hectares of arable farmlands and water bodies. The spill destroyed farmlands, vegetations, contaminated surface water which resulted in the death of fishes and other marine lives (Staigen, 2008). According to Badejo and Nwilo (2005), oil spill is a major environmental problem in Nigeria. Their study adduced that as a result of oil spillages the resultant degradation of the surrounding environment causes significant tension between the people living in the region and multinational oil companies operating in the area. Gbadagesin (1997), indicated that apart from loss of fishing ponds and farmlands, oil spills have led to extensive deforestations which in effect has shortened fallow periods, compounded land use degradation and led to loss of soil fertility and consequently erosion of the top soil.

Oil spill has led to the destruction of fauna and resort centres, pollution of domestic and industrial water, destruction of properties and lives as well as regional crisis in the Niger Delta region, where the bulk of oil production and exploration takes place. Oil spilled on water surface could prevent natural aeration and leads to the death of fishes and other marine organisms trapped below and in some cases fish ingest the spilled oil or other foods impregnated with oil thus leading to their death. They are also passed on to humans along the food chain.

According to Choker (2004), fishing is the major source of income and means of livelihood for the rural populace of the Niger Delta region and one determinant of socio-economic wellbeing of the people within the study area. Pollution of surface water, a major economic asset where fishing takes place as a source of livelihood of the people of Ughelli is a serious threat to the communities. Egboh (2010), identified that oil spill affects the socio-economic lives of man in a number of ways, such as loss of farmlands, cash crops, economic trees, fishing ground, destruction of main source of livelihood such as fishing in Niger Delta region. Therefore this study examines the effects of oil spillage on water quality and fish production in Out – Jeromi and its environs in the Niger Delta area of Nigeria and how future occurrence could be minimized or prevented.

STUDY AREA

Otu-Jeremi, the study area is located in Delta State of Nigeria and its Latitude is approximately 4° 45′ and 5° 15′ North of the Equator, and between Longitude of 5° 31′ and 5° 59′ East of the Greenwich Meridian. Otu-Jeremi which is the headquarters of Ughelli South Local Government Area of Delta State, is bounded in the North by Uvwie Local Government Area, on the South by Udu Local Government Area, on the East by Burutu and Patani Local Government Areas and on the West by Ughelli North Local Government Area (Fig.1.1). The area is situated on lowland bordering the Forcados River and Okpara Creek hence the people of these communities are engaged in fishing activities as their source and means of livelihood.

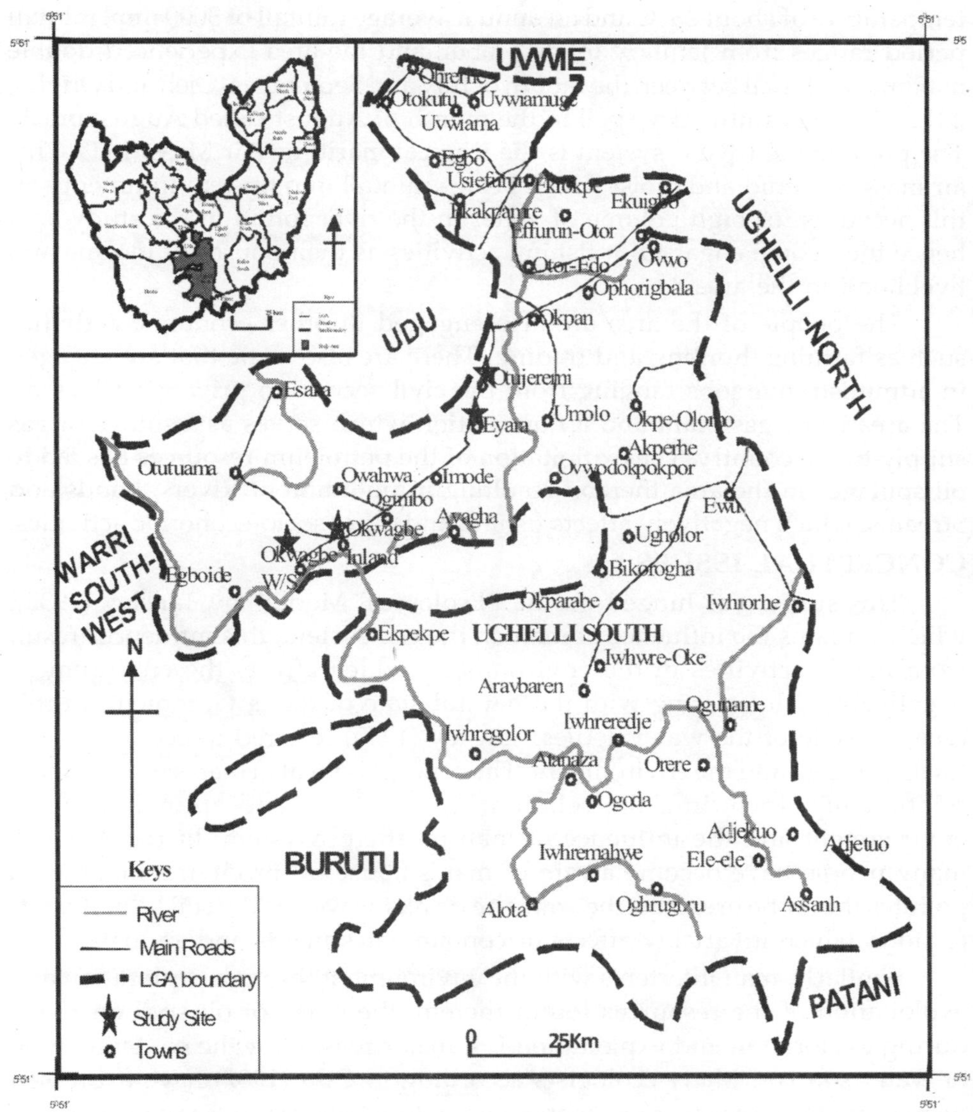

Fig. 3.1: Map of Ughelli-South Showing Otu-Jeremi and Environs

Source: Modified after Ministry of Lands, Survey and Urban Development Asaba, 2008

Otu-Jeremi lies on a coastal plain, which is generally low with lowland rising to 15 metres above sea level, the area has a high water table especially during the wet season, it is drained by the Forcados River and Okpara Creek. Also the area is riddled with an intricate system of natural water channels and valleys culminating in the dominance of fishing as the major economic activities. Otu-Jeremi and its environs experience an average monthly temperature of about 28° C and an annual average rainfall of 3000 mm, rainfall period ranges from January to December, and the area experienced double maxima of rainfall between the mouth of July and September (Ojeh and Origho, 2012). There is a little dry spell in the month of August called August break. The predominant wind system is the tropical maritime Air Mass (MT). This air mass is humid and moist which brings rainfall into this environment and this accounts for high volume of water in the river found in the study area hence the people engaged in fishing activities as their source of income and livelihood in the area.

The people of the area are also engaged in other economic activities such as farming, hunting and trading. There are also some that are engaged in administrative jobs ranging from the civil service to private businesses. The area has a gas plant and a flow station which serves as a source of gas supply to the country. The exploitation of the petroleum resources has led to oil spillages in the area thereby resulting in pollution of Rivers, Ponds and Streams, which negatively affects fishing and other socio-economic activities.

CONCEPTUAL ISSUES

This study was hinged on the "Ecological Model" by Tansley (1935), which explains the influence of man on the eco-system, this influences result from man's activities in the environment, which affects the environment negatively by interfering with the natural state of the environment, in this case the state of the water bodies. Tansley (1935) referred to ecology as the totality of man and the environment. The concept is ideal in man's environment relationship, including the relationship of plants and animals to their environment and the influence of man on the ecosystem. In recent years many people have become aware of man's abuse of his environment; man pollutes the air he breathes, the water he drinks as well as the soil he cultivates for food which invariably affects or contaminates plants and animals.

Similarly, man interferes with the environment through exploration and exploitation of the resources found therein, the effect of oil spill on rivers during exploration and exploitation is a major reason for the contamination of water sources. Many ecologists according to Odu (1987) have expressed dismay at the increasing rate of indiscriminate act of oil spills in rivers without any consideration on its effect on the ecosystem, especially surface water and marine lives. Agboola (1985) looked at the environment as the sum of all elements that influence man on a regular basis, the continuous interaction of man with the natural environment has resulted into environmental problems. Further support for this view comes from Isichei and Sanford (1976), Which state that ''people live and run various kinds of business, extracting resources from the surrounding environment and discharging domestic wastes into the same environment, therefore as long as people's impacts stay within this ability, the ecosystem remains imbalance. This concept is relevant to this study because as man discharge oil into water bodies, they alter and pollute the water, making it unfit and unhealthy for fish to suvive and reproduce.

MATERIALS AND METHODS

The researcher adopted the experimental and ex post factor survey designs. This involved the administration of 244 copies of questionnaires aided with oral interview and the collection of water samples from polluted sites (Otu-Jeremi and Eyara Rivers) and non-polluted site (Okwagbe River) as control site for laboratory analysis. White polyethylene bottles ($750cm^3$) were used for collecting samples. The bottles were rinsed first with distilled water before filling, rinsed a further two or three times with the water being sampled, and then the water sample was taken.

Standard methods for the examination of water and waste water from the US Environmental Protection Agency (USEPA) (1986) were used for the determination of trace elements/compounds such as fluoride, lead, cadmium, zinc, copper, iron and nitrite. All these elements and nitrite was analyzed using atomic absorption spectrophotometer. Other parameters include BOD, COD, the pH, temperature, dissolved oxygen (DO), electrical conductivity (EC) and total dissolved solids (TDS) of the water samples were done in the field and results recorded in the field logbook to determine the quality of water from the rivers. The water quality parameters analysed, were compared with DPR guidelines for oil operating companies in Nigeria. In the process of the analysis, two sets of internal standard were run, one at the beginning and the other in between the analyses to have a check on the accuracy and precision of the results following Balaram (1992) method. Lenntech W.H.O/E.U drinking water standards were used for comparison. The parameters were determined three times and the mean was taken.

RESULT OF THE FINDINGS

Physico-chemical Properties of the Sampled Water

Table 3.1, (*See Table on next page*) presents the results of analysis on the physio-chemical properties of the water samples from Okwagbe River (the control site). The mean data as shown indicates that the chemical properties of water from the Okwagbe River is lower than the DPR limit which is also used as a standard of assessment for the quality of water effective for fish production. Although the acid concentration is near neutral in the Okwagbe River, it is also lower than the standard limit of the DPR.

The mean pH recorded in Okwagbe River, which was 6.66 falls within DPR standard of 6.5- 8.5 indicating that the acidic level of the water sample from the river is within acceptable limit as good quality water, fit for the effective production of fishes. The mean temperature recorded was 26.6°C while the DPR maximum limit is 30°C, thus, the observed value falls within

Table 3.1: Physio-chemical Results of Water Samples from Okwagbe River

Parameter	Okwagbe River (Control Site)						
	Sample 1	Sample 2	Sample 3	Sample 4	Sample 5	Mean	DPR Limit
P^H	6.7	6.6	6.7	6.6	6.7	6.66	6.5-8.5
Temp (°C)	26.6	26.7	26.5	26.6	26.6	26.6	30.0
EC (US/MC)	186.5	186.8	186.8	186.4	186.5	186.6	200.0
TDS (Mg/I)	483	484	483	483	483	483.2	500.0
Turbidity (NTU)	8.0	8.2	8.0	8.2	8.2	8.12	10.0
TSS (mg/I)	23.1	23.2	23.0	23.0	23.1	23.08	30.0
Salinity (Mg/I)	534.2	536.8	536.4	536.1	536.4	535.98	600.0
THC (Mg/I)	8.2	8.3	8.3	8.3	8.2	8.26	10.0
BOD (Mg/I)	8.4	8.8	8.5	8.5	8.4	8.52	10.0
COD (Mg/I)	8.3	8.2	8.4	8.3	8.4	8.32	10.0
Fe (mg/I)	0.73	0.72	0.73	0.73	0.72	0.726	1.0
Cr (Mg/I)	0.01	0.02	0.01	0.02	0.01	0.014	0.03
Cu (Mg/I)	1.20	1.2	1.2	1.3	1.3	1.24	1.5
Zn (Mg/I)	0.68	0.68	0.68	0.69	0.68	0.682	1.0
Pb (Mg/I)	0.04	0.05	0.05	0.04	0.04	0.044	0.05

Source: Fieldwork, 2011.

the tolerance level for fish production. The mean electrical conductivity recorded was 186.6us/mc while the DPR limit is 200us/mc, this falls within the DPR limits. The total dissolve solid mean recorded was 483.2 mg/l which is less than the DPR limit of 500 mg/l. The turbidity mean recorded was 8.12 as against DPR limit of 10mg/l. The mean of TSS recorded was 23.08 which is also within the DPR limit of 30 mg/l. The mean of salinity recorded was 535.98 mg/l while DPR limit is 600 mg/l; the mean recorded for THC, BOD, COD, Fe, Cr,Cu, Zn, Pb falls within DPR standard limits, this indicates that the water quality from this river is not polluted and therefore suitable for fish production in the study (Fig 3.2).

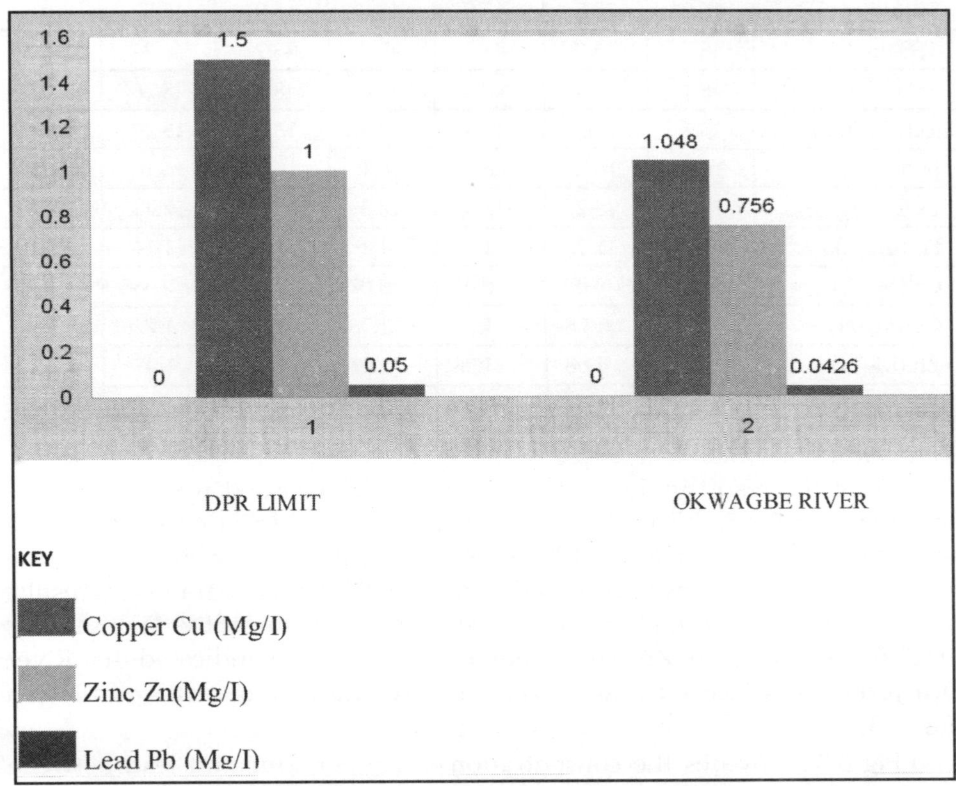

Fig. 3.2: Results of Water Quality from Okwagbe River

Figure 3.2, reveals that the concentrations of copper is highest followed by that of zinc, while the lowest concentration observed is lead. However, these concentrations were lower than the DPR standard limit.

Effects of Oil Spillage on Water Quality for Fish Production

The effects of oil spillage on the water quality as it affects fish production can be ascertained through the physio-chemical analysis of water samples from oil polluted rivers (Table 3.2).

Table 3.2: Physio-Chemical Results of Water Samples from Otu-Jeremi River

Parameter	Otu-Jeremi River						
	Sample 1	Sample 2	Sample 3	Sample 4	Sample 5	Mean	DPR Limit
PH	13.2	13.1	13.0	13.1	13.0	13.08	6.5-8.5
Temp (°C)	32.0	32.1	32.5	32.4	32.6	32.36	30.0
EC (US/MC)	300.0	320.1	310.5	315.0	318.0	312.72	200.0
TDS (Mg/I)	650.0	655.2	659.2	656.1	653.2	654.74	500.00
Turbidity (NTU)	16.0	15.5	15.9	15.8	15.9	15.82	10.0
TSS (mg/I)	48.5	48.0	48.2	48.3	48.2	48.24	30.00
Salinity (Mg/I)	748.1	748.4	748.3	748.4	748.1	748.26	600.00
THC (MG/I)	13.1	13.7	13.2	13.1	13.2	13.26	10.0
BOD (Mg/I)	16.0	16.2	16.3	16.1	16.2	16.16	10.0
COD (Mg/I)	17.7	18.2	17.1	18.3	17.4	17.74	10.0
Fe (mg/I)	1.2	1.2	1.1	1.1	1.1	1.14	1.0
Cr (Mg/I)	0.07	0.07	0.06	0.07	0.07	0.068	0.03
Cu (Mg/I)	1.78	1.78	1.77	1.78	1.77	1.776	1.5
Zn (Mg/I)	1.06	1.08	1.08	1.07	1.06	1.07	1.0
Pb (Mg/I)	0.07	0.08	0.07	0.07	0.07	0.072	0.05

Source: Field work, 2011.

From the result in Table 3.2, the mean pH recorded was 13.08 while DPR limit is 6.5-8.5, this indicates that the river has a higher concentration of acidic level and this is not suitable for fish production. The mean temperature recorded was 32.36°C as against DPR limit of 30°C. Others parameters results such as electrical conductivity, total dissolved solid, turbidity, TSS, salinity, THC, BOD, Fe, Cr, Cu, Zn, Pb exceeded DPR limits, this indicated that River Otu-Jeremi is polluted and therefore poses danger to fish production (Fig 3.3).

Fig 3.3 compares the concentration of copper, zinc and lead between Otu-Jeremi and the DPR limits. The concentration of copper was higher in Otu-Jeremi River than that of the DPR set limit. Amongst the three elements, chromium has the lowest concentration, having 0.03 mg/l at the DPR limit and a concentration of 0.068 mg/l and 0.063 mg/l in Otu-Jeremi and Eyara Rivers respectively. The concentration of lead is about the same range, having 0.05 mg/l at the DPR limit and a concentration of 0.072 mg/l and 0.066 mg/l in Otu-Jeremi and Eyara Rivers.

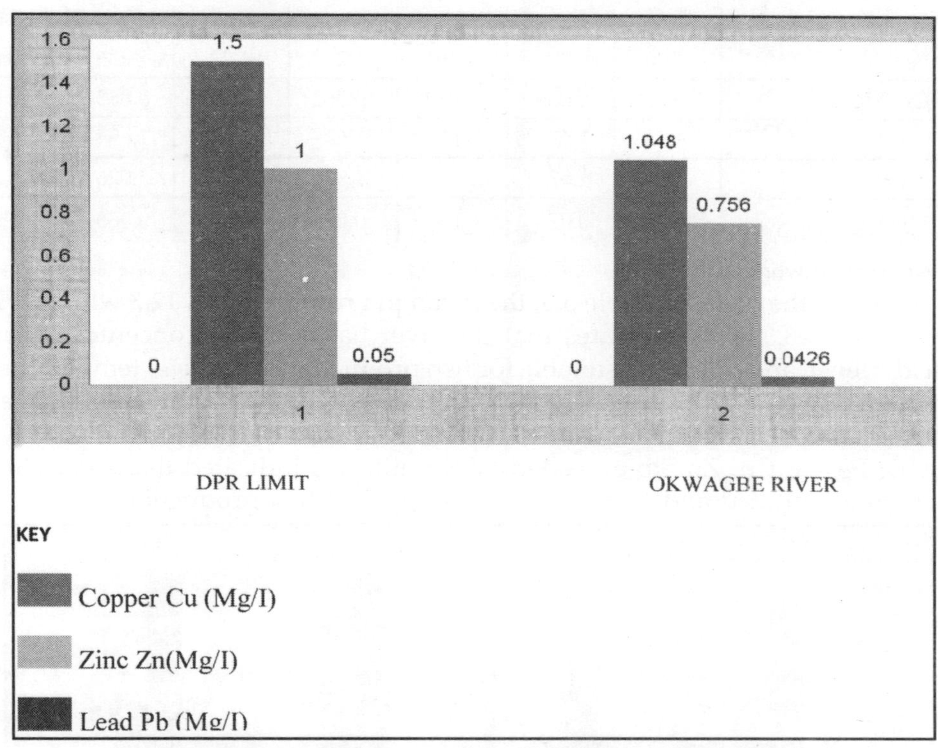

Fig 3.3: Results of Water Quality from Otu-Jeremi River

Table 3.3: Physio-Chemical Results of Water Samples from Eyara River

Parameters	Eyara River						
	Sample 1	Sample 2	Sample 3	Sample 4	Sample 5	Mean	DPR Limit
1	*2*	*3*	*4*	*5*	*6*	*7*	*8*
pH	12.4	12.2	12.5	12.2	12.2	12.3	6.5-8.5
Temp (°C)	35.1	35.2	35.1	35.1	35.3	35.16	30.0
EC (US/MC)	250.2	249.3	249.5	248.3	249.2	249.3	200.0
TDS (Mg/I)	550.1	552.3	560.2	551.0	550.0	552.72	500.0
Turbidity (NTU)	12.8	12.6	12.7	12.7	12.7	12.7	10.0
TSS (mg/I)	36.5	36.0	36.1	36.2	36.3	36.22	30.0
Salinity (Mg/I)	680.2	670.1	630.2	640.1	630.2	650.16	600
THC (MG/I)	12.2	12.4	12.3	12.4	12.5	12.36	10.0
BOD (Mg/I)	12.2	12.2	12.2	12.1	12.2	12.18	10.0
COD (Mg/I)	15.0	14.0	14.5	15.0	15.6	14.82	10.0

(Contd…)

1	2	3	4	5	6	7	8
Fe (mg/I)	1.22	1.25	1.26	1.23	1.22	1.236	1.0
Cr (Mg/I)	0.063	0.065	0.063	0.062	0.062	0.063	0.03
Cu (Mg/I)	1.66	1.63	1.62	1.63	1.63	1.634	1.5
Zn (Mg/I)	1.03	1.02	1.03	1.02	1.03	1.026	1.0
Pb (Mg/I)	0.06	0.07	0.06	0.07	0.07	0.066	0.05

Source: Field work, 2010.

From the result in Table 3.3, the mean pH recorded was 12.3 while DPR limit is 6.5-8.5. This indicates that the river has a strong concentration of acidic level, and this is not suitable for fish production. The mean temperature recorded was 35.16°C as against DPR limit of 30°C. Other parameters such as electrical conductivity, total dissolved solid, turbidity, TSS, salinity, THC, BOD, Fe, Cr, Cu, Zn, Pb exceeded DPR limit, this indicated that river Otu-Jeremi is polluted and therefore poses danger to fish production.

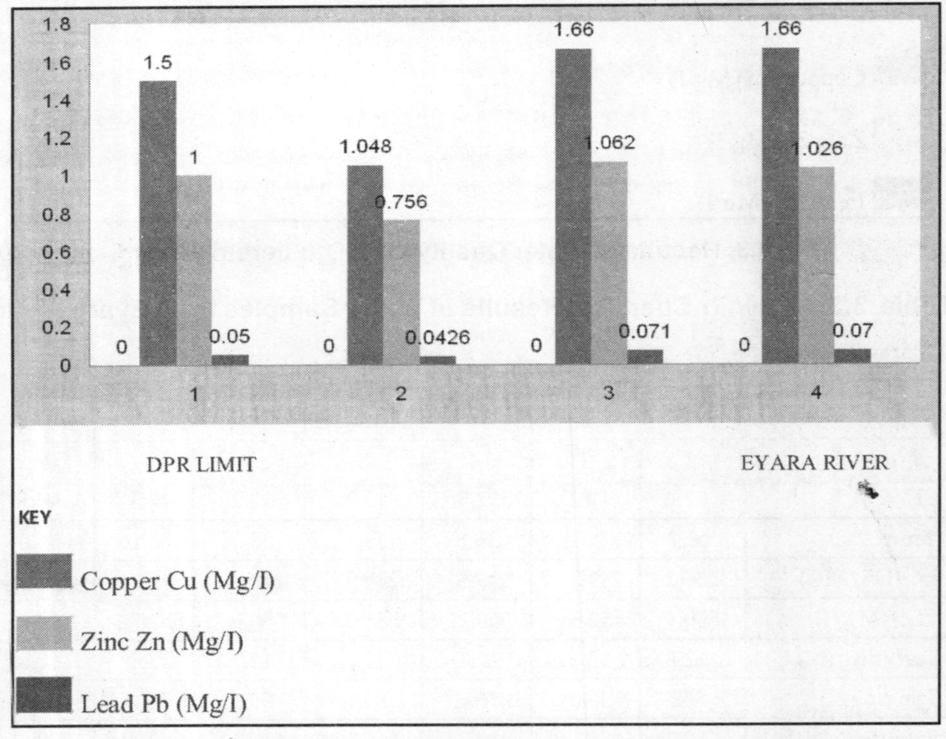

Fig. 3.4: DPR Limit/Results of Water Quality from Eyara River

Fig 3.4 compares the concentration of copper, zinc and lead between Eyara River and the DPR limit. The concentrations of copper were higher in Otu-Jeremi River than that of the DPR set limit. Amongst the three elements, lead has the lowest concentration followed by zinc and copper, having 0.066 mg/l, 1.026 mg/l and 1.634 mg/l as at the DPR limit of 0.05, 1.0 and 1.5 mg/ l respectively

A Comparative Analysis of Water Qualities Amongst the Rivers and the DPR Limits

The physio-chemical properties of water for fish production vary amongst the different rivers as well as the DPR limits. This is to be expected because Okwagbe River was used as a control site and has not been affected by oil spill. Although the physio-chemical properties of water in the Okwagbe River also differ from that of the DPR limit for fish production, the observed mean differences was not significant at the 5 per cent levels (Tables 3.4 and 3.5), which compares the mean differences of the physio-chemical properties of the different water samples for a consideration of the effects of oil spill, which could have impacted on the production of fishes.

Table 3.4: The Mean Physio-chemical Properties of Water Sample from Okwagbe, Otu-Jeremi, Eyara and DPR Limit

Parameter	Okwagbe	Otu-Jeremi	Eyara	DPR Limit
PH	6.66	13.08	12.30	6.5-8.5
Temp (°C)	26.60	32.36	35.16	30.0
EC (US/MC)	186.60	312.72	249.30	200.0
TDS (Mg/I)	483.20	654.74	552.72	500.0
Turbidity (NTU)	8.12	15.82	12.70	10.0
TSS (mg/I)	23.08	48.24	36.22	30.0
Salinity (Mg/I)	535.98	748.26	650.16	600.0
THC (MG/I)	8.26	13.26	12.36	10.0
BOD (Mg/I)	8.52	16.16	12.18	10.0
COD (Mg/I)	8.32	17.74	14.82	10.0
Fe (mg/I)	0.726	1.14	1.236	1.0
Cr (Mg/I)	0.014	0.068	0.063	0.03
Cu (Mg/I)	1.24	1.776	1.634	1.50
Zn (Mg/I)	0.682	1.070	1.026	1.00
Pb (Mg/I)	0.044	0.072	0.066	0.05

Source: Fieldwork, 2011.

The mean properties of water samples appeared similar as observed in the Eyara and Otu-Jeremi Rivers, and differ strikingly from the results observed in Okwagbe River as well as the DPR limit respectively. The concentrations of acid is higher in both Eyara and Otu-Jeremi Rivers than the concentration in Okwagbe River, which is near neutral and falls within the limit as indicated by the DPR standard. The temperature and BOD respectively are higher in both Otu-Jeremi and Eyara Rivers than the Okwagbe River as well as the DPR set limit.

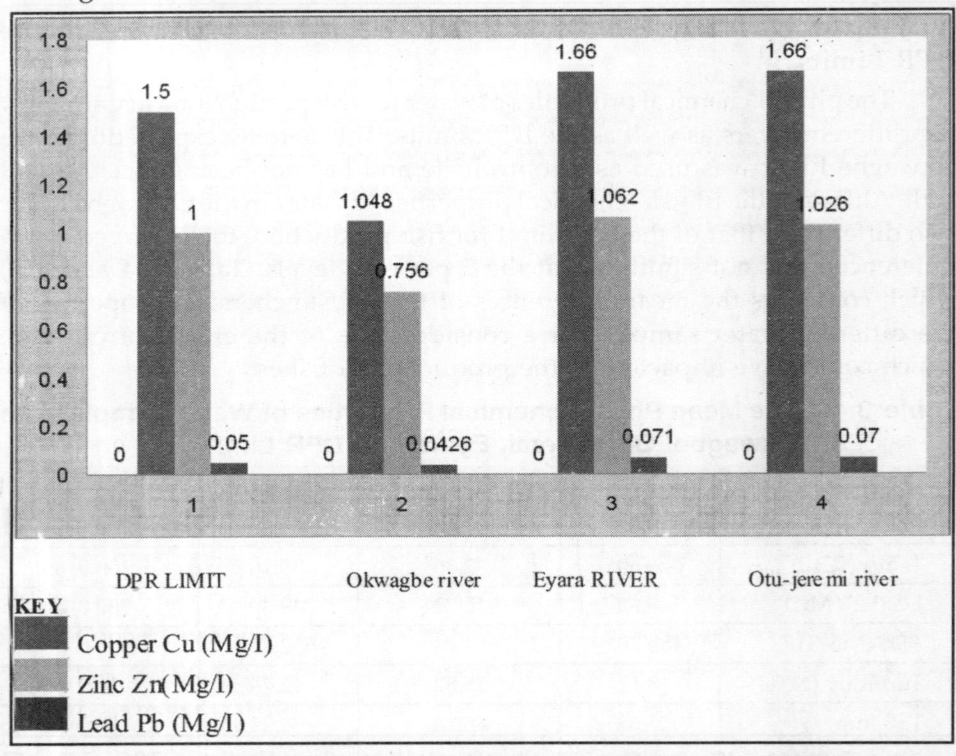

Fig. 3.5: DPR Limits/Results of Water Quality from Rivers Okwagbe, Eyara and Otu-Jeremi

Fig 3.5 compares the concentrations of copper, zinc and lead in all the rivers as well as the DPR limit. The concentrations of copper were higher in Eyara and Otu-Jeremi Rivers than that of the Okwagbe River and the DPR set limit. Amongst the three elements, lead has the lowest concentrations in all the samples, having 0.05 at the DPR limit and a concentration of about 0.07 in Eyara and Otu-Jeremi Rivers while that of Okwagbe River is about 0.04. These observed variations in the concentrations of chemical composition of water could be attributed to the effect of oil spill to the Rivers Otu-Jeremi and Eyara respectively. Therefore, it is possible to infer that effective fish production cannot be supported in these rivers which experienced oil spill overtime.

The results as presented in Tables 3.1-3.4, show that the physio-chemical properties of water vary amongst the different water bodies. The quality of water in terms of physio-chemical composition is similar in Rivers Otu-Jeremi and Eyara, and varies with that of the Okwagbe River, which has not been impacted by oil spill. However, the variation in the water qualities could possibly be attributed to the oil spill which possibly has affected the chemical properties of the waters in the affected rivers. It can therefore be inferred that the lower levels of observed physio-chemical properties in Okwagbe River, is because the water was not affected by oil spill.

Testing of Hypotheses I and II

Testing of Hypotheses I

HØ: There is no significant difference in water qualities for fish production between Otu-Jeremi and Eyara rivers and the DPR limit.

This hypothesis was tested with the analysis of variance statistics to ascertain if there was any significant difference in the physio-chemical compositions of water contained in the two oil polluted rivers, as well as the DPR set standard for effective fish production. However, the results of the analysis as presented in Table 3.5 and 3.6 show that there is a significant difference in the qualities of water from the oil impacted rivers and the DPR set standard for effective fish production.

Table 3.5 Descriptive Statistics

	N	Mean		Std. Deviation	Variance
	Statistic	Statistic	Std. Error	Statistic	Statistic
Otu-Jeremi	15	125.1004	63.85149	247.29574	61155.183
Eyara	15	106.1299	54.54536	211.25327	44627.942
Okwagbe	15	86.5361	46.02339	178.24781	31772.281
DPR Standard	15	94.7387	49.65329	192.30636	36981.734
Valid N (listwise)	15				

From Table 3.5, Otu-Jeremi River is most polluted with Statistical Mean = (125.1) and Eyara is less polluted with Statistical Mean = (106.1). Because of this, we can conclude that there is a statistically significant difference between the mean value for physio-chemical properties of the rivers Otu-Jeremi/Eyara and the DPR set standard with Statistical Mean = (94.7). However, Okwagbe River with Statistical Mean = (86.5) is within acceptable limit.

From Table 3.6, (*See Table on next page*) Physio-chemical properties differed significantly among the three groups. It is $F(5, 9) = 1548.5$, $p < .05$ for Otu-Jeremi and $F(5, 9) = 2992.6$, $p < .05$ for Eyara. However, the level of pollution between the two rivers is not statistically different. Thus we reject the H_0 and accept H_1 which says that there is significant difference in the quality of water between Otu-Jeremi/Eyara and DPR standard. This is to be expected since the two water bodies have records of oil spill overtime. This result corroborates Akah, Ezike, Offiah and Agbata (2009) findings. The implication of this result is that oil impacted water environments have high composition of both the physical and chemical properties of water of pollution, thus leading to water quality deterioration for human consumption as well as for aquatic live. This has negative effects on socio-economic developments in the study area and could lead to food insecurity if it is not properly managed.

Table 3.6: Analysis of Variance for the Quality of Water for Fish Production Between Otu-Jeremi/Eyara Rivers and the DPR Standard

ANOVA Table

		Sum of Squares	df	Mean Square	F	Sig.
Otu-Jeremi *	Between Groups (Combined)	855865.493	9	95096.166	1548.469	.000
DPR Standard	Within Groups	307.065	5	61.413		
	Total	856172.558	14			
Eyara *	Between Groups (Combined)	624675.224	9	69408.358	2992.622	.000
DPR Standard	Within Groups	115.966	5	23.193		
	Total	624791.190	14			

a Predictors: (Constant), DPR Standard: pH, Temp, EC,TDC, Turbidity, TSS, Salinity, THC, BOD, COD, Fe, Cr, Cu, Zn, Pb; b Dependent Variable: Mean value from Otu-Jeremi/Eyara Rivers

Testing of Hypothesis II

HØ: There is no significant difference in water qualities for fish production between Otu-Jeremi/Eyara Rivers and the control site (Okwagbe River).

This hypothesis was also tested using the T-test statistics to ascertain if there was any significant difference in the physio-chemical compositions of water contained in the two oil polluted rivers, as well as the control site (Okwagbe River) for effective fish production. The results of the analysis as presented in Table 3.7 show that there is a significant difference in the qualities of water from the oil impacted rivers (Otu-Jeremi and Eyara) and the control site (Okwagbe River) for effective fish production.

From Table 3.7, (*See Table on next page*) The Sig. values (p) are 0.07 for Otu-Jeremi/Eyara Rivers and 0.08 for Okwagbe River are less than t-values of 1.96, 1.95 and 1.89 for Otu-Jeremi/Eyara Rivers and Okwágbe River respectively. We can therefore, conclude that there is a statistically significant difference between the mean value for physio-chemical properties of the rivers Otu-Jeremi/Eyara and Okwagbe River. Therefore, we can on the strength of this statistic results rejects the null hypothesis (Ho) and accept H_1 which says that there is significant difference in the quality of water between Otu-Jeremi/Eyara and Okwagbe Rivers. This is also ascertained from the mean difference values. From the analysis, Otu-Jeremi has higher concentration of pollution than Eyara.

Table 3.7: T-test for the Quality of Water for Fish Production Between Otu-Jeremi/Eyara Rivers and the Control Site (Okwagbe River)

One-Sample Test

	Test Value = 0					
					95% Confidence Interval of the Difference	
	T	df	Sig. (2-tailed)	Mean Difference	Lower	Upper
Otu-Jeremi	1.959	14	.070	125.10000	-11.8479	262.0479
Eyara	1.946	14	.072	106.12993	-10.8582	223.1181
Okwagbe	1.880	14	.081	86.53640	-12.1739	185.2467

a Predictors: (Constant), Okwagbe River (Control): pH, Temp, EC,TDC, Turbidity, TSS, Salinity, THC, BOD, COD, Fe, Cr, Cu, Zn, Pb; b Dependent Variable: Mean value from Otu-Jeremi/Eyara Rivers.

The result implies that fishing as a socio-economic activity in the study area is limited in Otu-Jeremi and Eyara as a result of pollution levels of the rivers while Okwagbe is a choice area for the production of fish because of the good water quality of the rivers. This will generally affect the costs, demand and supply for fishes in the three areas respectively.

Relationship Between Oil Spillage and Fish Production

Table 3.8: Estimated Fish Production Before and After Oil Spill

Mean Kg of Fish Harvested	Otu-Jeremi		Eyara	
	Before	After	Before	After
75.5 kg	528.5	201.5	377.5	139.5
91 kg and Above	1274	364	728	182
Total	1802.5	565.5	1105.5	321.5

Source: Fieldwork, 2011.

From the above Table 3.8, the results revealed that before oil spill, an estimated fish production of 1802.5kg and 1105.5 kg in Otu-Jeremi and Eyara Rivers and an estimated quantity of 565.5kg and 321.5kg per month after oil spill were harvested by fishermen in the study area. From the analysis above, the researcher further employed an appropriate statistical test, (the paired t samples test) to test the stated hypothesis III which says that there no significant variation in the quantity of fish caught before and after oil spill in the area. Tables 3.8 and 3.9.

Testing of Hypothesis III

Ho: There is no significant variation in the quantity of fishes harvested before and after oil spillage in the study area.

Table 3.9: Paired Samples Test

		Paired Differences					T	df	Sig. (2-tailed)
		Mean	Std. Deviation	Std. Error Mean	95% Confidence Interval of the Difference				
					Lower	Upper			
Pair 1	Before – After	505.2500	299.2651	149.6325	29.0525	981.4475	3.377	3	.043

Table 3.9 shows that the calculated 't' (3.377) is greater than the critical 't' (2.353) at P<0.05. Therefore, the null hypothesis was rejected and the alternate hypothesis, which states that there is a significant variation in the total number of fishes harvested before and after oil spillage in the communities. The total number of fishes harvested reduced in the Otu-Jeremi and Eyara as result of oil spill on the rivers where these fishes are harvested. This brought the loss of not only household income and fish species caught for family usage but also loss of means of livelihood for these fishing communities.

Perception of the Impact of Oil Spillage on Fish Production

Sex and Marital Status

Table 3.10: Sex and Marital Status of Respondents

S.No.	Community	Sex		Marital Status			
		Male	Female	Single	Married	Divorce	Widowed
1.	Okwagbe	30	65	30	35	14	16
2.	Otu-Jeremi	20	48	18	28	7	15
3.	Eyara	17	32	9	28	6	6
	Total	67	145	57	91	27	37
	%	30.5%	65%	25.9%	41.4%	12.3%	16.8%

Source: Fieldwork, 2011.

Table 3.10, revealed that out of 212 respondents, 67 (30.5%), were male while 145 were female representing 30.5 per cent and 65.9 per cent. Also the marital status shows that 57 (25.9%) were single, 91 (41.4%) were married, 27 (12.3%) were divorced and 37 (16.8%) were widows in the study area. This means that there are more married people in the area. Also the results of the study show that there are more females than males in the study area. It is important to note that in these areas of Delta State, women are very much engaged in fish farming like the male counterparts. Women are seen with their canoes on rivers in the study area carrying out fishing activities to cater for the immediate needs of their families and for commercial purposes.

Age of Respondents

Table 3.11: Age of Respondents in the Study Area

S.No.	Community	Age 18-27	Age 28-37	Age 38-47	Age 48 above
1.	Okwagbe	17	39	20	19
2.	Otu-Jeremi	18	20	15	15
3.	Eyara	12	18	11	8
	Total	47	77	46	42
	Percentage	22.2%	36.3%	21.7%	19.8%

Source: Field work, 2011.

The age of respondents as shown in Table 3.11, indicates that out of 212 respondent, 47 (22.2%) were within the age of 18-27yrs, those within the age of 28-37 were 77 (36.3%), 46 (21.7%) were within the age of age 38-47 yrs, 42 (19.8%) were age 48 years and above. This implies that the study area has more of youthful population.

Level of Education of Respondents

Table 3.12: Level of Education in the Study Area

S.No.	Name of Community	Primary Education	Secondary Education	Tertiary Education
1.	Okwagbe	53	32	10
2.	Otu-Jeremi	38	18	12
3.	Eyara	27	16	6
	Total	118	66	28
	Percentage	55.7%	31.1%	13.2%

Source: Fieldwork, 2011.

Response on educational level as presented in Table 3.12 shows that 118 (55.7%) of the respondents had primary education, while 66 (31.1%) had secondary education, and 28 (13.2%) attended tertiary education. This implies that there was a general low level of educational attainment among the respondents. This corroborates with their occupation as subsistent fishing communities.

Types of Occupation in the Study Area

Table 3.13: Occupation of Respondents

S.No.	Name of Community	Farmers	Fishermen	Fishmongers	Traders	Civil Servants
1.	Okwagbe	22	29	10	18	16
2.	Otu-Jeremi	15	21	8	13	11
3.	Eyara	13	13	5	10	8
	Total	50	63	23	41	35
	Percentage	23.6%	30%	10.8%	19.3%	16.5%

Source: Field work, 2011.

Table 3.13, shows that 23.6 per cent are farmers, 30 per cent are fishermen, 10.8 per cent are fishmongers, 19.3 per cent are traders and 16.5 per cent are civil servants in the study area. This implies that the study area is mostly fishing community, compared to other occupations. This is made possible by the presence of the rivers in the area.

Oil Spill Occurrences in the Study Area

Table 3.14: Does Oil Spillage Occur in your Area

S.No.	Name of Community	(Yes)	(No)	No of Spill
1.	Okwagbe	–	95	–
2.	Otu–Jeremi	68	–	3
3.	Eyara	46	–	2
	Total	117	95	5
	Percentage	55.2%	44.82%	

Source: Fieldwork, 2011.

Responses to oil spill occurrences as presented in Table 3.14 revealed that 117 (55.2%) agreed that there were oil spill in Otu-Jeremi and Eyara, while 95 (44.8%) of the respondents insisted that there were no oil spill in Okwagbe. Moreso, Table 3.15 (*See Table on next page*) shows that the numbers of oil spill occurrence were 3 and 2 respectively in Otu-Jeremi and Eyara.

Table 3.15 shows that 77.9 per cent of respondents agreed that there was decline in fish production in Otu-Jeremi while 85.7 per cent of the respondents at Eyara also agreed that there is decline in fish production in the area. Meanwhile there was no response on the decline in fish production in Okwagbe.

Has there been Decline in Fish Production in the Study Area

Table 3.15: Decline in Fish Production

S.No.	Name of Community	(Yes)	%	No	%
1.	Okwagbe	0		95	0%
2.	Otu-Jeremi	53		15	77.9%
3.	Eyara	42		7	85.7%

Source: Fieldwork, 2011.

Causes of Decline in Fishing in the Study Area

Table 3.16: Is Oil Spill the Cause of Decline in Number of Fish Harvested?

S.No.	Name of Community	(Yes)	(No)	% of Yes Response
1.	Okwagbe	0	95	0
2.	Otu-Jeremi	64	4	94.1%
3.	Eyara	47	2	95.9%

Source: Fieldwork, 2011.

When the respondents were asked to comment on whether oil spillage was the causes of decline in fishing in the study area, 94.1 per cent responded in affirmative in Otu-Jeremi while 95.9 per cent agreed that oil spill was responsible for the decline in fish production in Eyara. At Okwagbe, the respondents do not see oil spillage as the causes of decline in the quantity of harvested fish. This may not be surprising since the people have not experience oil spillage in the community.

Assessment of Fish Harvest Before and After Oil Spillage

Table 3.17: Assessment of Fish Catch Before and After Oil Spillage According to Respondents Opinion

S.No.	Name of Community	Assessment of Fish Harvest Before Oil Spill			Assessment of Fish Harvest After Oil Spill		
		High	Medium	Low	High	Medium	Low
1.	Otu-Jeremi	21	–	–	–	3	18
2.	Eyara	13	–	–	–	4	9
	Total	34	–	–	–	7	27
	Percentage	100%				20.6%	79.4%

Source: Fieldwork, 2011.

From Table 3.17, 100 per cent of the respondents (21 at Otu-Jeremi and 13 at Eyara) confirmed that fish harvesting before oil spill was high. While 20.6 per cent says fish harvesting was of medium level after oil spillage, and 79.4 per cent confirmed that fish harvesting was low after oil spillage in the area.

Estimate of Fish Production in the Study Area

This section examines the estimates of fish harvested in kilogram in the study area.

Table 3.18: Estimate of Fish Harvest before Oil Spill

S. No.	Community Name	What is the Estimate of Fish Harvest Before Oil Spill			
		1-30 kg	31-60 kg	61-90 kg	91 kg Above
1.	Otu-Jeremi			7	14
2.	Eyara			5	8
	Total			12	22
	Percentage			35.3%	64.7%

Source: Fieldwork, 2011.

From Table 3.18, out of 34 respondents, 12 respondents (35.3%) revealed that their fish harvest per day before oil spill was between 61- 90kg, while 22 respondents representing 64.7 per cent revealed that their fish catch was between 91kg and above per day before oil spill.

Table 3.19: Responses to Estimate of Fish Harvest after Oil Spill

S.No.	Community	What is Estimate of Fish Harvest After Oil Spill Per Day			
		1-30 kg	31-60 kg	61-90 kg	91 kg and above
1.	Okwagbe				
2.	Otu-Jeremi	13	8		
3.	Eyara	9	4		
	Total	22	12		
	Percentage	64.7%	35.3%		

Source: Fieldwork, 2010.

From Table 3.19, out of 34 respondents, 22 respondents representing 64.7 per cent revealed that their fish harvest per day after oil spill is between 1- 30kg, while 12 respondents representing 35.3 per cent revealed that their fish catch is between 31kg-60kg per day after oil spill.

Otu-Jeremi and Environs at the event of oil spill in recent times, has suffered from pollution and contamination of surface water, a major asset where fish production takes place. These have resulted in poisoning and killing of fishes, periwinkle, crabs and other aquatic lives. In the case where some of the fishes survived the pollution, they migrate to other areas where the water is suitable for their existence, thereby causing reduction in the number of fish in the area.

The communities have also suffered reduction in the number and sizes of fish caught in the rivers due to oil spill, the fishermen revealed that the number of fish caught has reduced drastically in the study area as compared to when oil spill has not occurred in the area. The sizes of fish harvested have also been reduced, bigger fishes were caught prior to oil spill in the area. Also, the area now experience absence of some types of fish species that were present in the river before. The communities have also experienced contamination and destruction of fishing materials like boats, nets, hooks, traps and ponds. Commercial sale of commercial fishes have reduced. The communities also suffered deprivation of recreational activities as their swimming and diving activities have been rendered incapacitated due to oil spillage in the area.

Implications of Results

The results as presented in the different section show that both Eyara and Otu-Jeremi Rivers have been impacted upon by oil spill. The presence and concentrations of the different physio-chemical elements reveals a condition that is difficult for the adaptation of fishes to survive over time. However, a comparative analysis of the levels of the physio-chemical concentrations and that of the DPR (standard) shows that the oil impacted waters cannot support effective fish production. Thus, the observed low production of fishes in both Otu-Jeremi and Eyara rivers are as expected when compared with the DPR standard. However, the testing of hypothesis II shows that there is significant variation in the number of fish caught before and after oil spill in the study area. This revealed that effects of oil spill have a direct relationship on water quality for fish production in the study area. The result of this study, corroborate Akah *et al.,* (2009) findings in a study on the evaluation of the effects of crude oil on Tilapia *Guineesis* and *Sarothdron melanotheron* in Forcados area.

CONCLUSION AND RECOMMENDATION

The study found that the occurrences of oil spills in the study area accounted for the reduction in the number of fishes harvested, Thus oil spills led to poor performance experienced in the production of fish in these fishing communities thereby leading to decline in fishing and income in the study area. The rivers in the communities of Otu-Jeremi and Eyara were polluted and not fit for the production of fishes. At Otu-Jeremi River, values of recorded pollutants such as iron, chromium, copper, zinc and lead were as follows; 1.14, 0.068, 1.776, 1.07 and 0.072 while Eyara river recorded values as follows: 1.236, 0.063, 1.634, 1.026, and 0.066 as against DPR (standards) of 1.0, 0.03, 1.5, 1.0 and 0.05 respectively for the various parameters. These rivers exceeded the limit for DPR standard. This implies that the water was polluted and therefore harmful for fish production, thus leading to fish poisoning and increased mortality of fishes in the study area.

At the control site in Okwagbe River, values for iron, chromium, copper, zinc and lead were 0.17, 0.0014, 1.048, 0.756 and 0.0426 respectively. This was within the DPR stipulated safe limit of 1.0, 0.03, 1.5, 1.0 and 0.05

respectively. The result implies that the water from this river is of good quality since it is within the DPR limit. The pH value recorded in Okwagbe River was 6.66, which was within the DPR safe limit, while in Otu-Jeremi and Eyara rivers, it was 13.08 and 12.3 respectively. These are above the safe limit for DPR standard; increase in acidic content in water affects fish existences, metabolism and development which may eventually lead to increase in mortality rate in fish species in the river.

Based on the result of the findings of this study, the following recommendations are hereby presented. Firstly, operators of oil companies should strictly adhere to safety policies and best practices in oil exploration. Secondly, Corrosion control/ maintenance of oil pipelines and storage facilities should be regularly carried out. Thirdly, equipment used in the oil industries should be inspected to ensure that good and high quality equipments are used in oil exploration activities in the study area.

Environmental awareness and education should be promoted in all aspects of our national lives through public enlightenment campaigns. Jingles in the media houses such as televisions and radios should be aired regularly. Sabotage/vandalizers of oil pipeline and facilities should be discouraged at all levels. The public should be made to know that the effects of oil spill is more deadly and devastating than the compensation and temporal pleasure they achieved in vandalization of oil pipelines. Oil spill prevention target of zero tolerance should be set and enforced, and incentives given to achievers of the set goals. Recouping of rivers with fish fingerlings should be carried out to restock rivers in the study area. This will increase fish population which will enhance fish production in the study area.

REFERENCES

Agboola, T. A. (1985). 'Review of the Environmental Component in Nigeria's National Development Plans, 1940-1986', Paper Presented at the Policy Seminar on Environmental Issues and Management in Nigerian Development Under the Auspices of the Department of Geography and Regional Planning, University of Benin, Nigeria, 25th -27th November.

Akah, P.A,Ezike, C.A, Offiah, N and Agbata C.C. (2009) Evalution of the Acute Toxicity of Corexit 95271 Forcados Crude Oil Mixture on Tilapia Guineenses and Sarothedron Melanotheron, *Sustainable Human Development*, Vol. No 4, pp. 157-178.

Badejo O.T and Nwilo, P.C (2005). *"Management of Oil spill along the Nigeria Coast Areas"*. An Article to the Department of Surveying and Geo-informatics, University of Lagos.

Choker, B.A (2004). "Perception and Response to the Challenges of Poverty and Environmental Resources Degradation in Rural Community in Nigeria" *Journal of the Environmental Psychology*, 2(1): 16 -29.

Egboh S.H.O. (2010). Water Pollution and Control Chapter 4 in *"Man, His Environment and Sustainable Development"*. University Press, Delsu, Abraka.

Ekekwe, E. (2010). "Environment and Social Economic Impact Oil Spillage in the Riverine Areas of Nigeria" *Proceeding of International Seminar on the Petroleum Industry and the Environmental*, (Lagos: NNPC, FEPA).

Eteng, I A. (2007). The Nigerian State, *Oil Exploration and Community Interest: Issues and Perspective*, Port-Harcourt, University Press.

Gbadagesin, A. (1997). *The Impact of Exploration and Production Activities on the Environment: Implications for the Peasant Agriculture"* Seminar Paper on Oil and the Environment Organized by Friedrich Ebert Foundation's in Port Harcourt.

Ikporukpo, C.O. (1998). Managing Oil Pollution in Nigeria: Towards an Interactive Approach, pp. 224-229.

Isichei, A.O. and Sanford, W.W. (1976). "The Effect of Waste Gas Flares on the Surrounding Vegetation of South-Eastern Nigeria", *Journal of applied Ecology* 13(2): 69-74.

Odu, C.T.I. (1987). *"Oil Pollution and the Environmental"*, Business Science Association, 10(2): 30-35.

Ojeh, V.N and Origho, T (2012). Socio-economic Development of Rural Areas in Nigeria Using the Growth Pole Approach: A Case Study of Delta State University in Abraka. *Global Advanced Research Journal of Geography and Regional Planning* Vol. 1(1) pp. 007-015.

Staigen, P. (2008). Crude Oil in Water, *The Punch*, Friday, March 7, 2008.

Tansley, (1935). *The Use and Abuse of Vegetation Concepts and Terms, Forest Ecology and Management* 16, 284-307.

CHAPTER – 4

Status of Biodiversity in Man-made Wetlands Along Coastal Areas of Kachchh District Gujarat, India

Nikunj B. Gajera, ***India*****; Arun Kumar Roy Mahato,** ***India***
V. Vijaykumar, ***India***

ABSTRACT

Kachchh district is fall under arid zone of India and lying with long coastline with the Gulf of Kachchh and Arabian Sea. This district is characterized by the presence of various types of ecosystem which possess rich diversity of life forms. Wetlands of this region are one of the rich ecosystems in term of biodiversity, which are facing several kinds of threats by ongoing developmental activities and by the effects of climate change. Several man made wetlands are created by several agencies to meet the water requirements of this district. These wetlands are made along the coastline to fulfill the water needs and checking salinity of the land along the long coastline.

A study was conducted on the man-made wetlands situated along the coastline to assess the status of biodiversity. A total of 42 wetlands and surrounding areas were surveyed using block count and line transects to assess the status of floral and faunal biodiversity. A total of 306 species plant belonging to 63 families and 207 genera were recorded in and around the existing coastal wetlands/ study areas, of which 242 species were dicot and 64 species of monocot. Among the recorded plant species, 11 species were threatened species. The faunal diversity of these coastal wetlands constitutes; 20 species of herpeto-fauna belonging to 11 families and 20 genera, 199 species of birds belonging to 116 genera of 46 families and 13 species of mammals belonging to 10 families and 13 genera were recorded from different coastal wetlands. Among the birds, 127 species were terrestrial, 72 species were aquatic and 82 species were migratory in nature. Out of the total recorded fauna, 16 species of birds, 2 species of herpeto-fauna and mammal fall under various threatened categories of IUCN red data book, 2011.

The above results concludes that all man-made wetlands serve the water needs for the people, livestock, agriculture and are very important to the existing biodiversity of the areas. These wetlands are proved to be a part of complex ecosystem as they link terrestrial and aquatic ecosystem of this region.

Keywords: Wetland, Biodiversity, Flora, Fauna, Coast, Manmade, Kachchh, Gujarat.

INTRODUCTION

Conservation of biodiversity occupies a very high ethical value in the backdrop of rapid pace of development. Globally, humans and its developmental activities exert dominant influence on ecosystem and biodiversity. The accelerated destruction of biodiversity in every corner of earth has led to the signing of international agreements, such as the Convention on Biological Diversity (CBD). CBD defines biodiversity as "the variability among living organisms from all sources, including *inter alia* terrestrial, marine and other aquatic ecosystems and ecological complexes of which they are part and this includes diversity within species, between species and of ecosystems".

Wetlands are one of the complex and interlinking ecosystems between aquatic and terrestrial habitat. In the wetland system, the environmental characteristics are determined largely by hydrologic processes which exhibit daily, seasonal or annual fluctuations, in relation to regional climate and geographic location. The geographical location, climatic condition and environmental factors responsible for the creation of great varieties of wetland types globally. The habitat features of wetland system have helped to flourish variety of living organisms includes all major groups of plants and animals present. Wetlands of tropical/subtropical areas considered to be rich centers of biodiversity. However, there are large variations in species numbers of different plant and animal groups and also considerable differences in total species richness and numbers of endemic species between different wetlands. The tropical/subtropical wetlands are under immense human pressure on the maintenance and protection of biodiversity.

The natural wetlands in each part of the globe are experiencing serious loss and threats from natural factors like climate change and from anthropogenic factor. As the wetland ecosystem degrading the dependent biodiversity (aquatic and terrestrial) are also facing threats for their survival. The conservation and management of wetland requires data on the rate of harvest of the natural resources, the overall status of natural resources (Torell *et al.*, 2001) and the marginal net benefits of alternative uses of the wetland resources (Whitten and Bennett 2005). For more than a century, coastal wetlands are very important and have been recognized for their ability to stabilize shorelines and protect coastal communities (Gedan *et al.* 2010) and dependent biodiversity. The coastal wetland vegetation is an effective shoreline buffer and their combining manmade structure has likely to increase coastal protection (Gedan *et al.* 2010).

As the wetland area is shrinking, their key functions (ecosystem services) are also affected. Four of the major functions performed by wetlands as described by Greeson *et al.* (1979) that wetland having global signiûcance and value as an "ecosystem service". The major functions of wetland are; biodiversity support, water quality improvement, ûood abatement, and carbon management. The presence of water, high plant productivity, and other habitat qualities attracts large numbers of animal species, many of which depend entirely on wetlands (Zedler and Kercher, 2005). The important biodiversity of wetland includes; waterfowl, ûsh and rare plants.

The wetlands occupy less than 9 per cent of the earth's land area, and are contributing so many renewable ecosystem services (Zedler and Kercher, 2005). Wetlands in India supply crucial water need of human and domestic animal for drinking, domestic uses, fodder, water purification, wildlife habitat, and flood control. Three quarters of India's population is rural, it places great demands on India's wetlands and losses continue to occur (Lee Foote *et al.* 1996).

Coastal wetlands include littoral zones, brackish water and estuarine regions, lagoons and coral reefs, which constitute 70 per cent of total wetlands of India (Anon, 1991). These habitats in the India and whole world have great ecological and economic significance. The estuarine and backwater regions contribute 44.6 per cent of the wetland, followed by open mudflats (32%), mangroves (8.8%) and beach/spit (7.8%) (Jagtap *et al.* 2001). Estimates of global wetland area range from 5.3 to 12.8 million km^2. About half the global wetland area has been lost, but an international treaty (the 1971 Ramsar Convention) has helped 144 nations protect the most signiûcant remaining wetlands (Jagtap *et al.* 2001). Still in India, most of the wetlands are waiting for their inventories. The changes in the quantity and quality of the wetlands by various climatic and anthropogenic factors cannot be tracked adequately.

Kachchh has a range of natural habitats such as the dry saline Ranns of Kachchh, grasslands, coastal area with mangroves, thorn and scrub forests and wetlands. The coast line of Kachchh district is more than 200 km which is facing severe salinity problems. In addition to the natural wetland various wetlands are constructed in the coastal areas of Kachchh district, Gujarat to supply water for various purposes to stakeholders. The man made wetlands constructed along the coastal areas are not only fulfilling water for human need, they also helpful in rejuvenating various life forms. In addition, different habitats and vegetation types support a large number of floral and faunal species, which are adapted physiologically, as well as ecologically to the local arid condition. Conversion of natural habitats and creation of manmade habitat in a given area is likely to change the existing biological diversity of that area. Therefore, it is very crucial to understand such changes, which would help us for better management and sustainable development. So, this study was undertaken to understand and evaluate the status of biodiversity in and around the coastal wetlands.

MATERIALS AND METHODS

Study Area

Kachchh is a largest district (45,652 km^2) of Gujarat State. It lies at 22° 44′11″ to 24° 41′25″ North Latitude and 68° 09′46″ to 71° 54′47″ East Longitude. It's an arid district of Gujarat covering 73 per cent of the total geographical area of the arid region of this state. This district shares its north and north-west boundary with the Sind province of Pakistan and the west and south-west boundary with Arabian Sea. The southern part of this district is limited by Gulf of Kachchh and Rajkot district and the eastern boundary with Banaskantha and Mehsana districts. Some portion of the boundary in north-east is shared with the Rajasthan State. Administratively, the district is demarcated into ten talukas namely; Bhuj, Mandvi, Mundra, Abdasa, Gandhidham, Lakhpat, Nakhatrana, Rapar, Bhachau and Anjar of which 7 talukas are in coastal side where the coastal wetlands located (Fig. 4.1).

Out of the total geographical area of Kachchh district, 51 per cent (23,310 km^2) is occupied by high saline unproductive desert (Greater Rann of Kachchh – GRK and Little Rann of Kachchh - LRK). Only 7,674 km^2 area of the district is under agriculture that too faces serious problems like low annual rainfall (district average 348 mm), high rate of evaporation (2.25m/year), less surface water availability for irrigation, alarming rate of fall of ground water table (1-3.5m/year) and increasing salinity. The district supports over 1.4 million livestock (73 animal/km^2) and 1.2 million human populations (65 persons / km^2). The coastal talukas of Kachchh are witnessing aggressive maritime related industrial development and urbanization.

Rainfall in Kachchh is extremely erratic and variable in distribution in time and space, leading to frequent droughts, which are a recurring phenomenon in this region. Between 1901 and 1996, 57 drought years were recorded that affected the soil parameters like moisture, water balance and organic matter, thereby resulting in increased surface runoff and soil erosion. The coast of Kachchh, between Jakhau and Kandla have irregular and dissected configuration while in Mandvi and Jakhau the coast is comparatively plain and sandy in nature. The coast between Mundra and Kandla is marked by extensive tidal flats which merge with Rann of Kachchh to the east.

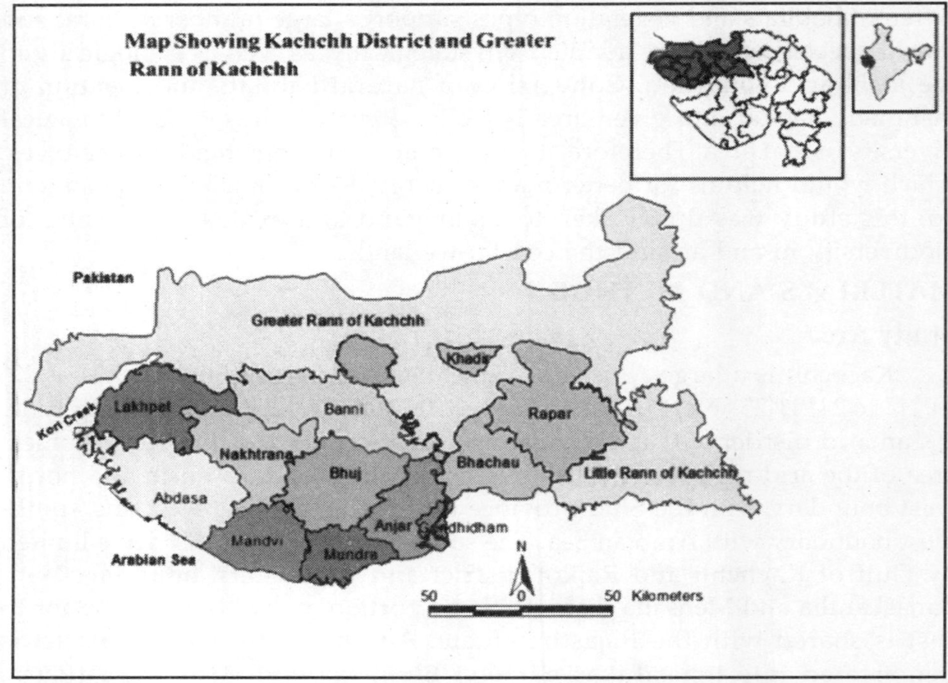

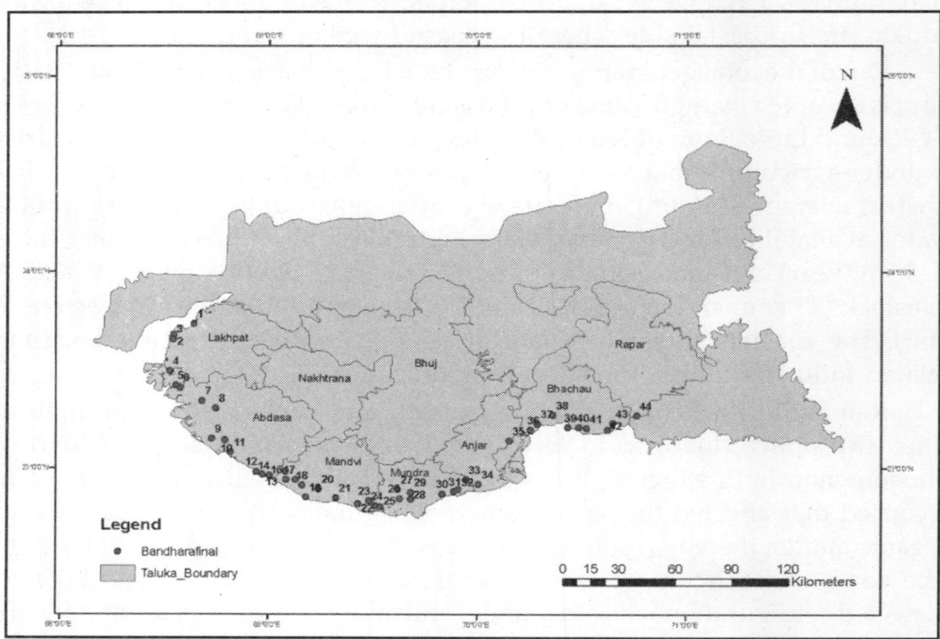

Fig. 4.1 (A-B): Locations of Coastal wetland in Kachchh District, Gujarat, India

Soils of Kachchh are mostly sandy to sandy loam and silty to clay-loam, and are highly salty especially in the northern and northeastern sectors where two Ranns are present. The coastal stretch of Kachchh district extends for about 406 km constituting the whole northern coast of Gulf of Kachchh. Mudflats and mangroves are the larger ecosystems occupying about 2500 and 775 km^2 respectively with other diverse habitats such as sandy shores and a network of creek systems.

Kosa Vadzar

Lathedi

Bhadreswar (TR)

Bhadreswar

Similar to the inland talukas, annual rainfall in the seven coastal talukas of Kachchh is also poor, ranging from 250-350 mm and which is often irregular. Rainfall during monsoon is confined to only 15-20 days and occurs as an instant downpour. Freshwater input into the near coastal waters is quite meager. Winter and summer temperatures range from 7-48°C with an average humidity of 60 per cent/yr and increase to 80 per cent during south-west monsoon and decrease to 50 per cent during November-December. Average wind speed is 4.65 m/s/yr with a maximum wind speed of 10.61 m/s during June. The phenomenon of drought is common with 2 drought year in a cycle of 5 years. As a characteristic of arid zone, annual temperature fluctuation in the district is extreme, ranging from 4°C to 48.5°C.

Northern coastal stretch from Kandla to Mundra in the interior Gulf region is marked by narrow beaches and wide mudflats with predominantly muddy alluvial substrate. Coastal stretch from Kandla to Mundra is dissected with creek systems forming extensive mudflats. Minor seasonal streams emptying freshwater run-off during monsoon months also characterize this coastal belt. The coastal stretch from Mandvi to Pingleshwar is an open coast, characterized by sandy beaches and sand dunes. The sandy intertidal belt is marked by sedimentary rocky outcroppings.

METHODOLOGY

In order to understand the status of biodiversity (flora and fauna) in different habitats in and around the coastal wetlands, field survey was carried out from September 2010 to March 2011. A total of 42 coastal wetlands were surveyed and 398 sample plots were laid down along the existing coastal wetlands in different coastal talukas. Before the intensive study a rapid assessment survey was carried out in all coastal wetlands to identify potential sampling sites for evaluating phyto-sociology of various floral and faunal species.

A filed survey on each coastal wetland area was conducted to identify the major habitat types existing in an around and to document the floral and faunal species. The area encompassing 2 km radius from the coastal wetland was designated for sampled area. The field data collection mainly included biodiversity status assessment of different life forms of floral elements such as trees, shrubs, herbs and grasses. Faunal diversity was assessed by inventorying the major taxa like herpetofauna (amphibian and reptiles), birds (both aquatic and terrestrial) and mammals.

Presence of different faunal species was also substantiated by interviewing the local people and experts with pictorial representation. All the nomenclature and scientific names have been referred from standard flora (Shah 1978; Bhandari 1990) and pictorial guides for fauna (Daniels, 1992; Daniel, 2002; Daniels 2005; Ali, 2002; Grimmett, *et al.* 2006; Prater, 2005).

Floral Status

Status of floral species was assessed in the representative habitats covering wetland and its surrounding habitats like forest, grassland, scrubland, wastelands and openland. Quantitative data was collected using Standard Quadrate Sampling Methods followed by Mueller-Dombois and Ellenberg (1967), Kershaw and Wright (1980). Status of tree, shrub, grass, creepers and herbs were quantified using square shaped plot of size 10m, 1m, 25cm respectively.

Faunal Status

The various groups of faunal species including mammal, bird, reptile and amphibian were assessed in the representative locations and habitat including wetland and its surrounding habitats like forest, scrubland, openland, wasteland, cropland etc.

Herpeto-fauna (Amphibian and Reptile)

Intensive search were made along the hedges of water bodies to quantify the amphibian species. Status of other herpeto-fauna was monitored and assessed by intensive survey by using standard methods (Campbell and Christman, 1982; Welsh, 1987; Corn and Bury, 1990; Heyer *et al.* 1994)

Birds

Avifaunal status was assessed both in terrestrial and aquatic habitats. Total count or flock count method (Sridharan, 1989; Bhupathy, 1991; Thompson, 2002; Steinkamp *et al.*, 2003) were adopted to monitor and assess the aquatic birds in all wetlands and waterlogged areas. Point centre count method/perambulation techniques (Hutto *et al.*, 1986; Bibly *et al.*, 1992; Rosenstock *et al.*, 2002) were applied to monitor and assess the status of terrestrial bird species. Additional efforts were made to locate/identify the presence of breeding/nesting sites of avi-faunal species.

Mammals

Status and distribution of different mammal species were monitored and quantified by direct count while walking along the Line transect in various types of habitat (Burnham *et al.*, 1980; Sale and Berkmuller, 1988; Rodger, 1991).

In addition, 20 m radius circular plots were laid in each sampling location along transects to survey the indirect evidences for the presence of mammalian species and quantification of relative density and abundance. The indirect survey of the mammalian fauna was conducted using standard methods (Thompson *et al.*, 1989; Daniel, 1992; Henke and Knowlton, 1995; Allen *et al.*, 1996).

RESULT AND DISSCUSION

Floral Status

Species Richness

In total, 306 plant species belonging to 63 families and 207 genera were recorded in and around the existing coastal wetlands/ study areas, of which 242 species were dicots and 64 monocots (Fig. 4.2). Among the coastal wetlands, Modkuba coastal wetland reported maximum 199 species and they belong to 154 genera and 53 families followed by Navinal coastal wetland with 176 species (125 genera and 40 families), whereas lowest species richness was reported in Budia coastal wetland (66 species). Next to Budia coastal wetland, Panchotia and Mopar reported 71 species each. Within the project area overall the estimated species diversity was H′ 2.47. Among the coastal wetlands, Modkuba estimated highest diversity of H′ 3.097 and Chhadvara estimated lowest floral diversity H′ 1.171 (*See Table Table 4.1 on next page*).

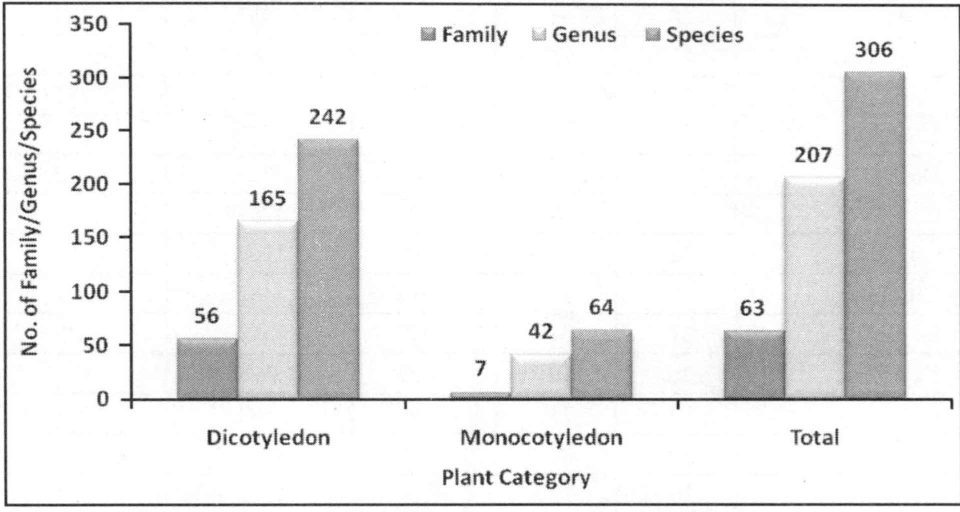

Fig. 4.2: Taxonomic Diversity of Flora of Coastal Wetlands

Floral Habit/Life form

Based on the taxonomical classification all the 306 plant species reported from the study area fall under 5 types of life forms. Among the life forms, the study area identifies maximum of 87 herb species, 29 tree species and 28 shrub species from Modkuba coastal wetland and minimum of 21 herb species from Budia coastal wetland, 1 tree species from Kosa Vadzar and 9 shrub species recorded from Bada Coastal wetland. Maximum of 39 grass species recorded from Navinal coastal wetland and minimum of 12 grass species recorded from Mopar coastal wetland (*See Fig. 4.3 on page 97 and Table 4.2 98*).

Table 4.1: Taxonomical Status of Vegetation in and around Coastal wetland Study Area

Coastal Wetland	Family	Genus	Species	Abundance	Species Diversity
1	2	3	4	5	6
Ambliyara	24	65	81	1150	1.539
Bada	26	62	78	1794	1.732
Bambhadai	38	111	150	1726	1.848
Bhachau	29	77	106	1243	2.001
Bhadia Nana	32	94	134	977	1.876
Bhadreshwar	33	90	126	705	1.974
Bhadreshwar (TR)	30	81	110	1167	1.532
Bharapar	35	95	126	1038	2.419
Budia	26	54	64	1757	2.172
Charopadi Moti	27	72	92	1289	1.29
Chhadvara	28	76	102	1451	1.171
Dhrub	35	91	134	680	2.025
Dhuvai	30	78	102	708	1.912
Golay	34	79	104	1264	2.111
Gunau	32	68	95	1249	1.704
Gundiyali	35	86	115	1482	2.204
Jangi	31	84	115	1515	1.618
Kadoli	28	66	79	2598	1.983
Khirsara	30	74	96	683	2.314
Khuda	34	82	108	1578	2.381
Kori Creek	26	72	100	1987	1.451
Koriyani	28	76	96	618	2.906
Kosa Vadzar	24	59	72	1189	1.391
Kukadsar	35	97	137	1750	1.37
Lakhapar	24	65	84	1051	2.256
Lathedi	29	69	87	2399	2.124
Luni	36	107	157	975	2.228
Modkuba	53	154	199	950	3.097
Modvadar	37	103	143	1524	2.614
Mopar	25	59	71	2169	1.565

(Contd...)

1	2	3	4	5	6
Mota Layja	40	115	144	754	2.338
Moti Chirai	27	69	88	1324	1.849
Mundra	35	99	137	1112	2.085
Nani Chirai	24	67	87	1864	1.29
Narayan Sarovar	32	89	127	807	1.786
Navagam (Manaba)	35	94	118	1070	1.617
Navinal	40	125	176	1079	1.578
Panchotia	26	56	71	1758	1.729
Sindhodi	25	66	84	2014	2.405
Vira	38	102	144	632	2.32
Wandhia	34	93	132	1648	1.549
Zarpara	37	106	154	960	2.358
Overall	**63**	**207**	**306**	**55688**	**2.47**

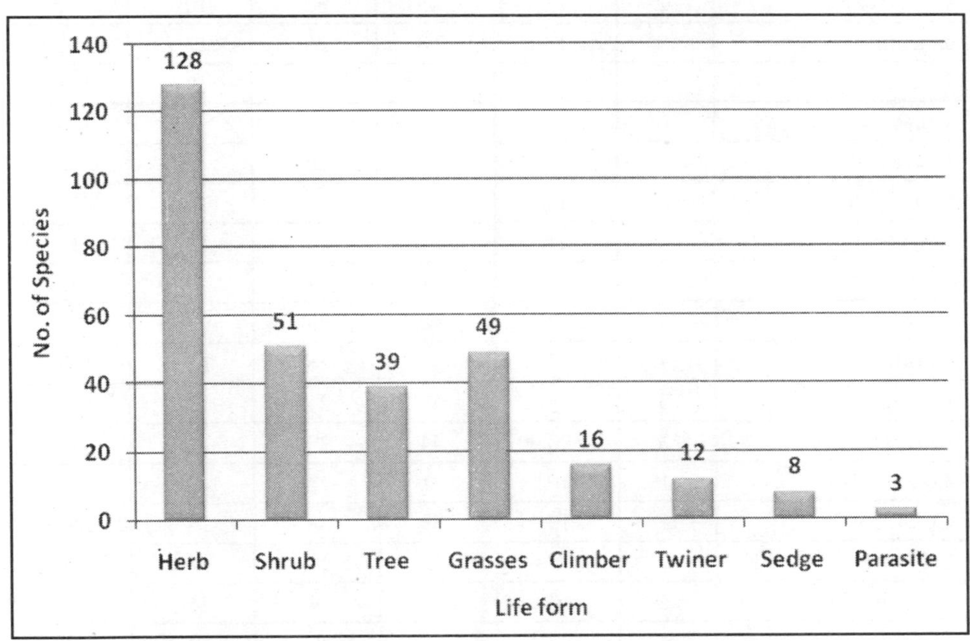

Fig. 4.3: Diversity of Plant Forms in Coastal Wetlands of Kachchh

Table 4.2: Habit/life form Status of Floral Component of the Coastal Wetland Study Area

Coastal Wetland	Major Habit/Life Forms					Total
	Tree	Shrub	Herbs	Grass	Others	
1	2	3	4	5	6	7
Ambliyara	2	13	36	22	8	81
Bada	2	9	35	20	12	78
Bambhadai	7	23	74	31	15	150
Bhachau	4	13	54	25	10	106
Bhadia Nana	8	18	56	34	18	134
Bhadreshwar	6	13	59	32	16	126
Bhadreshwar (TR)	6	12	50	28	14	110
Bharapar	8	14	56	31	17	126
Budia	4	14	21	17	8	64
Charopadi Moti	2	16	37	27	10	92
Chhadvara	2	15	45	30	10	102
Dhrub	9	18	68	26	13	134
Dhuvai	5	13	48	26	10	102
Golay	6	14	52	23	9	1,04
Gunau	6	14	48	20	7	95
Gundiyali	10	14	48	27	16	115
Jangi	2	11	61	28	13	115
Kadoli	2	7	37	24	9	79
Khirsara	4	12	48	25	7	96
Khuda	4	15	47	28	14	108
Kori Creek	3	18	48	24	7	100
Koriyani	3	13	44	25	11	96
Kosa Vadzar	1	10	31	22	9	72
Kukadsar	11	19	59	33	15	137
Lakhapar	2	15	32	28	7	84
Lathedi	3	10	44	19	11	87
Luni	9	20	73	36	19	157
Modkuba	29	28	87	33	22	199
Modvadar	9	18	61	35	20	143
Mopar	8	10	33	12	8	71

(Contd...)

1	2	3	4	5	6	7
Mota Layja	20	18	64	29	12	143
Moti Chirai	3	11	38	25	11	88
Mundra	15	17	. 64	26	15	137
Nani Chirai	3	14	37	24	9	87
Narayan Sarovar	6	20	55	33	13	127
Navagam (Manaba)	3	16	58	30	11	118
Navinal	11	25	83	39	18	176
Panchotia	4	11	28	19	9	71
Sindhodi	4	11	31	24	14	84
Vira	5	18	69	31	21	144
Wandhia	6	15	66	33	12	132
Zarpara	13	17	73	29	22	154
Overall	**39**	**51**	**128**	**49**	**39**	**306**

Threatened Floral Species

Eleven plant species categorized as "Threatened" by the World Conservation Monitoring centre (WCMC 1994) and also listed under various threat categories in the Red Data Book of Indian Plants (Nayar and Sastry, 1988) were recorded in the study areas. During this study, a total of 11 threatened plant species were reported from the study area. Out of these, maximum of six species were recorded from wasteland/open scrub, followed by five species each in agriculture hedges, wetland and Prosopis thickets.

Among these, *Ammannia desertorum, Citrullus colocynthis, Dactyliandra welwitschii, Indigofera caerulea* var. *monosperma* and *Convolvulus stocksii* had very low numbers i.e. 2, 3, 3, 3 and 6 individuals, respectively and it had highly restricted distribution in study areas. *Helichrysum cutchicum, Heliotropium rariflorum, Commiphora wightii* and *Ipomoea kotschyana* showed wider distribution and had 71, 62, 23 and 21 individuals, respectively (*See Table 4.3 on next page*). Out of the eleven species, ten are herbaceous life form and maximum of four threatened species were reported in Bambharayi and Khuda. In most of the coastal wetlands one or two species were reported.

In general plant diversity seems to be much higher in the coastal wetland surroundings than the other areas nearby which is obviously due to increased water availability and soil moisture content which promotes higher range of natural vegetation. However, there was no data on before the construction of coastal wetlands. Hence there was no comparison made and this information can be baseline date for future monitoring.

Table: 4.3: Status of Threatened Plant Species in and Around Studied Coastal Wetlands

S. No.	Species	Open Scrub	Agri. Hedge	Wetland	Waste Land	*Prosopis* Dominant	Open Grassland	Total
1.	*Ammannia desertorum*			2				2
2.	*Citrullus colocynthis*	3						3
3.	*Dactyliandra welwitschii*		3					3
4.	*Commiphora wightii*		7	3	10	3		23
5.	*Heliotropium bacciferum*			5		5	1	11
6.	*Heliotropium rariflorum*	3	8	3	34	13	1	62
7.	*Helicrysum cutchicum*		3	6	60	2		71
8.	*Indigofera caerulea*				3			3
9.	*Convolvulus stocksii*		2		4			6
10.	*Ipomoea kotschyana*				2	19		21
	No of species	2	5	5	6	5	2	
	Overall	6	23	19	113	42	2	205

Faunal Status

Herpetofaunal Staus

Species Richness: Overall 20 species of herpetofauna belonging to 11 families and 20 genera were recorded from different coastal wetlands. Out of the total species, four are amphibians, 15 reptiles and one species is turtle (Fig. 4.4). Maximum of seven species were recorded from two coastal wetlands i.e. Modkuba and Bhadia Nana. Panchotia, Luni and Vira coastal wetlands had richness of only one species while no species were recorded from Bhadreshwar coastal wetland (Table 4.4). One schedule-I species and three schedule-II species were recorded and their Threatened status is given in Table 4.4.

Abundance: This list of herpetofauna resulted with total count of 448 animals, of that maximum of 71 animals were counted from Modkuba coastal wetland followed by 32 in Bharapar and 26 in Sindhodi. Minimum of five coastal wetlands i.e., Dhrab, Dhuvai, Lathedi, Luni and Zarpara reported minimum of only two animals each. In addition to 448 animals 17 indirect evidences were reported to confirm the presence of some of these species (*See Table 4.4 on next page*).

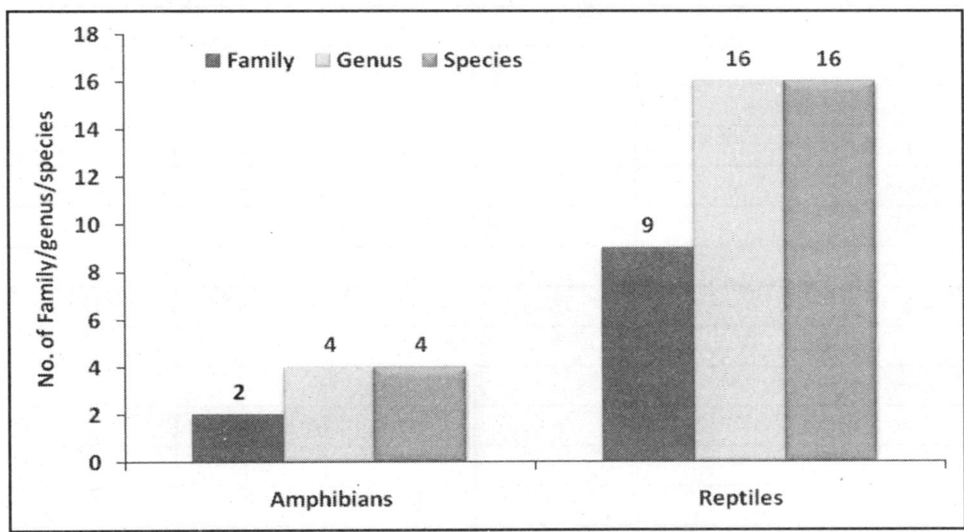

Fig. 4.4: Taxonomic Diversity of Herpetofauna in and Around Coastal Wetlands

Conservation Status

Among the 20 species only one species Indian Flap-shelled Turtle (*Lissemys punctata*), fall under the endangered category of Indian Wildlife Protection act. Hardwicke's Short Tail Agama (*Brachysaura minor*), Monitor Lizard (*Varanus bengalensis*), Indian Rat Snake (*Ptyas mucosa*) are schedule II or vulnerable species (*See Table Table 4.5 on page 103*).

Table 4.4: Taxonomical Status of Herpetofauna in and Around Coastal Wetland

Coastal Wetland Name	Family	Genus	Species	Abundance
1	2	3	4	5
Ambliyara	4	6	6	10
Bada	2	4	4	3(3)
Bambhadai	2	3	3	3(4)
Bhachau	3	3	3	4
Bhadia Nana	5	7	7	24(4)
Bhadreshwar	0	0	0	7
Bhadreshwar (TR)	2	2	2	3
Bharapar	3	4	4	32
Budia	2	2	2	11
Charopadi Moti	4	4	4	22
Chhadvara	3	3	3	9
Dhrabh	1	2	2	2
Dhuvai	2	2	2	2
Golay	6	6	6	7
Gunai	3	3	3	4
Gundiali	2	2	2	9
Jangi	4	4	4	18
Kadoli	3	3	3	23
Khirsara	4	4	4	4
Khuda	5	5	5	17
Kori Creek	3	3	3	20
Koriyani	6	6	6	17
Kosa Vadzar	6	6	6	17
Kukadsar	4	5	5	6
Lakhapar	4	5	5	5
Lathedi	1	2	2	2
Luni	1	1	1	2
Modkuba	6	7	7	71(1)
Mopar	4	4	4	3(2)
Morvadar	3	4	4	8
Mota Layja	5	5	5	12

(Contd...)

1	2	3	4	5
Moti Chirai	3	4	4	5
Mundra	6	6	6	12
Nani Chirai	3	6	6	7
Narayan Sarovar	6	6	6	11
Navagam (Manana)	3	3	3	3
Navinal	2	2	2	4
Panchatia	1	1	1	1(3)
Sindhodi	2	2	2	26
Vira	1	1	1	6
Wandhia	5	6	6	6
Zarpara	2	2	2	2
Overall	**11**	**20**	**20**	**448(17)**

Table 4.5: Conservation Status of Herpeto-fauna Recorded in Coastal Wetlands during the Survey

S. No.	Family and Scientific Name	Common Name	IUCN Status	IWP Act 1972
1	2	3	4	5
	Bufonidae (Toads)			
1.	*Bufo stomaticus*	Marbled Toad	LC	Schedule IV
	Ranidae (Frogs)			
2.	*Euphlyctis cyanophlyctis*	Skittering Frog	LC	Schedule IV
3.	*Tomopterna breviceps*	Indian Burrowing Frog	LC	Schedule IV
4.	*Hoplobatrachus tigerinus*	Indian Bull Frog	LC	Schedule IV
	Gekkonidae (Lizards)			
5.	*Hemidactylus leschenaultii*	Bark Gecko	LRlc	
	Agamidae (Agamids)			
6.	*Calotes versicolor*	Indian Garden Lizard	LRnt	Schedule IV
7.	*Sitana ponticeriana*	Fan-Throated Lizard	LC	Schedule IV
8.	*Uromastyx hardwikii*	Spiny Tailed Lizard	VU	Schedule II, Part I
9.	*Brachysaura minor*	Hardwicke's Short Tail Agama	DD	
	Scincidae (Skinks)			
10.	*Mabuya carinata*	Common Keeled Grass Skink	LC	

(Contd…)

1	2	3	4	5
11.	*Mabuya macularius* **Lacertidae (Lacertides)**	Eastern Bronze Skink	LC	
12.	*Acanthodactylus cantoris*	Indian Fringe-Toad Lizard	LRnt	
13.	*Ophisops jerdonii*	Jerdon's Snake-Eye	LC	
	Varanidae (Monitor lizard)			
14.	*Varanus bengalensis*	Monitor Lizard	LC	Schedule II, Part I
	***Colubridae* (Snake)**			
15.	*Ptyas mucosa*	Indian Rat Snake	LRnt	Schedule II, Part I
16.	*Xenochrophis piscator*	Checkered Keelback Water Snake	LRlc	Schedule IV
17.	*Coelognathus Helena*	Common Indian Trinklet Snake	LRnt	Schedule IV
	***Elapidae* (Snake)**			
18.	*Naja oxiana*	Black Cobra	CR	Schedule II, Part I
	***Viperidae* (Snake)**		DD	
19.	*Echis carinatus*	Indian Saw-Scaled Viper	NT	Schedule IV
	***Trionychidae* (Turtle)**			
20.	*Lissemys punctata*	Indian Flap-shelled Turtle	LRlc	Schedule I, Part II

CR: Critically Endangered, DD: Data Deficient, LC: Least Concern, LRlc: Lower Risk Least concern, LRnt: Lower Risk near threatened, NT: Near Threatened, VU: Vulnerable

BIRDS

Species Richness

A total of 199 species of birds belonging to 116 genera of 46 families were recorded during the survey. Out of the total recorded species, 127 species were terrestrial, belonging to 77 genera under 32 families (Fig. 4.5) and 72 species were aquatic birds belonging to 39 genera under 18 families (Fig. 4.6). During this survey Manaba (Rapar) coastal wetland had highest number (75) of bird species whereas Bhadreshwar had lowest number (32) of bird species.

Overall the coastal wetland study area estimated species diversity of H′ 4.486 showed the habitats in and around the manmade coastal wetland supported high diversity of bird species. Among the coastal wetland, Dhuvai coastal wetland estimated highest diversity of 3.86, followed by 3.84

Bambhadai and 3.79 Budia coastal wetlands. Lakhapar coastal wetland supported very low species richness and abundance and hence it had estimated low species diversity of H 2.025 among the coastal wetlands (Table 4.6).

Abundance Status

Number of birds counted within the study area reached to a total of around 14,000 birds. Among the coastal wetlands, Navagam (Manaba) had counted maximum of 1109 birds, followed by Kosa Vadzar 991, Lakhapar 692 and Khuda 689 birds. Bhadia Nana coastal wetland was counted minimum of 78 birds (Table 4.6).

Table 4.6: Overall Avifaunal Status in and Around Coastal Wetlands

Coastal Wetland	Family	Genus	Species	Abundance	Species Diversity
1	2	3	4	5	6
Ambliyara	22	30	35	168	3.287
Bada	21	32	36	156	3.184
Bambhadai	29	50	64	272	3.842
Bhachau	25	35	45	259	3.363
Bhadia Nana	22	28	34	78	3.33
Bhadreshwar	17	25	32	123	3.569
Bhadreshwar (TR)	27	43	57	356	3.234
Bharapar	24	41	45	205	3.417
Budia	26	47	65	422	3.791
Charopadi Moti	25	33	39	258	3.244
Chhadvara	22	36	45	231	3.527
Dhrub	22	35	45	228	3.482
Dhuvai	26	49	63	490	3.86
Golay	28	36	47	270	3.503
Gunau	25	35	41	211	3.142
Gundiyali	28	40	43	229	2.995
Jangi	22	35	43	227	3.474
Kadoli	26	39	55	320	3.68
Khirsara	21	33	38	177	3.494
Khuda	26	39	52	689	3.18
Kori Creek	28	37	45	361	3.225
Koriyani	31	52	67	455	3.783
Kosa Vadzar	32	47	57	911	2.325
Kukadsar	25	37	43	195	3.362
Lakhapar	23	31	39	692	2.025

(Contd...)

1	2	3	4	5	6
Lathedi	21	38	47	438	3.441
Luni	28	45	59	335	3.601
Modkuba	27	46	54	365	3.214
Modvadar	27	46	63	592	3.53
Mopar	24	36	46	225	3.571
Mota Layza	24	38	41	129	3.423
Moti Chirai	24	36	46	373	3.398
Mundra	22	35	43	211	3.469
Nani Chirai	26	43	56	235	3.793
Narayan Sarovar	30	42	53	366	3.567
Navagam (Manaba)	29	54	75	1109	3.678
Navinal	25	37	48	214	3.579
Panchotia	31	47	60	418	3.392
Sindhodi	30	43	57	363	3.743
Vira	24	38	46	211	3.345
Wandhia	19	29	33	187	3.233
Zarpara	25	43	59	307	3.79
Overall	**46**	**116**	**199**	**14,061**	**4.486**

Migratory Status

Out of the total 199 recorded species, 114 were residents and 82 species were migratory (Table 4.7).Out of resident species 89 are terrestrial and 25 are aquatic in nature. Among the migratory species 35 are terrestrial while 47 species fall under aquatic species (Table 4.7).

Table 4.7: Overall Migratory Status of the Recorded Avifauna in and Around Coastal Wetlands

Migratory Status	Terrestrial	Aquatic	Total
P	3	0	3
R	89	25	114
Rp	2	0	2
RW	13	15	28
V	2	3	5
W	16	29	45
WP	1	0	1
?	1	0	1
Total	**127**	**72**	**199**

R = *widespread resident;* r = *very local resident;* W = *widespread winter visitor;* w = *sparse winter visitor;* P = *widespread migrant;* p = *sparse migrant;* V = *vagrant or irregular visitor;* ? = *requires status confirmation.*

Conservation Status

Among the recorded avian fauna, 16 species have been listed in the threatened category of IUCN red list (BirdLife International 2010) (Table 4.8). Out of these threatened species, nine were aquatic bird species (Black-necked Stork, Painted Stork, Spot-billed Pelican and Black-tailed Godwit, etc.) and seven were terrestrial bird species (Long-billed Vulture, White-rumped Vulture, European Roller, Black-headed Ibis and White-browed Bush chat, etc.).

Table 4.8: Overall Status of Recorded Avifauna in and Around Coastal Wetlands

IUCN-2010	Terrestrial	Aquatic	Total
CR	2	0	2
VU	1	1	2
NT	4	8	12
LC	120	63	183
Total	**127**	**72**	**199**

CR= Critically Endangered, LC= Least consent, NT= Near threatened, VU= Vulnerable.

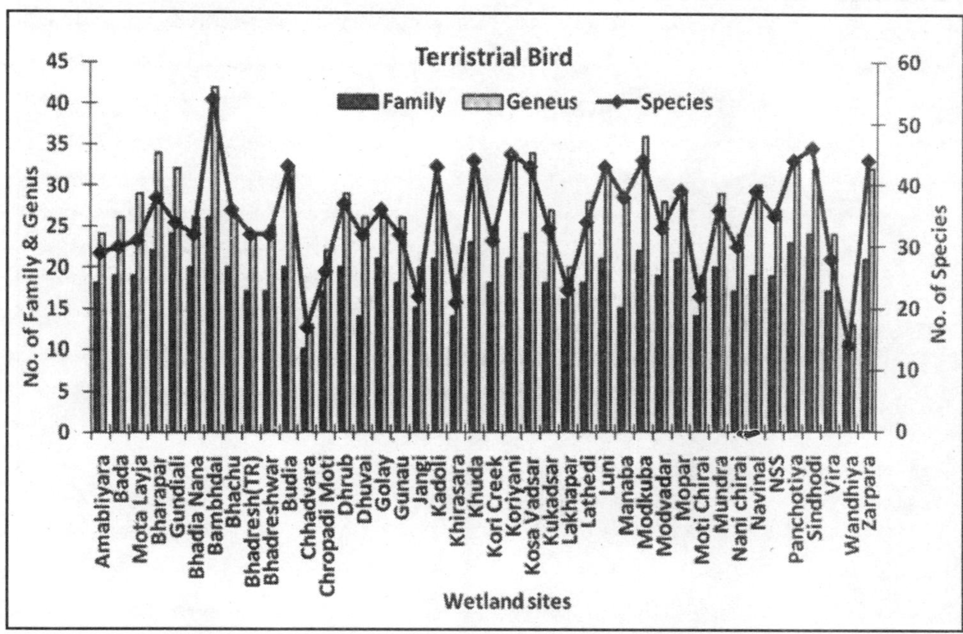

Fig. 4.5: Taxonomic Diversity of Terrestrial Birds of Coastal Wetlands of Kachchh

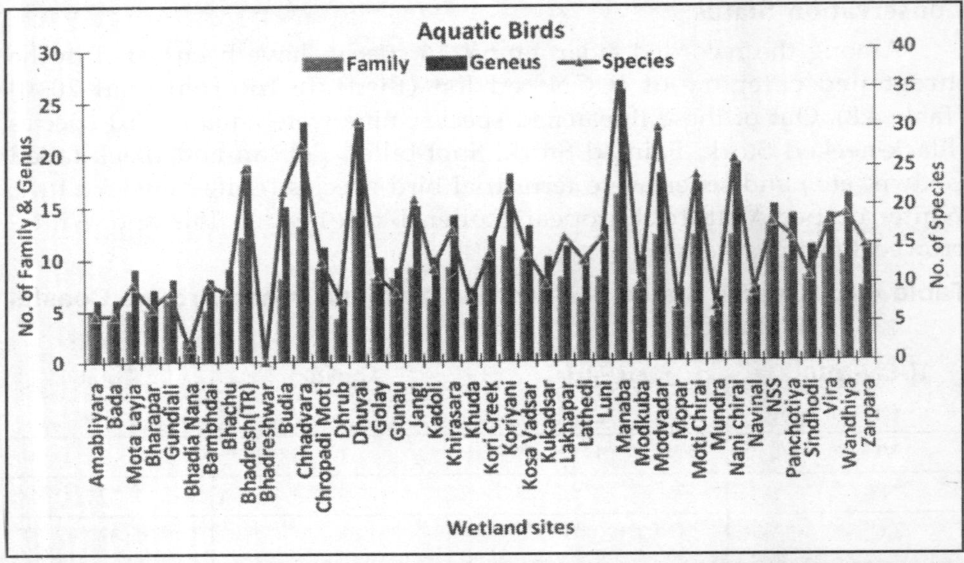

Fig. 4.6: Taxonomic Diversity of Aquatic Birds of Coastal Wetlands of Kachchh

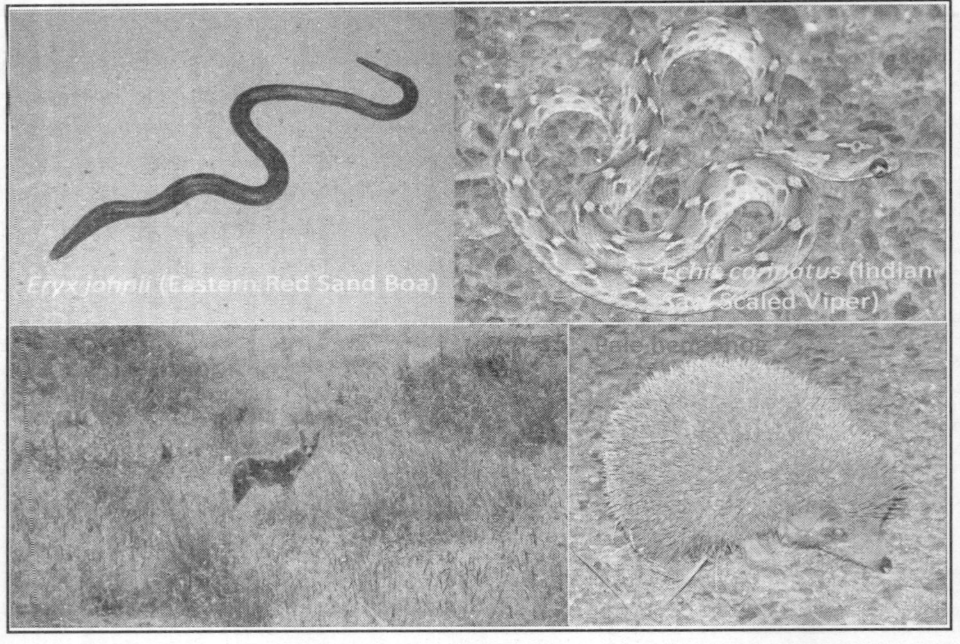

Painted Stork

Pied Kingfisher

Spotted Owlet

Black-nacked Stork

Small Blue Kingfisher

Green Bee-eater

MAMMALS

Species Richness

Overall 13 species of mammals belonging to 10 families and 13 genera were recorded from different coastal wetlands. Out of the total species, seven are Carnivore, three are artiodactyla and rodentia and one species of Logomorpha (Fig. 4.7). Maximum 11 species were recorded from Panchotia coastal wetland while only one species was recorded from each coastal wetland of Kadoli, Zarpara, Vira, Chhadvara, Ambliyara, Wandhia, Gunai, Khirsara and Navagam (Manaba). No mammal species were recorded from Bhadia Nana and Jangi coastal wetland.

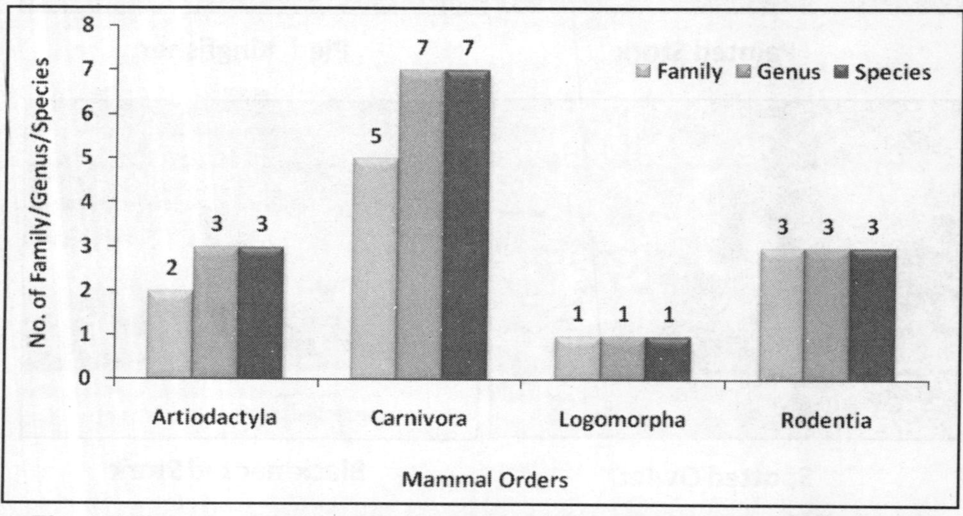

Fig. 4.7: Taxonomic Diversity of Mammalian Orders in Coastal Wetlands

Abundance Status

Survey of mammalian fauna in the project area recorded 217 animals. Among the species maximum of 44 Indian Hare were reported followed by 38 Nilgai, 35 Indian Gerbill, 21 Chinkara, 19 Jungle Cat, 15 wild boar, 14 common Mongoose and 13 Jackal (*See Table 4.9 on next page*).

Conservation Status

Out of 13 mammalian fauna reported from the study area, Leopard (*Panthera pardus) and* Chinkara or Indian Gazelle (*Gazella gazelle) were the two species belong to* Schedule –I of Indian Wildlife protection Act. Presence of Leopard was conformed based on the indirect evidence i.e., Pug mark, while Chinkara was reported based on both direct sightings and indirect evidences like pellets and hoof marks. These faunal lists include three schedule II species (Jackal, Jungle Cat and Indian Fox or Bengal Fox) and threatened status of mammals is given in Table 4.10 (*See Table on page 112*).

Table 4.9: Taxonomical Status of Mammalian Fauna in and Around Coastal Wetland

Coastal Wetland Name	Family	Genus	Species	Abundance
1	2	3	4	5
Ambliyara	1	1	1	0(3)
Bada	8	8	8	7(3)
Bambhadai	2	2	2	2
Bhachau	2	2	2	2
Bhadia Nana	0	0	0	0
Bhadreshwar	4	5	5	15
Bhadreshwar (TR)	4	5	5	7
Bharapar	2	2	2	2
Budia	2	2	2	4(1)
Charopadi Moti	5	6	6	20
Chhadvara	1	1	1	0(9)
Dhrab	4	4	4	4(2)
Dhuvai	2	2	2	4(1)
Golay	4	4	4	4
Gunai	1	1	1	1
Gundiyali	4	4	4	7(2)
Jangi	0	0	0	0
Kadoli	1	1	1	1
Khirsara	1	1	1	1
Khuda	5	6	6	17
Kori Creek	3	3	3	10
Koriyani	3	3	3	3(2)
Kosa Vadzar	4	5	5	6
Kukadsar	2	2	2	3(1)
Lakhapar	3	3	3	3
Lathedi	2	3	3	3
Luni	2	2	2	4
Modkuba	8	9	9	8(4)
Mopar	4	4	4	4
Modvadar	6	6	6	17
Mota Layja	2	2	2	2

(Contd...)

1	2	3	4	5
Moti Chirai	2	2	2	2
Mundra	3	3	3	6
Nani Chirai	3	4	4	3(5)
Narayan Sarovar	4	5	5	9(1)
Navagam (Manaba)	1	1	1	4
Navinal	3	3	3	2(2)
Panchotia	9	11	11	17(2)
Sindhodi	6	7	7	10(3)
Vira	1	1	1	1
Wandhia	1	1	1	1
Zarpara	1	1	1	1
Overall	**9**	**13**	**13**	**217(37)**

Table 4.10: List and Status of Mammalian Species Recorded in Coastal Wetlands during the Survey

S. No.	Order, Family and Scientific Names	Common Name	IUCN Status	IWP Act 1972
1	2	3	4	5
	ARTIODACTYLA			
	Bovidae			
1.	*Boselaphus tragocamelus*	Nilgai or Blue bull	LC	Schedule III
2.	*Gazella gazelle*	Chinkara or Indian Gazelle	VU	Schedule I, Part I
	Suidae			
3.	Sus scrofa	Wild Boar	LC	Schedule III
	CARNIVORA			
	Canidae			
4.	Canis aureus	Jackal	LC	Schedule II, Part II
5.	Vulpes bengalensis	Indian Fox or Bengal Fox	LC	Schedule II, Part II
	Felidae			
6.	*Felis chaus*	Jungle Cat	LC	Schedule II, Part II
7.	*Panthera pardus*	Leopard	NT	Schedule I, Part I
	Herpestidae			
8.	*Herpestes edwardsii*	Common or Grey Mongoose	LC	Schedule IV
	Hyaenidae			

(Contd…)

1	2	3	4	5
9.	*Hyaena hyaena*	Striped Hyaena	NT	Schedule III
	LAGOMORPHA			
	Leporidae			
10.	*Lepus nigricollis*	Indian Hare	LC	Schedule IV
	RODENTIA			
	Hystricidae			
11.	*Hystrix indica*	Indian Porcupine	LC	Schedule IV
	Sciuricidae			
12.	*Funambulus pennantii*	Five-Striped Palm Squirrel	LC	Schedule IV
	Muridae			
13.	*Tatera indica*	Indian Gerbil	LC	Schedule V

CR: *Critically Rare*, DD: *Data Deficient*, LC: *Least Concern*, LRlc: *Lower Risk Least concern*, LRnt: *Lower Risk near threatened*, NT: *near Threatened*, VU: *Vulnerable*.

Threatened Biodiversity

IUCN conservation status and Indian Wildlife Protection Act schedule –I flora and fauna species status was analysed in all the coastal wetlands and it found that a total of nine species were recorded. *Commiphora wightii*; is the only plant species in IUCN conservation status recorded in nine coastal wetlands. Under herpatofauna, Wildlife Protection Act schedule –I species was Indian Flag shell Turtle was reported only in Mota Layja. Avifauna list included five schedule –I species and they include: Indian Peafowl recorded in most of the coastal wetlands whereas Long-billed vulture and White-rumped vulture was recorded only in Kori creek coastal wetland (Table 4.11).

In the absence of biodiversity status before the construction of coastal wetland, the impact or influence of coastal wetland on biodiversity values are not comparable. Hence the current biodiversity status can be used as bench mark data base for future monitoring.

Table 4.11: Overall IUCN and IWPA –Schedule-I Species Status in and Around Coastal Wetlands

Coastal Wetland	Flora	Birds					Mammals		Herpatofauna
	C.w	I.P	L.V	Os	WS	W.V	Ch	Le	FT
Amabliyara		3					–	–	
Bada		4					–	–	
Bambhdai	4	4					–	–	
Bhachau							–	–	
Bhadia Nana		4					–	–	

(Contd...)

Coastal Wetland	Flora	Birds					Mammals		Herpatofauna
	C.w	I.P	L.V	Os	WS	W.V	Ch	Le	FT
Bhadreshwar	2						1	–	
Bhadreshwar (TR)							2	–	
Bharapar							–	–	
Budia							–	–	
Charopadi Moti		3					3	–	
Chhadvara		4					–	–	
Dhrub		20			4		–	–	
Dhuvai							–	–	
Golay		4					1	–	
Gunau		4		1			–	–	
Gundiali					1		–	–	
Jangi		4					–	–	
Kadoli							–	–	
Khirasara							–	–	
Khuda							1	–	
Kori Creek		4	4			2	–	–	
Koriyani		14					3(2)	–	
Kosa Vadsar		7			4		1	–	
Kukadsar	6						–	–	
Lakhapar		17		2			–	–	
Lathedi							1	–	
Luni	2						–	–	
Manaba							–	–	
Modkuba	9						0(3)	–	
Modvadar							1	–	
Mopar	8	8					3	–	
Mota Layja							–	–	1
Moti Chirai		3					–	–	
Mundra							–	–	

(Contd...)

Coastal Wetland	Flora	Birds					Mammals		Herpatofauna
	C.w	I.P	L.V	Os	WS	W.V	Ch	Le	FT
Nani chirai	3	4					1	–	
Narayan Sarovar	5						1	–	
Navinal		8					–	–	
Panchotiya		7					1	1	
Sindhodi		8					1	–	
Vira							–	–	
Wandhiya	5	4					–	–	
Zarpara		3					–	–	

I.P – *Indian Peafowl*, L.V- *Long billed Vulture*, Os- *Osprey*, Ws- *White stork*, W.V- *White rumped Valture*, Cw- *Commiphora wightii*, Ch-*Chinkara*, Le-*Leopard*, F.T- *Flag shell turtle*

REFERENCES

Ahmad, L. (1972): Coastal Geomorphology of India. Orient Longmans Ltd. New Delhi.

Ali, S. (2002): Book of Indian Birds. Bombay Natural History Society. p. 345.

Allen L, Engeman R and Krupa H (1996): Evaluation of Three Telative Abundance Indices for Assessing Dingo Population. *Wildlife Research*. 23: 197-206.

Anon, (2001): District Census Handbook- Kachchh District. Government of India Publication, New Delhi.

Begon, M., Harper J.L. and Townsend, C.R. (1996): A Text Book on Ecology: Individuals, Populations and Communities, by Blackwell Science Publications, *2nd* Edition.

Bhandari, M.M. (1990): Flora of the Indian Desert. MPS Reports, Jodhpur.

Bhupathy, S. (1991): Population and Resources Utilization of Waterfowl in Keoladeo National Park, Bharatpur. Ph.D. Thesis. Rajasthan University, Jaipur.

Bibby, C.J., Burgess, N.D. and Hill, D.A. (1992): Bird Census Techniques. Academic Press, London.

BirdLife International, (2010): The BirdLife Checklist of the Birds of the World, with Conservation Status and Taxonomic Sources. Version 3. Downloaded from http://www.birdlife.org/datazone/species/downloads/BirdLife_Checklist_Version_3.zip [.xls zipped 1 MB].

Burnham, K.P., Anderson, D.R. & Laake, J.L. (1980). Estimation of Density from Line Transect Sampling of Biological Populations. Wildlife Monographs. 72: 1-202.

Corn & Bury, R.B. (1990). Sampling Methods for Terrestrial Amphibians and Teptiles. In A.C. Carey & L.F. Ruggiero (eds.), Wildlife-Habitat Relationships: Sampling Procedures for Pacific North-west Vertebrates, pp. 1-28. U.S. Dept. Agri. For. Serv., Gen. Tech. Rep. PNW-GTR-256.

Daniel, J.C. (2002): The Book of Indian Reptiles and Amphibians. Bombay Natural History Society and Oxford University press. p. 238.

Daniels, R.J.R. (1992): Environmental Impact Assessment of Ecological Resources: Lesson from the Proposed Konkan Railway Project. Energy Env. Monitor. 8. (2): 67-70.

Daniels, R.J.R. (2005): Amphibians of Peninsular India. Universities Press (India) Private Limited. First Edn. p. 267.

Dieni, J.S. and Jones, S.L. (2002): A Field Test of the Area Search Method for Measuring Breeding Birds Populations. Journal of Field Ornithology, 73: 253-257.

Gedan, K.B., Kirwan, M.L. and Wolanski, E. (2010): The Present and Future Role of Coastal Wetland Vegetation in Protecting Shorelines: Answering Recent Challenges to the Paradigm. Climatic Change. DOI 10.1007/s10584-010-0003-7.

Gopal. B. and Krishnamurthy. K. (1993): Wetlands of the World I. (Ed D.F. Whigham, et al. (eds.). Kluver Academic Publishers, Netherlands, pp: 345-414.

Greeson P.E., Clark J.R. and Clark J.E., eds. (1979): Wetland Functions and Values: The State of Our Understanding. Minneapolis, MN: Am. Water Resour. Assoc.

Grimmett, R., Inskipp, C. and Inskipp, T. (2006): Pocket Guide to the Birds of the Indian Sub-continent. Oxford University Press, New Delhi. p. 384.

Henke, S.E. and Knowlton, F.F. (1995): Techniques for Estimating Coyote Abundance. pp. 71-78. In: Proceedings of the Symposium: Coyotes in the Southwest. Parks and Wildlife Department: Austin, Texas.

Hutto, R.L., Pletsechel, S.M. and Hendrick, P. (1986): A Fixed Radius Point Count Method for Non Breeding Season Use. *The Auk.* 103: 593-602.

Jagtap, T.G., Naik, S. and Nagle V.L. (2001): Assessment of Coastal Wetland Resources of Central West Coast, India, using LANDSAT Data. Journal of the Indian Society of Remote Sensing, 29(3): 140-150.

Kershaw, K.A. (ed) (1973): Sampling Test of Comparison and Application of Quadrate Measures pp. 21-39. In: Quantitative and Dynamic Plant Ecology. Second Edition. William Clowes and Sons Limited, London.

Lee Foote A., Pandey Sanjeeva and Krogman Naomi T. (1996): Processes of Wetland Loss in India Environmental Conservation 23(1): 45-54.

Mueller-Dombios H and Ellenberg (1974): Aims and Methods of Vegetation Ecology. John Wiley and Sons, New York. p. 547.

Nayar, M.P. and Sastry, A.R.K. (eds.) (1990): Red Data Book of Indian Plants. Vol. 3. B.S.I., Howrah.

Prater, S.H. (2005): The Book of Indian Animals. Bombay Natural History Society and Oxford University press 12th Edn. p. 316.

Rodgers, W.A. (1991): Techniques of Wildlife Census in India: A Field Manual. Wildlife Institute of India, Dehra Dun.

Sale, J.B. and Berkmuller, K. (1988): *Manual of Wildlife Techniques for India*. FAO, United Nation's India Establishment of Wildlife Institute of India Dehra Dun.

Sarkar, S.K. and Bhattacharya, A.K. (2003): Conservation of Biodiversity of the Coastal Resources of Sundarbans, Northeast India: An Integrated Approach Through Environmental Education. Marine Pollution Bulletin 47: 260-264.

Shah, G.L. (1978): Flora of Gujarat State. University Press, Sardar Patel University. Vallabh Vidyanagar.

Sridharan, U. (1989): Comparative Ecology of Resident Ducks in Keoladeo National Park. Bharatpur, Ph.D. Dissertation, University of Bombay, Bombay.

Thommpson, I.D., Davidson, I.J., O' Donnell, S. and Brazeau, F. (1989): Use of Track Transect to Measure the Relative Occurrence of some Arboreal Mammals in Uncut Forest and Regeneration Stands. Canadian Journal of Zoology. 67: 1816-1823.

WCMC, (1994): Status Report as of 24 November 1994, Gujarat, Printout from Plant Database BG- BASE. World Conservation Monitoring Centre.

Welsh, H.H. Jr. (1987): Monitoring Herpetofauna in Woodland Habitats of North Western California and South West Oregon: A Comprehensive Strategy. pp. 203-213. In: Multiple-use Management of California's Hardwood Resources. (Eds.) T.R. Plumb, and N. H. Pillisbury Gen. Tech. Rep. PSW-100. US Dep. of Agri., Forest Service.

Welsh, H.H. Jr. and Lind, A. (1991): The Structure of the Herpetofaunal Assemblage in the Douglas-fir/hardwood Forests of Northwestern California and South Western Oregon. pp. 395-411. *In: Wildlife and vegetation of unmanaged Douglas-fir forests.* (Edt. LF Ruggiero, KB Aubry, AB Carey and MH Huff) Gen. Tech. Rep. PNW-GTR-285. Portland, OR: U. S. Dep. of Agri., Forest Service.

Zedler, J.B. and Kercher, S. (2005): Wetland Resources: Status, Trends, Ecosystem Services, and Restorability. Annu. Rev. Environ. Resour. 30: 39-74.

CHAPTER – 5

Impact of Fipronil on the Aquatic Environment

S.K. Gupta, *India*; N. Saharan, *India*; Akriti Gupta, *India*
K.K Sharma, *India*; A.K. Prusty, *India*

ABSTRACT

Fipronil is a highly effective, broad-spectrum first generation phenylpyrazole insecticide used in agricultural and domestic surroundings for controlling various insect pests in crops, lawns, public hygiene, amenity, veterinary pests and residential structures. It is a potent disrupter of the insect central nervous system via interference with the passage of chloride ions through the GABA regulated chloride channel. It is highly effective against a variety of insect pests such as ants, beetles, cockroaches, fleas, ticks, termites, mole crickets, thrips, rootworms, weevils, and other insects. The degradated products of fipronil are highly toxic to rainbow trout, bluegill sunfish, and freshwater invertebrates. The fipronil-sulfone and fipronil-desulfinyl metabolites are more toxic to freshwater invertebrates than the parent compound. There is evidence that fipronil and its degradates fipronil-sulfone and fipronil-sulfide may bioaccumulate, particularly in fishes. Fipronil poses a long term risks to nutrient cycling and soil fertility as some of the beneficial species like termites are severely affected due to toxicity, which indicates that fipronil may be unsuitable with locust IPM.

Due to development of resistance and cross-resistance and impending bans on the application of dieldrin, lindane and DDT in india, use of fipronil is gaining considerable attention in recent years. Risk assessment predictions have shown that some fipronil formulations present a risk to endangered bird, fish and aquatic and marine invertebrates. The application of fipronil requires careful consideration where contamination of the aquatic environment is expected, because of its high toxicity to some fishes and aquatic invertebrates. Also, growing concern on the use of the fipronil need further research to assess enantiomer-specific effects on non-target aquatic organism. Use of the single active enantiomer, need careful attention for safety of the environment. Further studies on chronic toxicity are needed to evaluate the risks associated with the current use pesticide (CUP) pesticide that may provide a greater insight into the potential teratogenic or other physiological effects of fipronil in aquatic organism.

Key Words: Fipronil, Bioaccumulation, Aquatic, Toxicity, Environment, Metabolite.

INTRODUCTION

Aquatic pollution has become an important global concern in recent times due to tremendous increase in the use of agrochemicals for control of insect pests of crop plants. Burgeoning and widespread use of pesticides primarily in the agricultural sector leads to pollution of aquatic environment which becomes hazardous to the aquatic life. Some of these pesticides find their way into neighboring water bodies through surface run-off, spray drift, soil or seed treatment and accidental spillage. On reaching the water bodies pesticides experience different fates, some of them persists and some of them degrades into metabolite.

In India as much as 70 per cent of the chemical formulations employed in agricultural practices are believed to affect non target organism and to find their way to water bodies, ultimately polluting the water (Bhatnagar et al., 1992). Kilgore and Mingyuli (1975) reported that concentration of pesticide residues were found to be more in aquatic ecosystem rather than in terrestrial ecosystem. The overall impact is more in aquatic environment as residues of pesticides and other harmful agrochemicals gets transported to greater distances in the hydrosphere. On reaching the water bodies, pesticide adversely affect non-target aquatic organisms that are bathed in the medium containing toxicant. Furthermore, indiscriminate use of pesticides in the agriculture and its occurrence in the water magnifies the stress mediated factors in aquatic organism, thus posing a hazard of the possibility of getting into the food chain. The adverse effect leads to bioaccumulation and biomagnifications through entry into the food chain besides direct consumption of contaminated edible aquatic organism.

Aquatic animals inhabiting polluted water may tend to accumulate toxic chemicals in higher concentration even when the ambient environment concentrations are low. Accumulation of pesticides is not only hazardous for these animals but it may also weaken immunity of non-target aquatic animals to make them more prone to various diseases. Consumption of pesticide contaminated aquatic organisms such as fishes, shrimps, oysters and crabs has been reported to affect the immune response and causes severe health problems in human beings. Different pesticides have markedly different effects on aquatic life which makes generalization very difficult. The important point is that many of these effects are chronic and often not noticed by casual observers, yet have consequences for the entire food chain.

Detrimental effect of the pesticide on the aquatic organisms may be expressed by either their mortality or the alteration in the growth and development, Cancers, tumours and lesions on fish and animals, reproductive inhibition or failure, suppression of immune system, disruption of endocrine (hormonal) system, Cellular and DNA damage, teratogenic effects (physical deformities), poor fish health marked by low red to white blood cell ratio, excessive slime on fish scales and gills, intergenerational effects (effects are not apparent until subsequent generations of the organism), other physiological effects such as egg shell thinning etc. It also affects the survival of the juvenile fishes and reduce the availability of table size fish and which leads to reduction in fish catch for the fisher folks. These effects are not inevitably caused by exposure to pesticides or other organic toxicants but in fact, it is a cumulative and synergistic effect of many stressors like temperature, heavy metals, crowding, pesticides, low dissolved oxygen, eutrophication and pathogens.

Among these stressors, pesticides are of prime concern as far as agriculture industry is concerned. These associated stresses need not be sufficient to have a synergistic effect with organic contaminants. Studies on pesticide residues in fish for lipophilic compounds and determination of exposure of fish to lipophobic pesticides through liver or bile analysis is mainly restricted to research programmes. Therefore, it is difficult to determine the pathways and fate of pesticides that are now used in many parts of the globe. In contrast, the ecosystemic affects from older, organochlorine pesticides has became readily evident which has resulted in the banning of these pesticide for agricultural activities.

The problem of pesticide management in developing countries is to some extent different than those of the industrialized nations which includes severe groundwater contamination and public health crises due to dumping of pesticides by unqualified people; improper destruction of old stores of pesticides; handling and application by untrained users, leading to improper application with environmental consequences; inadequate legislation and enforcement of pesticide regulations; disposal, storage and handling is a major problem, including leakage from old barrels and deliberate dumping of surplus pesticide mixtures into water courses; use of pesticides for inappropriate purposes, such as killing of trash fish; use of old pesticide drums for drinking water, cooking, etc.

Pescticides, heavy metals and fertilizers are the major sources of aquatic pollution. Among the pesticides, insecticides are one of the chemicals which play an important role in controlling different types of insects. Unsystematic use of insecticides on crops causes serious environmental hazards. Unfortunately, most of the insecticides are non biodegradable and tend to persist for years together in soil and water. The residues of insecticides from soil and water may concentrate into bodies of plants, micro-organisms, invertebrates and arthropods and which may get transported into the bodies of higher organisms through the food chain. Problem associated with the use of insecticides in particular over a long period is the development of cross-resistance in insect pests. It is generally observed that when an insect develops resistance to a particular insecticide, it automatically becomes resistant to all the other insecticides having the same activity. Hence, current use pesticides (CUP), fipronil was developed as its mechanism of action on the insect pests is different from the other conventional insecticides.

FIPRONIL

Fipronil is relatively new, broad-spectrum, insecticide, first approved in 1996 for use on a number of crops in the Unites States, discovered and developed by Rhone-Poulenc. It is a member of a small class of pesticides, the phenyl pyrazoles, which are principally chemicals with an herbicidal effect (Rhone-Poulenc, 1995). Fipronil acts as an insecticide with contact and stomach action. It is highly effective against a variety of insect pests such as ants, beetles, cockroaches, fleas, ticks, termites, mole crickets, thrips, rootworms, weevils, and other insects. Even minute concentration of fipronil is highly effective against various insects and pests (Mulrooney, Wolfenbarger, Howard, Goli & Goli 1998) owing to its lipophilicity and persistency properties. While fipronil is effective in insect control at comparable potencies to organophosphorous (OP) and carbamate insecticides, its use is expected to increase relative to other classes of pesticides because of developing species resistance to (OP) insecticide and (Hosie *et al.* 1995). It is being actively commercialized throughout a wide gamut of industrialized and developing countries. In India, fipronil is commercially sold in the market under various trade names like regent, termidor. Because of impending bans on application of dieldrin, lindane and DDT in india, use of fipronil is gaining considerable attention in recent years.

Fipronil is used to protect paddy crop from the attack of various pests in paddy-cum fish integrated farming system and also to control bund-destroying crabs in rice field. Thus there is potential threat on non-target aquatic organism. It is used on the water surface for killing of predatory bugs from the families Gerridae and Veliidae and killing of predatory bugs and beetles from the families Corixidae, Haliplidae (larvae), Dytiscidae, Notonectidae, Belastomatidae, Naucordiae, Gyrinidae, and Hydrophilidae (larvae). Moreover, the various fipronil degraded product, which are similar and even higher in potency to parent compound (Fenet *et al.* 2001; Schlenk *et al.* 2001) and more environmentally persistent (Walse *et al.* 2004; US EPA 1997), may lead to long term effects on non-target species.

STRUCTURE OF FIPRONIL

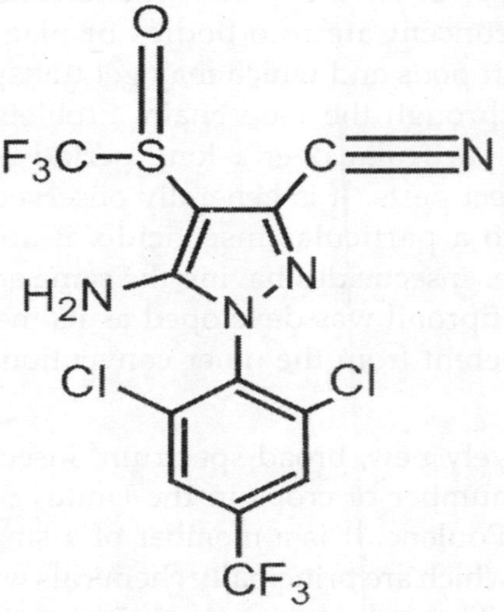

Fipronil: (±)-5-amino-1-(2, 6-dichloro-α, α, α-trifluoro-p-tolyl)-4-trifluoromethylsulfinylpyrazole-3-carbonitrile

CHARACTERISTICS OF FIPRONIL

Physical

White powder with a mouldy Odour (USEPA, 1996)

Molecular Formula

$C_{12}H_4Cl_2F_6N_4OS$

Melting Point

Stable to heat (MP=200-201°C), Density: 1.6262 g/ml at 20°C

Vapour Pressure

2.8 × 10-9 mm Hg at 25°C Octanol/Water Partition Coefficient

Solubility

Sparingly soluble in water (ACP, 1999), solubility in acetone is 545.9 gl^{-1} at water pH 9.0.

Stability

Stable at normal temperatures for one year but not stable in the presence of metal ions. Degrade slightly by sunlight, to produce a variety of metabolites, one of which (fipronil-desulfinyl) is extremely stable and is more toxic than the parent compound (USEPA, 1998a).

MODE OF ACTION

Fipronil represents the second generation of insecticides which exhibits neurotoxic activity by blocking the gamma-aminobutyric acid (GABA) receptor system as a noncompetitive blocker. The polychlorocycloalkanes are the first generation of such insecticides, that include α-endosulfan and lindane (Hainzl *et al.*,1998). Fipronil is an extremely active molecule and toxic to insects by contact or ingestion. Fipronil is a potent disrupter of the insect central nervous system via interference with the passage of chloride ions through the GABA regulated chloride channel (Rhone-Poulenc, 1996). This results in uncontrolled activity of central nervous system and the result is excessive neuronal activity. At sufficient doses fipronil causes paralysis and insect death (FAO, 1998). Some of the toxicity of fipronil observed in mammals also appears to involve interference with normal functioning of the GABA receptor (FAO, 1998). Fipronil sulfone, the biological metabolite of fipronil, is reported to be 20 times more active at mammalian chloride channels than at insect chloride channels.

TOXICITY OF FIPRONIL ON AQUATIC ORGANISMS

Fipronil applications can impact aquatic environments at low concentrations (US EPA 2001; US EPA 1997), thus there is potential for adverse effects on non-target species. The application of fipronil requires careful consideration where contamination of the aquatic environment is expected, because of its high toxicity to some fishes and aquatic invertebrates. It is classified as "dangerous to fish and other aquatic life" on certain product labels. Further, after getting into the field even at lower concentarion it may show chronic effects to aquatic organisms due to slow arte of dissipation. The only major established route of entry of fipronil to aquatic habitat is through direct use. A simulation model study undertaken by environmental protection agency (EPA) revealed that run off may be likely from in channel treatments (USEPA, 1996). Fipronil is classified by the FAO's Locust Pesticide Referee Group (LPRG) as low risk to aquatic invertebrates when applied at the recommended dosage rate for both barrier and blanket treatments for the control of locusts (LPRG, 1999).

Based on an acute toxicity study on *Daphnia* using fipronil, and three supplemental studies using its metabolites, fipronil was characterized as highly toxic to aquatic invertebrates (USEPA, 1996). Fipronil have an effective concentration (EC50) of 190 ppb for *Daphnia*. An invertebrate life cycle study of *Daphnia* showed that the least observable effective concentration (LOEC) and the maximum allowable toxicant concentration (MATC) was as 20 ppb and 14 ppb respectively (USEPA, 1996). Fipronil is highly toxic to oysters with an EC50 of 0.77 mg/l and very highly toxic to mysid shrimp with a 96-hour LC50 of 140 ng/l. Exposure to less than 5.0 ng/l fipronil affected mysid growth, reproduction and survival.

ACUTE TOXICITY STUDY IN FISHES

Median lethal concentration (LC_{50}) is the most widely accepted basis for acute toxicity test and it is the concentration of a test chemical which kills 50 per cent of the test organisms in a particular length of exposure (96 hours). Tests have been carried out to find out fipronil toxicity to different fish species and other aquatic organisms, such as shrimps and water fleas. Scientists have discovered that fipronil is highly toxic to sea and freshwater fishes and freshwater invertebrates. Two fipronil metabolites were also tested in freshwater fish and invertebrates and were more toxic than parent compound. The acute toxicity values of some species are as follows:

Species	Acute Toxicity	References
Oreochromis niloticus	(29-60) mg/l [96h]	Diallo *et al.*,1998
Bluegill sunfish	0.083 ppm [96h] 'very highly toxic'	USEPA, 1996
Rainbow trout	0.246 ppm [96h] 'highly toxic'	USEPA, 1996
Sheepshead minnow	0.13 ppm	USEPA, 1996
Japanese Carp	(LC50 (96 h) 0.34 ppm	(Colliot *et al.*, 1992)
Cyprinus carpio	(LC50 (96 h) 0.428 ppm	(Gupta *et al.*, 2012)

The degradated products of fipronil are highly toxic to rainbow trout, bluegill sunfish, and freshwater invertebrates. The sulfide degradate is 1.9 times more toxic to freshwater invertebrates. The results of a fish early life-stage toxicity study in rainbow trout show that fipronil affects larval growth with a non observable effective concentration (NOEC) of 0.0066 ppm and an least observable effective concentration (LOEC) of 0.015 ppm. Fipronil-sulfone is 6.3 times more toxic to rainbow trout and 3.3 times more toxic to bluegill sunfish (USEPA,1996) than the parent compound. The fipronil-sulfone and fipronil-desulfinyl metabolites are 6.6 and 1.9 times more toxic to freshwater invertebrates, respectively, than the parent compound. When applied to water, fipronil varies greatly in its toxicity and potential to bioaccumulate in aquatic arthropods, depending on the species.

Fate of Fipronil in the Environment

SOIL

Fipronil is readily transformed into desulfinyl derivatives when exposed to sunlight, with a half-life of 34 days. No evidence of volatility of fipronil or its metabolites have been observed (USEPA, 1996; Mulrooney *et al.*, 1998). Fipronil sticks tightly to soil and does not mix very well with water. Therefore, It is relatively immobile in soil and is not expected to percolate into groundwater. The sulfone and the amide are the two major degradates that was found at greater amounts than the limit of detection in field studies conducted under temperate climatic conditions (Belayneh, 1998).

Fishes Collected from the Fipronil Contaminated Water Bodies

Sample Collection for Analysis of Zooplankton from the Water Bodies Polluted with Fipronil

Degradation of the Aquatic Habitat due to Pesticide Pollution

A Garra Sps, Tolerant to Pesticide Contaminated Water Bodies

A field report advocated that fipronil degrades faster under tropical conditions than temperate with the majority of the metabolites belonged to the photodegradate desulfinyl (Belayneh, 1998). In soil, fipronil tends to dissipate by soil binding along with gradual microbial breakdown; however, on the soil surface photolysis may also be important. Fipronil has a half-life of 3.63 hours when exposed to a xenon light source in the laboratory. There is no evidence that fipronil or its breakdown metabolites evaporate from soil or water into the air. Fipronil is not well absorbed by plants when it is applied to soil.

MICROBIAL DEGRADATION

The by-products resulted from the microbial degradation of fipronil in the soil is found to be more active. Half lives for technical grade fipronil were relatively longer on bare soil than turfed soil, which suggests that microbial degradation may be responsible. Since fipronil adversely affect the nontarget aquatic species so as a curative measure, decontamination of the contaminated sites through bioremediation process offers viable alternative.

WATER

Hydrolysis of fipronil is important in alkaline conditions in direct proportion to increasing pH values. Fipronil is stable in the water at mild acidic pH and neutral. Fipronil reacts with water to break down into smaller chemicals when water becomes less acidic. The hydrolysis half-lives for pH of 12 and 9 in aqueous solutions were 0.1 and 32 days, respectively. Fipronil exposed to sunlight in water has a half-life of 3.6 h with the major degradates being desulfinyl (Belayneh, 1998). The reported solubilities for fipronil in water are 2.0-2.4 ppm (U.S EPA 1996; Kidd and James 1991; Ayliffe 1998).

The reported half-life for fipronil under aerobic aquatic conditions is about 14.5 days. The major metabolite (sulfide degradate) represented 74 per cent of the total radioactive residues after 30 days. The remaining minor metabolites identified by HPLC as the amide degradate, the carboxamide, and the desulfinyl photodegradate. The sulfide degradate was a major metabolite in anaerobic aquatic conditions while under aerobic soil conditions the amide and the sulfone were identified as the main degradation products (Feung and Yenne, 1997).

AIR

Fipronil does not readily volatilize due to relatively low vapor pressure and a low Henry's law constant. Consequently, except for drift that may occur during spray applications, fipronil is not likely to be found in the air (The British Crop Protection Council, 1997; U.S. EPA, 1996). There is no confirmation that fipronil or its breakdown products evaporate from soil or water into the air. Fipronil is not well absorbed by plants when it is applied to soil. If fipronil does get into plants, it can partially break down.

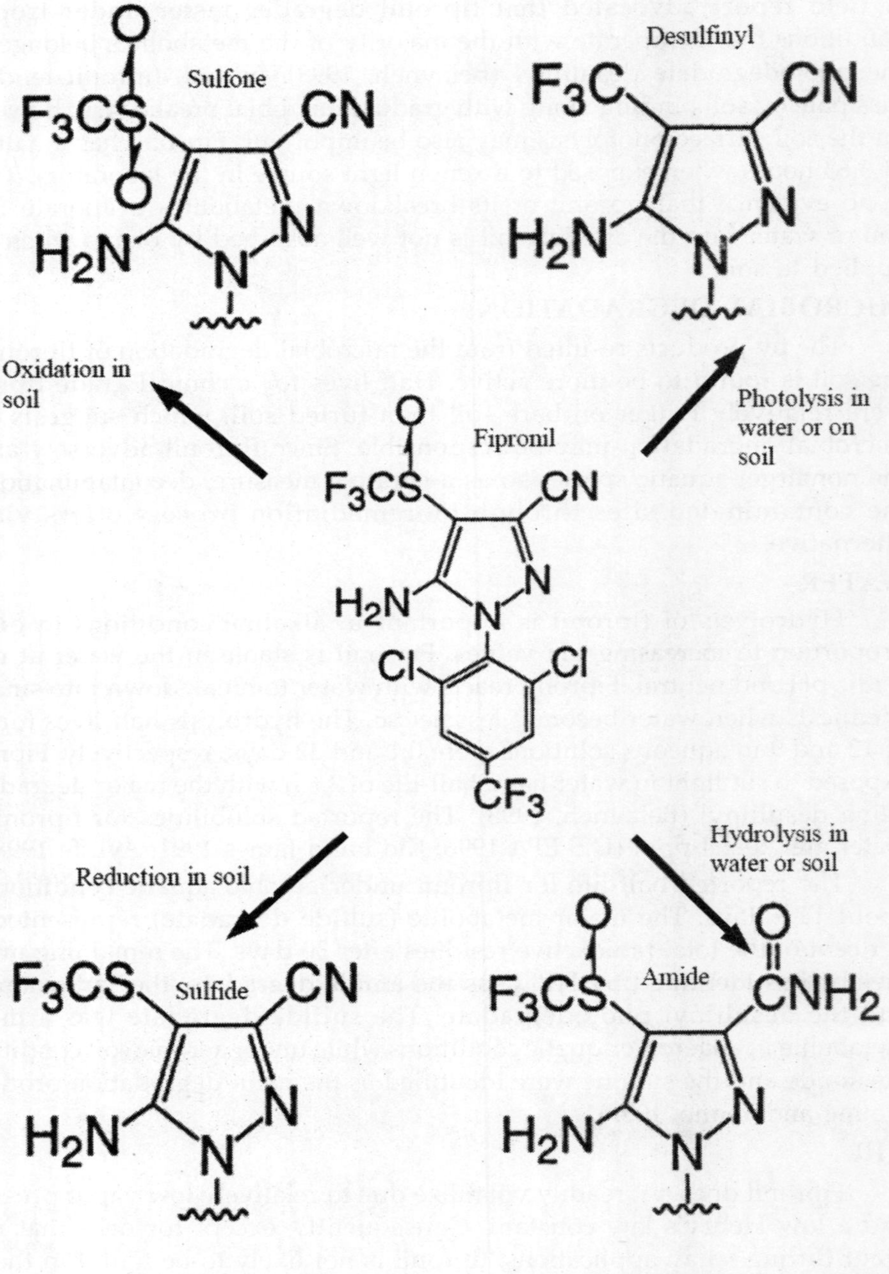
Sulfone
F3CS
O
O
CN
N
H2N
N
Desulfinyl
F3C
CN
N
H2N
N
Oxidation in soil
Photolysis in water or on soil
Fipronil
O
F3CS
CN
N
H2N
N
Cl
Cl
CF3
Reduction in soil
Hydrolysis in water or soil
F3CS
Sulfide
CN
N
H2N
N
O
F3CS
O
Amide
CNH2
N
H2N
N

Fig. 5.1: Degradation Pathways of Fipronil in Soils. (Adapted from Bobe et al. 1998)

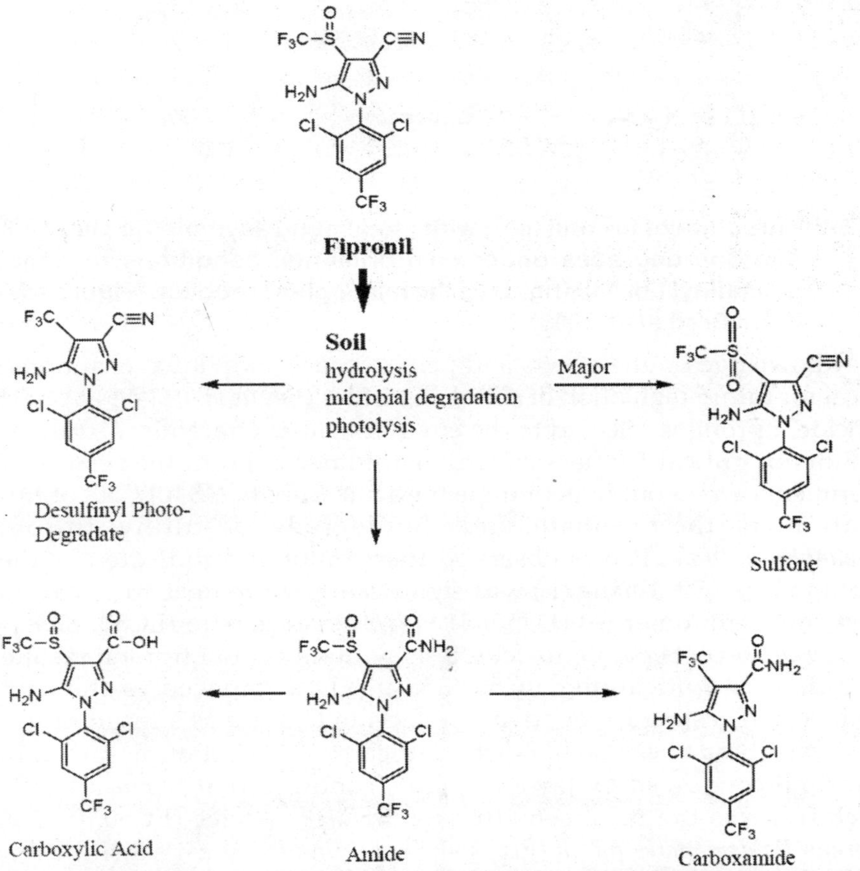

Fipronil

Soil
hydrolysis
microbial degradation
photolysis

Major

Desulfinyl Photo-Degradate

Sulfone

Carboxylic Acid

Amide

Carboxamide

Fig. 5.2: Degradation pathways of fipronil (Adapted from Pete Conelley 2001)

ENANTIOSELECTIVE EFFECTS OF FIPRONIL

Fipronil is one of the approximately 25 per cent of current-use pesticides that are chiral (Fig. 5.3) (Key *et al.*, 2003). Chiral molecules form nonsuperimposable mirror images and thus exist as enantiomers, which are designated as (+) and (–) based on their rotation of plane-polarized light. The most common cause of chirality in an organic molecule is a carbon atom with four different atoms or groups bonded to it. This carbon atom is called astereogenic, chiral, or asymmetric center. The manufacture of chiral chemicals results in a mixture designated as racemic (±), which contains equal parts (50%) of an optically active isomer and its enantiomer which is the they typically released into the environment. The physical and chemical properties as well as abiotic degradation rates of enantiomers are identical but they differ in their toxicity, biological activity and microbial degradation rates from each other (Bradbury *et al.*, 1987; Garrison *et al.*, 1996; Kodama *et al.*, 2002).

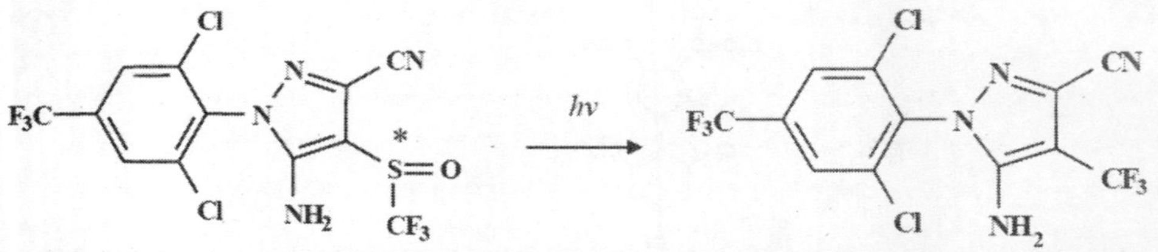

Fig. 5.3: Structure of fipronil (left) with * indicating asymmetric chiral center. Fipronil degrades under environmental conditions to nonchiral desulfinyl fipronil (right) as the major photoproduct. (Figure adapted from Brad *et al.* 2005)

Knowledge on the effects and persistence of individual enantiomers is critical for future regulation of chiral pesticides (Lewis *et al.*,1999). As a chiral pesticide, fipronil is released to the environment as a racemic mixture (equal amounts of optical isomers called enantiomers). From the results of the experiment carried out to determine the acute toxicity (48 h LC50) of fipronil enantiomers, the racemate, and photdegrade, desulfinyl fipronil in *Ceriodaphnia dubia*, it was observed that compound indicated as the (+) enantiomer (LC50, 10.3µg/l) was significantly more toxic to *C. dubia* than either the enantiomer (–) (LC50, 31.9µg/l) or racemate (LC50, 17.7 µg/l) (Brad *et al.* 2005). Separate toxicity tests with desulfinyl fipronil resulted in more than 20-fold higher LC50 (355 µg/l) compared to the fipronil racemate, suggesting lesser adverse effects to *C. dubia* as a result of fipronil photolysis (Brad *et al.* 2005). Further, research on effect of racemic mixture of fipronil conducted by Jay *et al.*, (2007) showed that *Simulium vittatum* (black fly) was the most sensitive freshwater species (LC50, 0.65 µg/l) whereas *Palaemonetes pugio* (grass shrimp) was the most sensitive marine species (LC50 = 0.32 µg/l). *Procambarus clarkii* (crayfish) were significantly more sensitive to the (S,+) enantiomer while larval *P. pugio* were significantly more sensitive to the (R,–) enantiomer. Enantioselective toxicity was not observed in the other organisms such as *Xenopus laevis* (African clawed frog), *Mercenaria mercenaria* (hardshell clam) and *Dunaliella tertiolecta* (phytoplankton) (Jay *et al.*, 2007).

Thus increasing concern on the growing use of the fipronil need further research to assess enantiomer-specific effects on the chronic toxicity in non-target organism . Identification of its enantiomer-specific effects on a variety of organisms may specify that manufacture and use of the single active enantiomer, need careful attention for safety of the environment.

INTEGRATED PEST MANAGEMENT (IPM) COMPATIBILITY IN AGRICULTURAL ENVIRONMENT

Conflicting concerns have been raised about the suitability of fipronil for use in IPM, and the results from a wide gamut of studies suggested that this must be assessed on a case by case basis. Depending on the species, doses, local environment, areas, methodologies and the timing of application its acute toxicity may vary widely, even in animals within the same groups. This indicates that the toxicological results on standard test animals are not necessarily applicable to animals in the wild, particularly in the more arid ecosystems (van der Valk, 1997). This is particularly true for birds, fish, amphibians and reptiles. Testing on local species seems important in determining suitability of fipronil-based products for registration in different countries or habitats and the potential risk associated with non-target wildlife. Fipronil poses a long term risks to nutrient cycling and soil fertility where some of the beneficial species like termites are affected due to toxicity. Termites have significant importance as a food source to many higher animals; hence the ecological risks associated with the termites must be evaluated. The risk of slowing biogeochemical cycles (notably nitrogen) and decreasing fertility of soil could not be ignored (Balança & De Visscher, 1995).

Results of the field study suggested that fipronil has good selectivity for certain beneficial insects and has lower toxicity than (the highly toxic) methyl parathion and endosulfan (Hamon *et al.*, 1996). Fipronil is relatively highly toxic to the ectoparasite *Catolaccus grandis* [Hymenoptera: Chalcidoidea], a natural enemy of cotton boll weevil (Elzen *et al.*, 1999) and *Cotesia marginiventris* [Hymenoptera: Braconidae], a natural foe of cotton pests (Tillman & Scott, 1997). Predators beneficial to agricultural production generally seem to show fewer adverse effects from fipronil than the other insecticides. The ground-dwelling predatory beetles particularly Carabidae do not seem to be generally adversely affected by fipronil, (Balança & De Visscher, 1995; 1997b; Danfa *et al.*, 1999). Fipronil is reported to be non-toxic to spiders by Rhone-Poulenc researchers, who reported that even foliar spraying did not led to decline the populations of predators (Bostain & Long, 1997).

Fipronil also showed more detrimental and longer lived impacts than chlorpyrifos on epigeal beetles and soil arthropods (Danfa *et al.*, 1999). The finding that fipronil is toxic to both *Beauveria bassiana* and *Metarhizium anisopliae*, two fungi used in biological control of locusts and grasshoppers (Moino & Alves, 1998) advocates that it is unsuitable to be employ in areas where these mycopesticides have been applied as part of preventative locust control operations. This indicates are that fipronil may be unsuitable with locust IPM, therefore requires further imperative examination.

BIOACCUMULATION

"Bioaccumulation is defined as the accumulation of chemicals in the tissue of organisms through any route, including respiration, ingestion, or direct contact with contaminated water, sediment, and pore water in the sediment." (USEPA 2000). Fipronil does not accumulate in the abiotic environment. However, relatively longer persistence of some metabolites, such as the desulfinyl, have been observed. Some level of accumulation is likely to occur if repeated applications were to be carried out in the same sites every year (Belayneh, 1998). Though it has a short persistence in the environment, the excess use of the insecticide may result in its accidental introduction in natural waters with damage to non-target organisms, particularly fish which are highly sensitive even to a very low concentration of fipronil.

There is evidence that fipronil and some of its degradates may bioaccumulate, particularly in fishes. The primary metabolites in fishes are fipronil-sulfone and fipronil-sulfide. The accumulation study showed that fipronil appears to bioaccumulate in fish when exposed to treated water at a concentration of about 900 nanograms for 35 days. The data indicate that the residues are almost completely eliminated 14 days after being transferred to clean water. Bioconcentration factors were 321, 164, and 575 for whole fish, edible tissue and non-edible tissue, respectively. When applied to water, fipronil varies greatly in its toxicity and potential to bioaccumulate in aquatic arthropods, depending on the species. One of its main degradation products, fipronil desulfinyl, is generally more toxic to a variety of animals than the parent compound and is very persistent. Further investigation on bioaccumulation in fishes needs to evaluated, especially for the desulfinyl degradate. Maximum residue levels (MRLs) in food products range from 0.01 to 1.5 ppm depending on the animal or crop product; whilst the Acceptable Daily Intake (ADI) of 0.00003 mg/kg body weight/day (prospective) for fipronil desulfinyl and range between 0.0002-0.00025 mg/kg bw/day was recorded for fipronil in humans.

RESIDUE ANALYSIS

The biochemical equipments used for the determination of fipronil residues are Gas chromatography (GC) with Mass spectrometry (MS) and Electron capture (EC) detection using an HP-1701 capillary column by means of a temperature controlled programme held at 250°C for 16 min. High pressure liquid chromatography (HPLC) with a reversed phase ultrasphere C^{18} column using methanol/water as the mobile phase used to determine polar metabolites in aqueous fractions from mice faeces (Hainzl & Casida, 1996). GC with EC failed to produce an interpretable chromatogram for residues less than or equal to 0.002 mg/kg, as did Mass Selective (MS). Vegetation samples for fipronil residue analysis with florisil using solvent elution was found to be ineffective, giving meager recoveries (<30%) of fipronil from samples. Gel permeation chromatography (GPC) was ultimately found to give satisfactory results, particularly with grass and leaves containing high levels of chlorophyll and other colored pigments (King and Aigreau, 2000).

STRESS AMELIORATION IN AQUATIC ORGANISM

Recent studies on the fish immune system have indicated that immunostimulants can activate various immune functions, even in stressful situations, and therefore reverse the deleterious effects mediated by stress (Ortuno *et al.*, 2003). To overcome different kinds of stress, a number of natural and synthetic compounds viz. vitamin C (Sarma *et al.*, 2009), alpha-tocopherol (Belo *et al.* 2005), tryptophan (Tejpal *et al.* 2008), and pyridoxine (Akhter *et al.*, 2009) etc. have been tried. It is, therefore, important to mitigate the immunosuppressive effect of pesticide in cultured fish by modulating its immune system through dietary manipulation, which has become an important area of research. Recently Gupta *et al.*, (2012) concluded that, dietary supplementation of levan (an immunostimulant) at 0.75 per cent level ameliorated fipronil induced stress and helped to augment immunity in *Cyprinus carpio* fry. This amelioration method can be potentially suggested especially for commercial culture of common carp, where fish are exposed to sub lethal contamination of fipronil and thus it provides appropriate management option to overcome fipronil induced stress.

CONCLUSION

Fipronil is a highly effective, broad-spectrum first generation insecticide with potent ability to control a broad range of crop, public hygiene, amenity and veterinary pests. Application of fipornil even in the minutest dose is sufficient enough to achieve effective pest control. The development of resistance and cross-resistance are potential threats arising from the overdoses of any pesticides but fipronil is relatively new so presently free from this problem. Risk assessment predictions have shown that some fipronil formulations present a risk to endangered bird, fish and aquatic and marine invertebrates. Great attention needs be paid for using these products to save the endangered wildlife animals. Moreover, conflicting issues has been voiced out about the use of fipronil in relevanance to human health risk.

From data on human exposure to the product, a preventive direction may be warranted especially in developing countries where lack of education and container disposal system, poor knowledge of the ecological fauna and use of insecticide drums for water and food storage, increase the risk of human contact with the product at above recommended dose rates. The use of some fipronil based formulations on domestic animals is not suggested where owner spend time on grooming of domestic animals. In general, it would appear imprudent to use fipronil based insecticides without environmental monitoring.

FUTURE DIRECTION

Further work is needed on the impacts of fipronil on non-target fauna (amphibia, reptiles, and mammals) before the risk to wildlife from this insecticide can be adequately assessed. Studies on chronic toxicity are needed to evaluate the risks associated with the current use pesticide. Eexperiments that may provide a greater insight into the potential teratogenic or other physiological effects of fipronil in aquatic organism needs to be explored. Further investigation into the fate of the fipronil in other aquatic species at developmental stages would provide a better overall picture as a test subject. It will be appropriate to include their metabolites (particularly the fipronil sulfone) as test substances during the toxicity testing method.

REFERENCES

Atwell R, Sillar R, Jeanin P, Postal JM & Consalvi PJ (1996). The Effects of Fipronil on *Ixodes holocyclus* on Dogs in Northern NSW. Australian

Balança G, and de Visscher MN. (1997a). Effects of Very Low Fipronil Doses on Grasshoppers and Non-target Insects Following Field Trials for Grasshopper Control. Crop Protection 16(6): 553-564.

Belo MAA, Schalch SHC, Moraes FR, Soares VE, Otoboni AMMB and Moraes JER (2005). Effect of Dietary Supplementation with Vitamin E and Stocking Density on Macrophage Recruitment and Giant Cell Formation in the Teleost Fish, *Piaractus mesopotamicus*. Journal of Comparative Pathology, 133 (2 & 3): 146-154.

Bobe A, Meallier P, Cooper JF & Coste CM (1997). Kinetics and Mechanisms of Abiotic Degradation of Fipronil (Hydrolysis and Photolysis). Journal of Agricultural & Food Chemistry, 46(7): 2834-2839.

Brad JK, Aaron TF, Arthur WG, Jimmy KA and Marsha CB (2005). Acute Enantioselective Toxicity of Fipronil and its Desulfinyl Photoproduct to *Ceriodaphnia Dubia*. Environmental Toxicology and Chemistry, 24: 9, 2350-55.

Bradbury SP, Symonik DM, Coats JR, Atchison GJ. (1987). Toxicity of Fenvalerate and its Constituent Isomers to the Fathead Minnow, *Pimephales Promelas*, and Bluegill, *Lepomis macrochirus*. Bull Environ Contam Toxicol 38: 727-735.

Cambell LH & Cook AS (Eds.) (1997). The Indirect Effects of Pesticides on Birds. Joint Nature Conservation Committee, Peterborough.

Cary TL, Chandler GT, Volz DC, Walse SS & Ferry JL (2004) Phenylpyrazole Insecticide Fipronil Induces Male Infertility in the Estuarine Meiobenthic Crustacean Amphiascus Tenuiremis. Environmental Science and Technology 38: 522-528.

Chadwick AJ (1997). Use of a 0.25 Per cent Fipronil Pump Spray Formulation to Treat Canine Cheyletiellosis. Journal of Small Animal Practice, 38(6): 261-262.

Christian M, Young H, Yang H & Olive L (1997). Fipronil Insecticide for Early Season Thrips Control Across the Cotton Belt. In: Herzog, G.A., Hardee (chairs), D.A., Ottens, R.J., Ireland, C.S., Nelms, J.V. & Ottea, J.A. (eds.) Proceedings Beltwide Cotton Conferences USA. Vol. 2. Jan 6-10 1997, New Orleans, LA. Cotton Insect Research and Control Conference. N.C.C., Memphis, TN. pp. 1168-1171.

Cochet P, Birkel P, Bromet-Petit M, Bromet N & Weil A (1997). Skin Distribution of Fipronil by Microautoradiography Following Topical Administration to the Beagle dog. European Journal of Drug Metabolism.

Cole LM, Nicholson RA and Casida JE (1993) Action of Phenylpyrazole Insecticides at the GABA-gated Chloride Channel. Pestic. Biochem. Physiol., 46(1): 47-54.

Collins HL & Callcott AMA (1998) Fipronil: An Ultra-low Dose Bait Toxicant for Control of Red Imported Fire Ants (Hymenoptera: Formicidae). Florida Entomologist 81(3): 407-415.

Colliot F, Kukorowski KA, Hawkins DW & Roberts DA (1992) Fipronil: A New Soil and Foliar Broad Spectrum Insecticide. Brighton Crop Protection Conference-Pests and Diseases 2(1): 29-34.

Diallo AO, Diagne M, Ndour KB and Lahr J. (1998) Laboratory Toxicity Tests with Eight Acridicides on *Oreochromis niloticus* (Pices, Cichlidae). *In*: (eds., Everts, J.W., Mbaye, D., Barry, O. and Mullie, W). Environmental Side-effects of Locust and Grasshopper Control. Vol. 3. LOCUSTOX Project-GCP/SEN/041/NET. FAO, Dakar, Senegal. pp. 188-204.

FAO (1998) Pesticide Residues in food – (1997). Report of the Joint Meeting of the FAO Panel of Experts on Pesticide Residues in Food and the Environment and the WHO Core Assessment Group on Pesticide Residues. Lyons, France. 22 Sept-1 Oct 1997. FAO Plant Production and Protection Paper 145. FAO Rome. 245 pp.

Fenet HE, Beltran B, Gadji JF, Cooper, Coste CM (2001) Fate of Phenylpyrazole in Vegetation and Soil Under Tropical Field Conditions. J Agr Food Chem 49: 1293-7.

Gant DB, Chalmers AE, Wolff MA, Hoffman HB, Bushey DF (1998) Fipronil: Action at the GABA Receptor. Rev Toxicol 2: 147-156.

Garrison AW, Schmitt P, Martens D, Kettrup A. (1996). Enantiomeric Selectivity in the Environmental Degradation of Dichlorprop as Determined by High-performance Capillary Electrophoresis. Environ Sci Technol 30: 2449-2455.

Grant DB, Chalmers AE, Wolff MA, Hoffman HB, Bushey DF, Kuhr RJ & Motoyama N (1998) Fipronil: Action at the GABA Receptor. In: Pesticides and the Future: Minimizing Chronic Exposure of Humans and the Environment. IOS Press, Amsterdam. pp. 147-156.

Gupta SK, Pal AK, Sahu NP, Saharan N, Mandal S, Chandraprakash, Akhtar MS & Prusty AK (2012) Dietary Microbial Levan Ameliorates Stress and Augments Immunity in *Cyprinus carpio* Fry (Linnaeus, 1758) Exposed to Sublethal Toxicity of Fipronil Aquculture Research 1-14, doi:10.1111/are.12030

Hainzl D, Cole LM, Casida JE (1998) Mechanisms for Selective Toxicity of Fipronil Insecticide and its Sulfone Metabolite and Desulfinyl Photoproduct. Chem ResToxicol 11: 1529-1535.

Harvey RG, Penaliggon EJ & Gautier P (1997) Prospective Study Comparing Firponil with Dichlorvos/Fenitrothion and Methoprene/Pyrethrins in Control of Flea Bite Hypersensitivity in Cats. Veterinary Record 141(24): 628-629.

Hosie AM, Baylis HA, Buckingham SD, Sattelle DB (1995) Actions of the Insecticide Fipronil on Dieldrin Sensitive and Resistant GABA Receptors of *Drosophila melanogaster*. Br J Pharmacol 115: 909-912.

Kilgore WW & Mingyuli (1975) Environmental Toxicolog. In: Insecticide Biochemistry and Physiology. Physiology (ed. by C. F. Wilkinson), Plenum Press, New York, NY, USA, 669 pp.

Jay PO, David RR, Jimmy KA, Garrison AW, Marie ED, Katy WC, Pete BK, Wilson WA, and Marsha CB (2007) Toxicity of Fipronil and its Enantiomers to Marine and Freshwater Non-targets. Journal of Environmental Science and Health Part B 42: 471-480.

Kodama S, Yamamoto A, Saitoh Y, Matsunaga A, Okamura K, Kizu R, Hayakawa K. (2002). Enantioseparation of Vinclozolin by g-cyclodextrin–modified Micellar Electrokinetic Chromatography. J Agric Food Chem 50: 1312-1317.

Lewis DL, Garrison AW, Wommack KE, Whittemore A, Steudler P, Melillo J. (1999). Influence of Environmental Changes on Degradation of Chiral Pollutants in Soils. Nature 401: 898-901.

Lockwood JA, Schell SP, Isu N, Norelius E, Schell S (1997) Field Tests of Fipronil: Large Scale Evaluations of Fipronil and Small Scale Evaluations of RPA 107382 for Control of Rangeland Grasshoppers in Wyoming (USA), with Implications for Reduced Agent/ Area Treatments, a Report to Rhone-Poulenc; 89 pp.

LPRG (1999). Evaluation of Field Trials Data on the Efficacy and Selectivity of Insecticides on Locusts and Grasshoppers. Report to FAO by the Locust Pesticide Referee Group. Eighth meeting, Rome 11-14 October 1999. 17 + xviii pp.

Mulrooney JE, Wolfenbarger DA, Howard KD and Goli D (1998). Efficacy of Ultra Low Volume and High Volume Applications of Fipronil Against the Boll Weevil. Journal of Cotton Science, 2:3, 110-116.

Ortuno, J., Esteban, M.A. and Meseguer, J., 2003. The Effect of Dietary Intake of Vitamins C and E on the Stress Response of Gilthead Seabream, *Sparus aurata*. Fish Shellfish Immunol, 14: 145-56.

Rainbird G & O Neil D (1993) Workrelated Diseases in Tropical Agriculture. A Review of Occupational Disorders Affecting Agricultural Workers in Tropical Developing Countries. Silsoe Research Institute, Bedfordshire, UK. 42 pp.

Rhone-Poulenc (1997). REGENT®, RHÔNE-POULENC AGRO's New Insecticide, Makes its Entry on the Indian Rice Market. Press Release, Paris, 17 April 1997. http:// www.rhonepoulenc. com/bodyu/nw970031.htm

Rhone-Poulenc, (1995) Atelier International Fipronil/lutte antiacridienne. Lyon 3-5 May 1995. Unpublished report. Rhone-Poulenc Agrochimie, Lyon, France.

Rhone-Poulenc, (1996). 'Fipronil' Worldwide Technical Bulletin. Rhône-Poulenc Agrochimie, Lyon, France. pp. 19.

Rodriguez OP, Muth GW, Berkman CE, Kim K, Thompson CM. (1997). Inhibition of Various Cholinesterases with the Enantiomers of Malaoxon. Bull Environ Contam Toxicol 58: 171-176.

Sarma K, Pal AK, Sahu NP, Ayyappan S and Baruah K (2009). Dietary High Protein and Vitamin C mitigates Endosulfan Oxicity in the Spotted Murrel, *Channa punctatus* (Bloch, 1793). Sci. Total Environ, 407: 3668-3673.

Schlenk D, Huggett DB, Allgood J, Bennett EJ, Rimoldi AB, Beeler D, Block D, Wolder AW, Hovinga R, Bedient P (2001) Toxicity of Fipronil and its Degradation Products to Procambarus sp.: Field and Laboratory Studies. Arch Environ Contam Toxicol 41: 325-332.

Scott WP, Snodgrass GL & Adams DA (1997). Mortality of Tarnished Plant Bug and Boll Weevils to Provado and Different Formulations of Fipronil. In: Herzog, G.A., Hardee (chairs), D.A., Ottens, R.J., Ireland, C.S., Nelms, J.V. & Ottea, J.A. (eds.) Proceedings Beltwide Cotton Conferences USA. Vol. 2. Jan 6-10 1997, New Orleans, LA. Cotton Insect Research and Control Conference. N.C.C., Memphis, TN. pp. 987-990.

Tillman, P.G. & Mulrooney, J.E. 1997. Tolerance of Natural Enemies to Selected Insecticides Applied at Ultra Low Volumes. In: Herzog, G.A., Hardee (chairs), D.A., Ottens, R.J., Ireland, C.S., Nelms, J.V. & Ottea, J.A. (eds.) Proceedings Beltwide Cotton Conferences USA. Vol. 2. Jan 6-10 1997, New Orleans, LA. Cotton Insect Research and Control Conference. N.C.C., Memphis, TN. pp. 1312-1313.

USEPA (U.S. Environmental Protection Agency) (1996) New Pesticide Fact Sheet, EPA 737-F-96-005, Office of Pesticide Programmes, Washington, DC.

USEPA (U.S. Environmental Protection Agency) (1997) Environmental Fate and Effects Section 3 Registration Decision for Fipronil: Use on Rice Seed, D235912. Environmental Fate and Effects Division, Office of Pesticide Programmes, Washington, DC.

USEPA (U.S. Environmental Protection Agency) (2001) Fipronil Environmental Fate and Ecological Effects Assessment and Characterization for a Section 3 for Broadcast Treatment with Granular Product to Control Turf Insects and Fire Ants (Addendum). Environmental Fate and Effects Division, Office of Pesticide Programmes, Washington, DC.

White GL, (1998). Control of the Leaf-cutting Ants *Acromyrmex octospinosus* (Reich), and *Atta cephalotes* (L), with a Bait of Citrus Meal and Fipronil. International Journal of Pest Management, 44(2): 115-117.

Williams A. 1996. Opportunities for Chiral Agrochemicals. Pestic Sci 46: 3-9.

CHAPTER – 6

Indo-Gangetic Riverine Fisheries
An Overview

A.K. Sahoo, *India*; D.K. Meena, *India*
Utpal Bhaumik, *India*; A.P. Sharma, *India*

ABSTRACT

Indo-Gangetic river systems form one of the world's most populous in the past 50 years and emerged into an intricate mosaic of interactions between man and nature, poverty and prosperity and problems and possibilities. Indo-Gangetic basin is found to be the most important because of the great alluvial crescent drawing from the Indus river and the Ganga river systems from a total of 28000 km^2. Both the river systems form a major portion for habitat and fisheries as a livelihood for millions of poorest of poor people. As per 2001 census, the basin population was 747 million and mostly depending for drinking water, irrigation, industries, fisheries and navigation.

The major tributaries of the Indus river systems are Beas, Sutlej, Jhelum, Ravi, and Chenab. While, Yamuna, Sone, Gandak, Ghagara, Mahananda, Kosi, Mahakali rivers form main tributaries of the Ganga river systems. From the fisheries perspective, the upper stretches of Indo Gangetic riverine system comprise mainly *Schizothorax* spp. and *Tor* spp.; middle stretches dominated by carps and catfishes, while lower stretches are dominated by estuarine fish and shell fishes such as *Harpodon neherius*, *Metapenaeus* spp. Hilsa, an anadromus fish form an important fishery in the lower stretches. Though fisheries form a major livelihood for millions in these river systems, threats are becoming a major concern for them, such as upcoming numerous hydel projects in the upper stretches, anthropogenic activities and pollution in middle stretches and siltation and heavy fishing pressure in lower stretches. This article will give insight into the details of fisheries of both riverine systems and the major threats for developing a management protocol for sustainable fisheries.

Key words: Indo-Gangetic basin; Hilsa; Fishing pressure; Humid fans; Harpodon neherius.

INTRODUCTION

Indo-Gangetic plains are not only one of the world's largest areas of Quaternary alluvial sedimentation; they also form the upper surface of one of the largest, still actively subsiding, foreland basins (Parkash and Kumar, 1991). They have therefore attracted international interest because of the examples they provide of very large river features, such as 'humid fans' (Collinson, 1986). However, because of the large size of the basin (about 3000 km, west to east), most basin scale maps provide little information about the rivers that supply and drain the Indo-Gangetic plains. The maps simply show a network of channels that converge on the main Indus and Ganges which, in turn, eventually flow into the Indian Ocean to the west and east, respectively, of the Indian peninsula Rivers form a major share of the inland freshwater resources covering almost 20, 05,453 km^2 drainage basin in India.

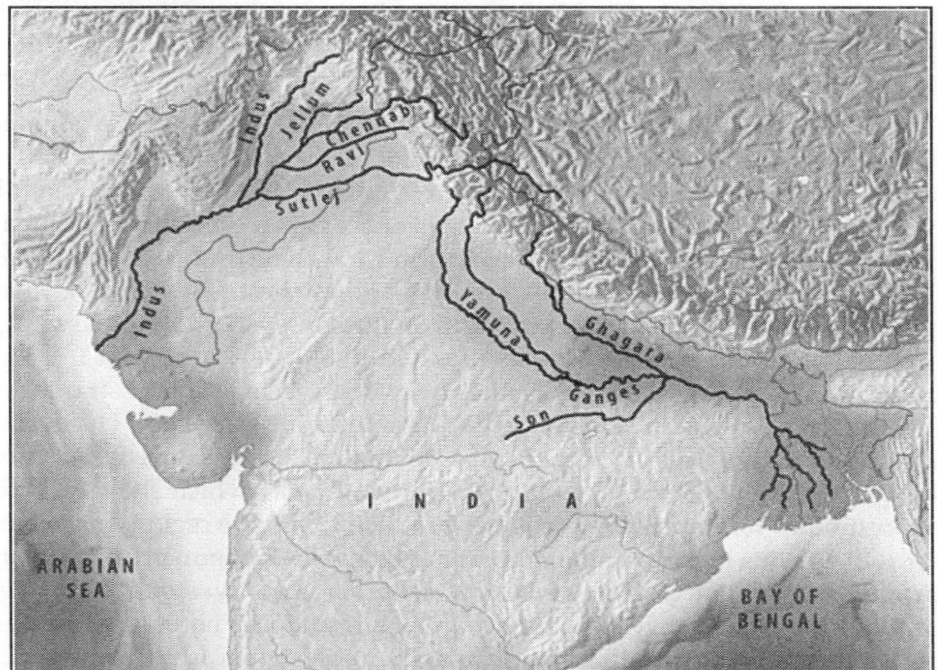

Fig. 6.1: Map Showing the Indo-Gangetic River Systems (*source:* www.whoi.edu/cms/images)

The origin of these rivers is believed to be of antecedent, where the drainage was established before uplift of the Himalaya and the rivers are older than the mountain ranges through which they flow. In geological term, in these cases generally erosion takes place at a faster rate than the upheaval of the Himalayas resulting in the formation of deep gorges. These rivers first flow for a considerable distance in longitudinal valleys and then suddenly cut across the mountains and reach the plains, as examples of India's mighty rivers of the north such as the Ganga, the Brahmaputra and the Indus.

TOPOGRAPHY

The IGB region is bounded by the Himalayas to the north, and by Vindhyan and Satpura range of mountains in the south. The western part is surrounded by the Thar Desert and Arabian Sea, whereas the eastern part is bounded by the Bay of Bengal. Due to its unique topography, this region can be summarized as a type of region, where, both anthropogenic and natural, aerosols show distinct seasonal characteristics and mixing (Guttikunda et al., 2003; Singh et al., 2004; Monkkonen et al., 2004; Massie et al., 2004; Jethva et al., 2005; Dey et al., 2008; Mishra et al., 2008). General seasonal abundance shows that the winter months are dominated by the fine-mode aerosols, produced by various anthropogenic sources from the IGB region, and pre-monsoon or summer months are dominated by the coarse-mode mineral dust, primarily from the Thar Desert region in the western Rajasthan and its frequent transportation over the IGB region.

WATER PRODUCTIVITY OF INDO-GANGETIC BASIN

In the lower parts of the Ganges basin in India and Bangladesh inland fisheries also forms a significant component of the agricultural production system. The Indus basin is quite productive in India and food surplus in this basin meets the food requirements of several other food deficits basins in India. However, there is a wide variation in agricultural productivity in different parts of the basin. It also reflects on how best water management practices are adopted at the farm and irrigation system levels. Average productivity of diverted water was reported to be 1.47 kg/m^3 and 1.11 kg/m^3 for Bhakra canal system of Kaithal Irrigation Circle in Indian and lower Jhelum Canal System in Pakistan (IWMI), respectively for wheat. The overall water productivity was reported to be 0.5 kg/m^3 for Pakistani Punjab and 1.0 kg/m^3 for the Bhakra system of the Indian Punjab which shows a lot of opportunities for improving the water productivity in the region. In general, the IGB exhibits high potential but with only low-to-medium actual primary productivity of agriculture, forestry, fisheries, and livestock. However, conditions are extremely heterogeneous; as a result, it is necessary to assess potential and actual productivity separately in the Upper Catchments (UC), Western Indo-Gangetic Plains (WIGP), and Eastern Gangetic Plains (EGP) (Table 6.1).

Table 6.1: Potential and Productivity Under Different Reaches of the Indus-Gangetic Basin (Sharma et al, 2008)

IG Basin Stretch	Agriculture		Forestry		Fisheries		Livestock	
	Potential	Productivity	Potential	Productivity	Potential	Productivity	Potential	Productivity
Upper Catchments	*Low-to medium*	*Low*	*High*	*Low-to medium*	*High*		*High*	*Low*
Western Indo-Gangetic Plains	*Medium to high*	*Medium-to high*	*Low*	*Low*	*Low*	*Low*	*High*	*Medium-to high*
Eastern Gangetic Plains	*High*	*Low*	*Medium*	*Low*	*High*	*Medium*	*Medium*	*Low*

INDUS RIVER SYSTEM

The Indus Basin is bounded on the east by the Great Himalayas, on the north by the Karakoram and Haramosh ranges, on the west by the Sulaiman and Kirtharranges and on the south by the Arabian Sea. The basin area of Indus is covering the States of Jammu & Kashmir, Haryana, Himachal Pradesh, Punjab, Chandigarh and Rajasthan. Though the Indus river is a large, only a small part flows through India and comprises of Jhelum, Ravi, Beas and Sutlej from the east. A part of Jhelum in India flows through Jammu and Kashmir. The river Ravi rises in Kulu, flows for about 370 km in India before meeting Sutlej. The Sutlej rises from Mansrovar lake at an elevation of 4,570 m. It enters into Indian Himalayas at Shipki, drains the Shiwalik Himalayas and enters into plains of Punjab at Ropar.

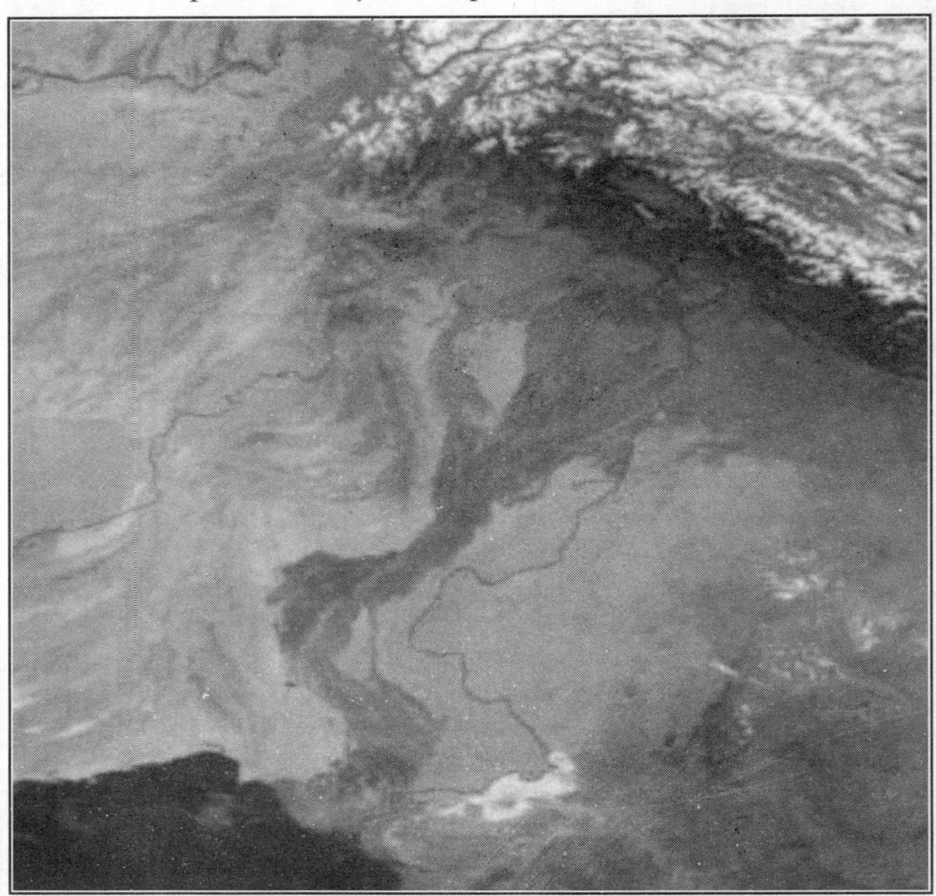

Fig. 6.2: Satellite Image of Indus River Basin
Source: **http://img1.photographersdirect.com)**

While river Beas rises near Rohtang Pass in Kulu at an elevation of 3,960 m and flows through a gorge from Larji in Talwara and then enters Punjab plains. The total length of river is 460 km with a catchment area of 20,303 km^2.

BEAS

The river Beas is an important contributory river of the Indus System confined to India. The river 460 km long originates from two sources, Beas Kund (4060 m asl) on the South and a caveran, Beas Rishi on the right of Rohtang Pass at an elevation of 4350 m asl within North; Western Himalaya. The two streams meet at Palchan village, 10 km north of Manali to form river Beas. The river was known as Arjiki in pre-mahabarat times and then onwards as Vipasa to ancient Indians. The catchment area of the river, 12130 km^{-2} is spread within Himachal Pradesh and it drains, 25900 km^2 of 2 states, H.P. and Punjab having maximum run of 295 km in former and 165 km in latter. The river is steep in Head waters and first 120 km have average fall of 1 in 40. Downstream it decreases rapidly 1 in 500 in Beas Valley. Along its course especially within Hiamalya zone river is fed by numerous streams. The main being Parbati, Spin, Malana Nala in the east; the Solang, Manalsu, Sujion, Phojal, Sarvati in the west. In district Mandi it is joined by the Tirthan, Hansa, Bakhli, Jiuni, Suketi, Panddi, Son and Bather from North side. In Kangra district, river is fed by the Kunah, Maseh, Khairan and Man from South and the Binwa, Neugal, Banganga, Cej, Dehr, Chakki from North side. The Northern and Eastern tributaries are perennial and snowfed, being drainage from southern slopes of Dhauladhar chain of mountains, while southern are seasonal with the result flow rate within river fluctuates widely. It being maximum during monsoons and minimum during winter. Total mean annual run off of Beas is 16,763 million cumecs (Sehgal, 1989) which is being utilized extensively for various purposes since the waters of the river are allotted to India along with that of river Sutlej and Ravi under Indus water treaty between India and Pakistan.

The river is subjected to first manipulation at village Pandoh in Mandi district within H.P. where it is dammed into Pandoh reservoir, the earth cum rock fill dam, 74.37 m high involving placement of 1.58 million cumecs of water and simultaneously a major chunk of its resources, 4716 cumecs of water diverted to river Sutlej through Beas-Sutlej Link canal in the form of tunnel (12.38 km long, 8.15 m. wide) and lined canal (11.8 km long, 9.14 m dia). The river is again damed at village Pong in Kangra district to form Pong reservoir, again a earth cum rock fill reservoir having water spread area between 6000-24000 ha. These changes allow the resources to be utilized for multipurpose activity mainly power generation. After leaving Pong Dam, river enters plains of Punjab at Talwara (Distt. Hoshiarpur) where it is immediately subjected to further manipulation for irrigation by carving a Canal-Shah Nehar Canal where in water in the range of 4170-8611 cusecs is diverted, dependini upon the season, leaving only 4.53-6.88 per cent of available water downstream between April-September and 12.18-39.0 per cent between October-March thereby denying the river natural monsoon flushing.

The river with depleted water resources takes a loop like course till it reaches Mirthal (Distt. Gurdaspur) in between traversing through foot hills of Himachal Nurpur. While in district Gurdaspur river regains some water resources made available from river Ravi through another Link Canal-Ravi Beas Link originating from Modhopur and a tributary Chakki coming from north side joining it around Mirthal and by another tributary Sarri joining at village Vhed Pattan. The river regains its resources fully at village Terrlkein (Distt. Hoshiarpur) through reinduction of Shah Nehar Canal. Thereafter river flows unrestricted for approximately 100 km to its culmination with Sutlej near village lohian at HariiKe-Pattan(confluence of 3 districts, Amritsar, Kapurthala and Firozpur)in between it receives many small Nallas amongst which two are important, an effluent loaded channel-Chakwal Nalla at village Chakwal (Distt. Hoshiarpur) below Terrikein and a seasonal tributary Kali or West Bein around its culmination point at Harike.

Fig. 6.3: Inlet of River Beas at Harike

An investigation made by CIFRI during 2000-2005 showed that the average water temperature was 23.3°C and transparency 29.5 cm. Dissolved oxygen was fairly rich (6.7 mg 1^{-1}) and pH was near neutral (6.8). Conductance, alkalinity, dissolved solids and hardness were comparatively lower in Beas (208 µmhos, 71.5, 103 and 89 mg1^{-1}) than the main river Sutlej before confluence and as a result a decreasing trend was observed below the confluence point. The river also showed poor nutrient status.

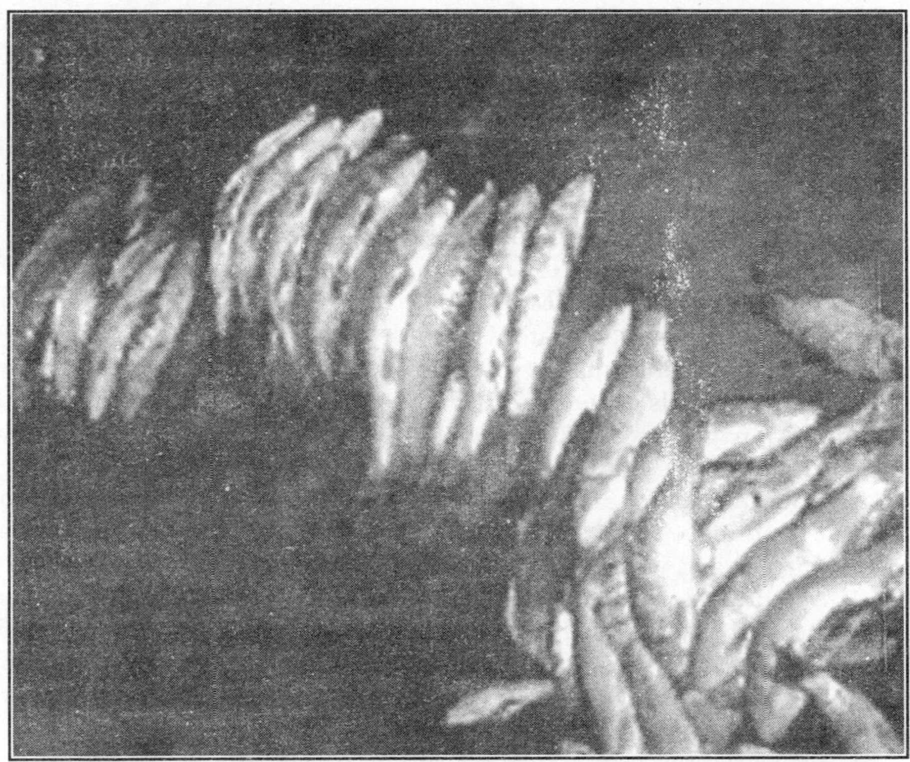

Fig. 6.4: Fish Landing at Pathankot Showing Abundance of Mahseer

Fishery present within Beas was observed to be formed by 53 species of which 31 are economically important. Its upper stretch running along foot hills of Himalayas hold cold water (*S. richardsonii*) to eurythermal carps. Lower stretch has *N. chital* and *M. aor*. Talwara centre having biomass of 12.0-24.5 t/y has dominance of *C. carpio* (66.67-84.50%) which may due to *(i)* Induction of common carp seed regularly by H.P. fisheries in Talwara Dam; and *(ii)* Conducive environments, lentic nature of river formed by existence of barrage at this site. The stretch contains eurythermal minor carps (12.24-25.0%) and *T. putitora* (0.03-1.30%) also mainly below barrage.

While in Pathankot centre having biomass range of 27.5-38.6 t/y, whose catchment area too is along foot hills of Shiwalik and seasonal mountainous tributary-ehaki, has dominance of cold water eurythermal minor carps such as *L. dero, L. dyocheilus* (84.97-90.03%). Presence of *T. putitora* (2.18-5.44%), mainly during winter and *S. richardsonii* (nil-2.35%) between winter to pre-monsoon. Mukerian centre, pure plain stretch having lotic environment, where Beas regains maximum water resources, has dominance of IMC (23.68-50.23%), although minor carps (18.72-40.14%) are also substantial. Regular presence of *T. putitora* (1.31-2.42%) during winter depict that Mahseer ascends upto Mukerian within Beas for its feeding. While in lower stretch between Amritsar to Harike where in river has good water resource, flow and depth contain mostly IMC (23.97-51.48%), large size catfishes (4.32-19.62%) and common carp (12.96-39.06%) - all important commercial fishery mainly because fish gets protected area within Harike wetland.

SUTLEJ

The river Sutlej is the longest of the five rivers in Indus basin with a total length of 1550 km. It flows through Punjab in northern India and originates from the snow filled Mansarovar Lake in Tibet and ends in Pakistani Punjab. The river is situated at an altitude of 20,000 feet above mean sea level. The river water is mainly used for power generation and irrigation and many large canals draw water from it. The water quality of river Sutlej between Roopnagar to Harike and below Beas confluence up to Ferozpur has been reported by CIFRI that the water temperature range from 22.0 to 24.0°C with transparency 39.5 cm in the upper zone but comparatively higher below the confluence. Dissolved oxygen was quite rich throughout the stretch (6.5 - 9.6 mg 1^{-1}) and water showed alkaline character with pH ranging from 7.5 to 7.8. Conductance, alkalinity, dissolved solid, hardness and chloride all were comparatively higher before Beas confluence (249 µmhos, 98.6, 150, 102 and 13.5 $mg1^{-1}$ respectively) and showed decline after the confluence (204 µmhos, 87.0, 103, 95 and 8.3 $mg1^{-1}$). The nutrient status of the river was poor (phosphate: 0.120-0.150 $mg1^{-1}$).

Based on CIFRI studies from a 280 km stretch of river Sutlej, the fish landings at five centres, viz., Roopnagar, Ludhiana, Sultanpur, Harike and Ferozpur were 37.47 t per month. Major carps and minor carps contributed 31.0 and 22.0 per cent. Among major carps *L. rohita* was dominant followed by *C. mrigala*. *T. putitora* was available only at Roopnagar (0.11%). Among large sized catfishes *A. seenghala* and *W. attu* were the main contributor, however, *A. aor* share was small (0.06%). Among exotics only *C. carpio* was observed and contributed significantly (14.4%).

Smaller species contribution was almost 1/4th of the total. There are several major hydroelectric projects on the Sutlej, e.g. the 1000 MW Bhakra Dam, the 1000 MW Karcham-Wangtoo and the 1650 MW Nathpa Jhakri Hydroelectric Dam. In addition to the dams, there has been a proposal to build a 214 km long heavy freight canal, known as the Sutlej-Yamuna Link (SYL), in India to connect the Sutlej and Yamuna rivers.

RAVI

The river Ravi originates in the Himalayas in the Chamba district of Himachal Pradesh and follows a north-westerly course with a total catchment area of 14,442 square km in India after flowing for a length of 725 km. It is the smallest of the five punjab rivers that rises from glacier fields at an elevation of 4,300 m, on the southern side of the Mid Himalayas.

Fig. 6.5: *Cyprinius carpio* (common carp)

It flows through Barabhangal, Bara Bansu and Chamba districts. The river is mostly fed by snow melt, as this region falls under rain shadow zone. Two of its major tributaries, the Budhil and Nai join 64 km downstream from its source. As per the report the river water clarity is slightly higher in the upper zone with an average water temperature 20.5° C to 21.5° C but the dissolved oxygen is quit high (6.4-7.1 mgl^{-1}) and pH is in the alkaline range (7.4-7.6). While considerable difference is observed in respect of conductance, alkalinity, dissolved solids and total hardness, all being comparatively lower between Shahpur and Madhopur (178 µmhos, 83.6, 89 and 113 mg 1^{-1}) but show sudden increase between Kathlour and Sakki (332 µmhos, 151, 160 and 154 mgl^{-1}, respectively). Chloride and Silicate are within the range of 12.4-16.2 and 4.2-6.8 mg $1^{-1,}$ respectively in the entire stretch.

The constructions of several hydropower projects are completed on the river. An oversees of the Hydropower potential of Ravi River system shows as 2294 MW. The hydropower potential developed since 1980s is through installation of Baira Suil Hydroelelectric Power Project of 198 MW capacity, the Chamera-I of 540 MW capacity commissioned in 1994, the Ranjitsagar Multipurpose Project (600 MW) completed in 1999 and the Chamera-II of 300 MW capacity in the upstream of Chamera-I commissioned in 2004. These are of major concern for the migratory fishes for both breeding and feeding purpose. In addition, subsistence fishery exists all along the course of Ravi with maximum at Ranjit Sagar dam. While the commercial fishery in Ravi is restricted to certain stretches only as it forms international border in many segments. During 2006-07, the average catch per month at Pathankot, Kathlour, Derababa and Amritsar were estimated as 2.68, 1.33, 0.92 and 1.10 t, respectively.

JHELUM

The river Jhelum rises from a spring at Verinag situated at the foot of south-eastern part of the valley of Kashmir in India. It flows through Srinagar and the Wular lake before entering Pakistan through a deep narrow gorge. The Jhelum enters the Punjab in the Jhelum District. From there, it flows through the plains of Pakistan's Punjab, forming the boundary between the Chaj and Sindh Sagar Doabs. It ends in a confluence with the Chenab at Trimmu in District Jhang. The Chenab merges with the Sutlej to form the Panjnad River which joins the Indus River at Mithankot.

The river also carries some water control structure named as Mangla dam, Rasul barrage and Trimmu barrage. Knowledge on selected aspects of physico-chemical and hydrobiological characters shows that pH varies between 7 to 7.6, water temperature reaches maximum 20 0C during July and August, total alkalinity 22-84 ppm, chloride 6-16 ppm and DO between 6.5 to 9.4 ppm (Vass et al., 1977). Major phytoplanktons are *Microcystis seruginosa, Navicula radiosa, Cymbela lanceolata, Tabeilaria fenestrate* and *Ceratium hirundinella*. While major zooplanktons *Daphnia longitermis, Bosmina longirostris, Moina* sp.,*Cyclops bicolour, Brachinous plicatilis* and *Diffugia lebes.*

The commercial fisheries of river Jhelum comprised mainly of six species of *Schizothorax* spp. such as *S. esocinus, S. micropahan, S. punctatus, S. curvifrons* and *S. longipinnis*. While other species such as *L. dero, L. dyocheilus, C. latius* and *P. conchonius* among Cyprinids, *G. kashmirensis* and *G. reticulatum* among Sisoridae and *B. birdi, N. kashmirensis, N. rupicola* and *N. marmoratus* among Cobitidae found occasionally. The exotic fish *C. carpio* (var. specularis and var. communis) was reported to contribute substantially to commercial catches of river Jhelum. It is estimated that during 1980's Schizothoracids constituted as much as 77.19 per cent and 77.86 per cent of the annual fish landed at Zerobridge and Chhatbal sites respectively.

FISH SEED RESOURCES IN INDUS RIVERS

The Indus River system is rather poor in seed resources. Only a small portion of the system comprising the Beas and the Sutlej and their tributaries is within India. Large scale egg collection is not done except in the upper reaches of the system which harbor only coldwater forms. A systematic collection of fish eggs has not been reported for the other major river systems of India.

THE GANGA RIVER SYSTEM

The river Ganga, a total length of 8,047 km is one of the largest river systems in the world with a drainage basin of 1.1 million km^2. The main river Ganga has its source from two headwaters at an altitude of about 6000 m in the Garhwal Himalaya, it flows through the Sivalik hills and entered the plains at Haridwar. Then it flows southwards, meandering over several hundred kilometers in the Indo-Gangetic plains in Uttar Pradesh, Bihar and West Bengal, ultimately to join the Bay of Bengal. The river has a large number of tributaries; to the south of the Ganga are the Yamuna and the Sone. The Yamuna flows to the west and south of the Ganga and joins it almost halfway down its course. The Sone has originated in the hills of Madhya Pradesh. To the north of the Ganga, the large tributaries are Ramganga, Gomti, Ghagra, Gandak, Kosi and Mahananda. Beyond the Mahananda the river enters its own delta, formed by its distributaries, and then merges into the combined delta of the Ganga, Brahmaputra and Meghna rivers.

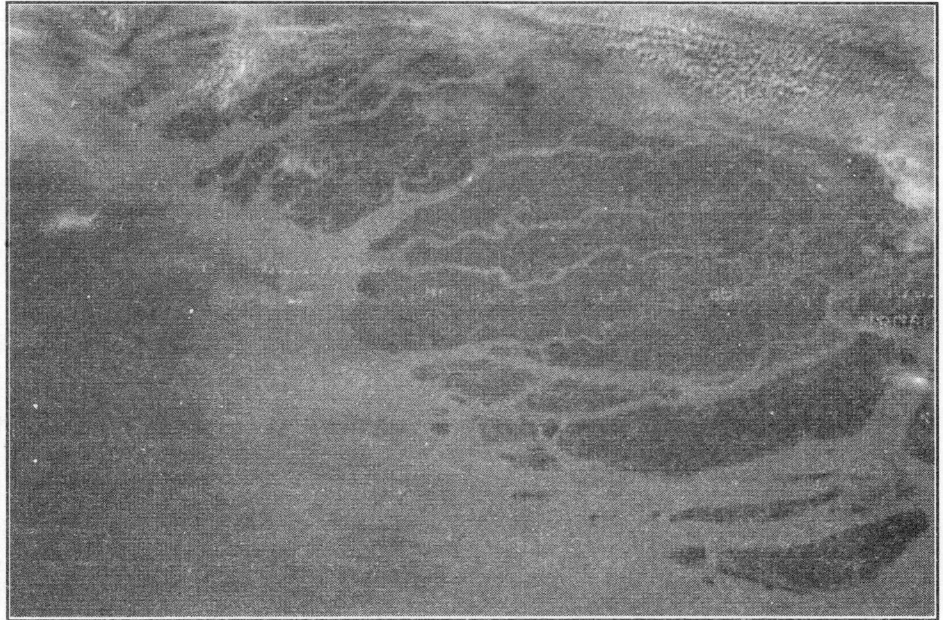

Fig. 6.6: Satelite Image of Ganga Basin

GANGA

The Ganges, which has held India's heart captive and drawn uncounted millions to her bank is now of major concern to the government of India because of severe pollution and anthropogenic activities. The river has been considered one of the dirtiest rivers in the world with degrading riverine ecology and biodiversity. Understanding the depth of concern CIFRI has been conducting studies on ecology including both biotic and abiotic parameters along the most populated stretched of the river Ganga. Our study mainly focuses the ecology and fisheries including water quality parameters.

The water quality parameters of Ganga in different zones have been presented in Table 6.2. Entire stretch of river was rich in oxygen (6.9-8.3 mg 1^{-1}) and poor in nutrients (nitrate: 0.017-0.050 and phosphate: 0.030-0.040 mg 1^{-1}). Due to strong buffering capacity of water there was no fluctuation in pH (8.1-8.2). Water temperature varied from 20.4 to 26.8°C and transparency was comparatively high in the upper zone (58.9 cm). On the basis of conductance, alkalinity, dissolved solids, hardness and chloride, Ganga appeared to be divided into three significant zones (upper zone: Deoprayag to Farrukhabad; middle Zone: Kannauji to Varanasi: Lower zone: Panta to Farakka). Upper zone showed minimum value of above parameters (206µmhos, 78.7, 104, 74 and 14.9 mg1^{-1}, respectively), while middle zone showed maximum values (456 µmhos, 150, 227, 148 and 30.8 mg1^{-1}, respectively).

Fig. 6.7: Lower Stretches of the River Ganga at Howrah

Table 6.2: Ganga Basin states in India

River System	Name of the Main Rivers	Approximate Length (km)	States
	Ganga	2525	Uttar Pradesh, Bihar, Jharkhand West Bengal
	Ramganga	569	Uttar Pradesh
	Gomti	940	Uttar Pradesh
	Ghagra	1080	Uttar Pradesh, Bihar
	Gandak	300	Bihar
Ganga	Kosi	492	Bihar
	Subarnarekha	395	Bihar, Jharkhand, West Bengal
	Yamuna	1376	Punjab, Haryana, Delhi Uttar Pradesh
	Chambal	1080	Madhya Pradesh, Uttar Pradesh Rajasthan
	Tons	264	Uttar Pradesh
	Sone	784	Uttar Pradesh
	Ken	360	Madhya Pradesh

Source: CIFRI.

The detailed account of soil quality of river Ganga, observed during an exploratory survey during 1995-96 by the CIFRI, based on holistic sampling at 43 centers from its origin to sea, showed that river-bed from Tehri to Patna (upper and middle stretch) is sandy with high percentage of sand (79 to 99.8%); clay being nil to 12 per cent. However, sand percentage decreased (34 to 79%) in the lower stretch (Sultanpur to Katwa) with corresponding increase in clay and silt load. It indicated that the stretch between Tehri and Patna suffered severely from textural deformities and sand drifting, through a number of tributaries (rivers Ramganga, Yamuna, Gomti, Ghagra, Sone, Gandak, *etc.*) in this region, heavily blanketed the river bed. The runoff from denuded catchments are also responsible for deformities of riverbed. Naturally, the blanketing of river-bed has prevented the contributions of soil to the aquatic productivity. Downstream of Patna, the tributaries of river Ganga are much more seasonal and Ganga passes through a predominantly clayey bed. As such, a sudden transformation in sediment texture was observed as the river flows in the lower.

In the upper stretch, between Tehri and Kanauj, the total plankton density varied from 58 to 1578 u l-1, 95 to 1050 u l-1 and 60 to 1435 u l-1 during summer, monsoon and winter months respectively. The bulk of it was phytoplankton. Zooplankton formed only 16.6 per cent. Bacillariophyceae being 83.4 per cent was the main representative of phytoplankton.

Table 6.3: Water Quality Parametres of Ganga River (Vass et al, 2010)

Zone	Water Temp (°C)	Transparency (cm)	DO (mgl^{-1})	pH	Total Alkalinity (mgl^{-1})	Conductance (μ mhos)	TDS (mgl^{-1})	Total Hardness (mgl^{-1})	Chloride (mgl^{-1})	Silicate (mgl^{-1})	Nitrate (mgl^{-1})	Phosphate (mgl^{-1})
Upper zone (Deoprayag-Farukhabad)	20.4	58.9	8.3	8.1	78.7	206	104	74	14.9	2.0	0.017	0.003
Middle Zone (Kannauj-Varanasi)	26.8	37.2	6.9	8.2	150.2	456	227	148	30.8	3.8	0.050	0.035
Lower Zone (Patna Farakka)	26.5	28.6	7.2	8.1	107.5	259	123	103	18.8	1.7	0.037	0.040

Zooplankton occupied 7.9 to 34.8 per cent of the total plankton in the stretch between Haridwar and Kanauj. Rotifers and protozoan made their first appearance at Anupsahar and Farukhabad respectively. The overall plankton density in the entire middle stretch varied from 24 to 782 u l^{-1}, 146 to 3649 u l^{-1} and 14 to 8049 u l^{-1} respectively during summer, monsoon and winter seasons. Maximum density is at Kanpur stretch (8049 u l^{-1}) during winter. On the whole, 18 taxa under phytoplankton and 11 taxa under zooplankton were encountered in the stretch between Kanpur and Allahabad. In the lower stretch, between Sultanpur and Farakka, the plankton density ranged between 34 and 1204 u l^{-1}. Of this, phytoplankton formed 70.9 to 89.2 per cent and the rest was zooplankton.

The total plankton production of the freshwater zone of Hooghly estuary varied from 26 to 935 u l^{-1}. In the marine zone of the estuary, the bulk of plankton was Bacillariophyceae (70-95%). Other phytoplankton groups observed were Chlorophyceae and Cyanophyceae. A decreased density of plankton in middle and lower freshwater stretches of river Ganga was observed during 1995-96 in comparison to what was reported in these centers in early sixties. But the qualitative composition of plankton witnessed little change. The pollution indicator species *Ankistrodesmus* sp., *Coelastrum* sp., *Pediastrum* sp., *Scenedesmus* sp., *Actinastrum* sp., *Cymbella* sp., *Cyclotella* sp., *Fragillaria* sp., *Anabaena* sp., *Lyngbya* sp., *Merismopedia* sp. *and Spirulina* sp. were recorded less in number in lotic waters of Ganga during 1995-96, indicating good water quality.

Macrobenthic population increased gradually from Tehri to Haridwar (189 to 628 u m^{-2}). Insects were the only component in the entire stretch. Chironomids appeared for the first time at Rishikesh. At Anupsahar, the benthos population was 644 u m^{-2}, 2108 u m^{-2}, and 811 u m^{-2} in summer, monsoon and winter respectively with 55.8 to 62.9 per cent annelids (Tubifex), 32.0 to 40.3 per cent insect larvae (Chironomids) and 3.9 to 5.1 per cent nymphs. The occurrence of gastropods was first observed in the stretch between Anupsahar and Kanauj, but they contributed very little. The insect population had a decreasing trend from the upper to middle stretch of the river. Bivalves formed the bulk of the benthic population in the middle stretch, represented by *Lamellidens marginalis* and *L. corrisnus*. Among gastropods *Melania striatella, M. plotia, Bellamia bengalensis* were the main forms. Insect population was represented by *Tricopteran* sp. *Chironomus* and stone fly nymph. In the freshwater zone of Hooghly the dominant forms were gastropods, followed by polychaetes, ligochaetes, decapods and bivalves. The annual production of macrobenthos in the marine zone of the estuary varied between 74 and 1472 nos. m^{-2}, mostly with a dominance of gastropods.

The periphyton flora in the riverine and estuarine stretches depicted almost similar trend of that of hytoplankton. Over the entire Ganga, Bhagirathi and Hooghly stretches, dominance of Bacillariophyceae was observed, followed by Chlorophyceae and Cyanophyceae. The average periphyton concentration in the upper stretch was between 512 and 2338 nos. cm^{-2}, of which 87 to 94 per cent by number, was Bacillariophyceae. In the middle stretch they formed 224 to 6080 nos. cm-2, the bulk of which being Bacillariophyceae. In the lower stretch also, Bacillariophyceae followed by Cyanophyceae and Chlorophyceae were the dominant forms. In the estuarine stretch the population of periphyton was lower than the freshwater stretches.

Table 6.4: Important Freshwater Fish Available in Ganga river (Vass *et al*, 2010)

River	Fish Species
The Ganga	**Carps:** *Catla catla, Labeo rohita, Cirrhinus mrigal, Labeo calbasu*
	Mahseers: *Tor putitora, T. mosal, T. Tor, Acrossocheilus hexagonolepis*
	Catfishes: *Osteobagrus aor, O. Seenghala, Silonia silondia, Wallago attu,Bagarius bagariu, Rita rita, Ompok bimaculatus Featherbacks: Notopterusnotopterus, N. chitala*
	Clupeids: *Hilsa ilisha, Gudusia chapra Setipinna phasa*
	Freshwater prawn: *Macrobrachium malcolmsoni, M. birmanicum*

From fisheries point of view Ganga is the most important river and source of livelihood for countless fishers inhabiting on its bank. Upper reaches (origin to Haridwar) is practically a non-fishing zone, however, species available in the stretch are *S. richardsonii, Tor* spp., *L. dero, L. pangusia, G. gotyla, C. latius, M. armatus*. The commercial fishing actually starts from district Bulandshahar (U.P.). The fishery in the potamon zone of the river is mainly represented by the species belonging to Cyprinidae and Siluridae families. The fishery from the river has shown serious structural changes and decline over the years. During 1958-61 the yield rate in different stretches of river varied from 480.4 to 2339.5 kg km^{-1}, being maximum at Kanpur and minimum at Bhagalpur. In the middle stretches the major carps contribution was around 50 per cent followed by large sized catfishes, but in Varanasi - Bhagalpur stretch the fishery was dominated by smaller species and hilsa.

During 1961-69 the yield rate dropped slightly (929.8 kg km^{-1}) with maximum at Patna (1811.3 kg km^{-1}) and minimum at Ballia (876.0 kg km^{-1}) with no significant change in fisheries structure. From 1972 onwards fishery from river started declining with sharp changes in stock structure. At Allahabad the yield rate came down from 935.39 kg km^{-1} of sixties to 368.01 kg km^{-1} for the present with a drastic decline in catches of major carps and large sized catfishes (*A. aor, A. seenghala, W. attu*). On the contrary, the catches of smaller species showed a marginal increase (211.96 kg km^{-1} to 223.41 kg km^{-1}) with slight changes in catch composition. The yield rate at Allahabad for different periods is presented in Table 6.5.

Table 6.5: Fish Yield Rate (kg /km^{-1}) in Different Periods at Allahabad (Vass *et al*, 2010)

Period	Major Carps	Large Catfishes	Hilsa	Exotics	Others	Total
1961-68	424.91	201.35	97.17	–	211.96	935.39
1972-80	135.17	98.55	9.66	–	197.86	441.25
1981-90	155.73	99.40	4.31	–	247.59	507.03
1991-00	28.91	62.74	4.51	–	178.20	274.36
2001-06	38.58	40.56	1.20	64.27	223.41	368.01

It is obvious from the table that all economic species followed a constant declining trend from 1972 onwards. However, the major carps fishery showed some improvement during 1981-90, which was due to good catches of *L. calbasu*, but during 1991-00 contribution of *L. calbasu* declined drastically and major carps share slipped to merely 28.91 kg km-l. During 2001-06, the fishery showed a general improvement, mainly due to invasion of exotic species, specifically *C. carpio* which is constantly increasing over the years.

Fig. 6.8: Hilsa (*T. ilisha*) Caught from River Ganga

During sixties hilsa fishery was the mainstay at Buxar contributing 744 kg km^{-1} in 1112.89 kg km^{-1} of the total. Again after 1972 the hilsa fishery suffered a serious setback and came down to only 22.37 kg km^{-1} in 1981-86. However, due to shift in fishing effort the fishery of rest of the species showed some improvement.

FISH SEED RESOURCES IN GANGES

Ganga bears the richest freshwater fish seed fauna of India ranging from the cultivable Gangetic (major) carps to Mahseers and other coldwater fishes of the Himalayas, the Hilsa. The Ganga system contributed to about 89.5 per cent of the total fish seed produced in the country during 1964-65. Bihar accounted for 2 010 million fry, while West Bengal contributed 1 200 million fry. As per CIFRI's investigation two breeding grounds of major carps are located in Bihar, which have been found to be extremely rich in major carp seed resources, with 90 per cent catla and 90 per cent rohu. In the lower section of the Ganga and its tributaries in West Bengal, large-scale spawn collection was carried out by private fishermen. Recent studies on Hilsa survey observed that huge numbers of hilsa juveniles of size 30-60mm were caught by various destructive gears which are of major concern for the native species.

YAMUNA

Yamuna is the second most important river of India, 1376 Km. long having a total catchment area of 3,425,848 Km^2, spread over seven Northern states. The river originates from Yamunotri Glacier situated on the western slope of Banderpunch peak of Himalayas at an elevation of 6387 m asl, passes through Tehri Himalayas of Uttaranchal, Haryana, Delhi, Uttar pradesh before joining Ganga at Allahabad (100 m asl), in between draining an area of 3,66,223 Km^2.

Fig. 6.9: Yamuna at Badwala

Based on geological and hydrological characteristics, Yamuna is classified into five distinct segments (GOI, 1993): *(i)* Himalayan segment; *(ii)* upper segment; *(iii)* Delhi segment; *(iv)* eutrophic segment; *(v)* diluted segment. Himalayan Yamuna extends from origin to Tajewallah barrage, covering a distance of 172 km, has a catchment area of 8280 km^2 which falls within Uttarkashi (Tehri region) and Dehradoon districts of Uttranchal and Sirmaur district of Himachal Pradesh. Many rivulets and tributaries join main river in this segment, important being Rishi Ganga, Kuntar, Hanuman Ganga in uppermost region and Tons, Giri, Asan, Lakhnar Amalnanda in lower region.

Along the lower region Lakhnar, Amalnanda and Tons meet Yamuna above Dakpather barrage at various points within greater Himalayas, while Giri and Asan join it along Shiwalik Himalayas and Doon valley range. Amongst all these tributaries Tons is largest. Yamuna contains more water in this zone due to high rainfall (150 cm) and is characterized by has an average flow of 116-645 kilo liters, average depth of 1.75 to 3 m. steep gradient of 59 in Greater Himalayas and 1 1.3 m/km in Shiwalik Himalayas (CPCB 89-90). Anthropogenic activity starts from this zone itself and is caused due to maneuvering of river for power generation and irrigation. Two barrages Dakpathar (1960) and Tajewallah (1899) and weirs at Kattapather and Ponta Saheb have been constructed for the purpose.

Upper segment of Yamuna extends from Tajewallah/ Hathnikund to Wazirabad barrage, covering a distance of 224 km, forming boundary between Haryana and Western U.P. Big cities like Saharanpur, Yamunanagar, Muzzafar nagar, Panipat are situated along its course, but all these cities are 20-25 km away from its banks and only three main drains one each from Panipat, Sonipat and Bhagpat enter into it carrying municipal effluents. Maximum abstraction of water resource takes place in this zone due to formation of two irrigation canals, namely Western Yamuna Canal (WYC) and Eastern Yamuna Canal (EYC). The river in this zone is very sluggish having an average flow of 9.8 to 38 Kilo liters and has average depth of 0.5 to 2.5 m, average width of 40 to 175 m and a gradient of 0.3 km/m only.

Ecology of Yamuna changes drastically from Delhi onwards under the impact of various types of effluent load. Delhi segment, 22 km stretch between Wazirabad and Okhla barrage is highly polluted (8.0.0. 160 M.T day (GOI 1993) due to offloading of 20 big drains and minimum water flow. The river remains as isolated entity barring monsoons, although Yamuna gets some water through Hindon cut in this region, but that water is mainly transmitted to "Agra Canal" above Okhla barrage. The river flow during monsoons varies between 25-616 Kilo liter has average depth of 1.25 to 3.5m and average width of 125-175 m.

Eutrophic segment, 490 km stretch between Okhla barrage to Chambal confluence harbours thickly populated cities like Mathura, Agra, Etawah discharging their domestic and industrial effluents mainly through 20 nallas,

1 from Shahdra (after Okhla barrage), 8 from Mathura, 10 from Agra and 1 from Etawah (GOI 1993). A tributary- Hindon joins Yamuna in this segment at Dadri (dist. Gautam Budh nagar U.P.) yet flushing by this does not help in recovering capacity due to lifting of its resources into Hindon cut above barrage. The flow rate of Yamuna along this stretch has been 2.5-692 kiloliters, has gradient of 0.22 to 0.08 mlkm only, average depth of 0.88-1.75m (CPCB 89-90).

Diluted segment, 468 km stretch of Yamuna between Chambal confluence (Panchnada) to Ganga confluence (Allahabad) receives maximum water supply from 4 main tributaries namely Chambal, Sind, Betwa and Ken. Amongst the 4, Chambal is the largest having 5-10 times more water flow than Yamuna and has a catchment area of 1,39.785 km^2 almost half of total Yamuna basin (CPCB 89-90). Maximum induction of water and minimum pollutional load (only 6 drains, 1 from Etawah and 5 from Allahabad) help in assimilation capacity of river. The river has an average depth of 1.75 to 6m, average width of 200-375m and attains flow rate of 214-5843m/sec (GOI 1993) thereby making it diluted segment.

Information was generated on hydrology and ecological parameters, flow pattern, potential energy resource and fishery in Yamuna river to formulate policies to achieve the goal of sustainable fishery from the system. The sediment was alkaline in reaction (pH 7.3-7.5) with dominance of sand (85-95.5%) in the upper stretch. Clay and silt were comparatively higher in the lower stretch. Organic carbon was poor (0.028-0.5%) but available phosphorus was high (4.3 to 9.0 mg/l 00 g). The water in upper most stretch Badwala was rich in dissolved oxygen (l0.4 mg/l) and showed comparatively lower values of alkalinity (72.6 mgl^{-1}), dissolved solids (93 mgl^{-I}), hardness (70 mgl–^{1}) and chloride (12.8 mgl–^{1}). From Yamuna Nagar the water quality started deteriorating due to discharge of effluents and reduction in flow rate. The condition was worst between Delhi and Etawah stretch where all the chemical parameters showed abrupt increase. The condition improved significantly below Hamirpur after the confluence of Chambal, Betwa, Ken and other tributaries.

The rate of energy transformation by producers indicated that the net energy was 1360 Cal m-z day-I at Badwala which increased gradually reaching maximum at Mathura (6400 Cal m-Z day-I), with fluctuations between Hamirpur and Arail. It is interesting to note that the water quality of the river showed maximum deterioration between Delhi-Etawah stretch, whereas, the energy transformation was much higher (4180-6400 Cal m-z day-I) reflecting positive impact of organic loading on energy fixation whenever the river was in a fluviatile condition. On the basis of energy transformation the estimated fish production potential was also observed to be high (145-221 kg ha-I) between Delhi and Etawah stretch. The average plankton population was maximum at Agra (1952 ul–^{1}) and minimum at Panipat

(113 ul^{-1}). Among phytoplanktons Bacillariophyceae was predominant followed by Chlorophyceae, and among zooplanktons rotifera and crustacea were predominant. The periphytic population was maximum at Badwala (9160 ucm^{-2}) and minimum at Arail (580 ucm^{-2}).

The dominant algal species were *Synedra* sp and *Navicula* sp. at all the centres. The benthic fauna investigations revealed abundance of macro benthic organisms, which were maximum at Mathura (2678 nm^{-2}) followed by Delhi (1059 nm^{-2}) and minimum at Badwala (169 nm^{-2}). Dominance of chironomids and tubifex in the middle stretch (Delhi-Etawah) clearly reflected organic loading in the system. Between Hamirpur and Arail the benthic population being dominated by molluscs (*Compeloma* sp., *Sphaerium* sp. and *Lymnea* sp.) indicated reduction in pollution load and improvement in water quality. Study in river Yamuna showed drastic decline in fishery, both in quality and quantity. Highly polluted stretch below Wazirpur in Delhi.

Major fishery within river was formed by agglomeration of various groups termed as other group forming 56.13 per cent of total biomass. Largest being cat fishes (14.23%), followed by minor carps (11.69%), IMC (6.64%) and common carps (5.20%). Fish composition depicted sectorial variation; uppermost segment- Yamunanagar contained commercially valuable fishes like, minor carps (21.45%), large size catfishes (18.46%). IMC (13.15%) and Mahseer (9.03%). Thereafter individual fishery behaved differently IMC contribution decreased from 13.15 to 3.67 per cent; minor carps from 21.45 to 7.82 per cent, Mahseer from 9.03-0.93 per cent, while the contributing percentage of Mahseer and minor carps may be affected due to thermal regimentation but that of IMC was surely due to less availability of water and siltation of river bed, as this group of fishes under conducive environment can withstand broad range of temperature.

Amongst IMC, *L. calbasu* was dominant and present throughout the stretch. *C. mrigala* and *L. rohita* were present equally. *C. catla* was least represented present mainly at Yamunanagar thereby showing that *C. catla* needs sufficient water column to thrive than other three species of IMC. Amongst large catfishes, *M. seenghala* and *W. attu* were of same magnitude and equally present. *B. bagarius* was less and mostly confined to Yamunanagar, while *R. rita* was present from Kamal onwards. The stretch showed presence of exotics mainly common carp. Invasion of common carp into Yamuna may be due to accidental entry during floods from the ponds at high altitude, where its culture is taken up on large scale, but its gradual increases show that fish is now sustaining in the system.

The other two genera *C. idella* and *A. nobilis* showed occasional presence. Length frequency estimation of commercial fishes showed that IMC were present mostly in 2nd group. *L. calbasu* being dominant (62.3%) in this group followed by *L. rohita* (51.0%) and *C. catla* (50%). Minimum presence of *C. catla* (7.2%) in 1st group showed its poor recruitment. Minimum presence 8.5

per cent of *L calbasu* in 3rd group shows that although this carp has efficient recruitment (29.2% in 1st group) than rest of carps, but it does not grow beyond a point. Highest presence of 30.3 per cent of 1st group Mahseer in Yamunanagar segment of river show recruitment in this specified area and its presence upto IV stage (2. 1%) clearly show the zones suitable for this fishery.

Fig. 6.10: Invasion of Tilapia in River Yamuna

Recent study by CIFRI (2009) in river Yamuna showed drastic decline in fishery both in quality and quantity. The fish landings at Sadiapur and Daraganj were estimated at 143.14 t and 37.79 t, respectively. At Sadiapur, common carp and Tilapia contributed to almost half and others contributed 34.4 per cent of the total catch. Major carps (12.1%) and large sized catfishes (7.1%) also contributed to the catch. As compared to preceding year, the fishery showed an increase of 62.5 per cent with three times higher landing of common carp; Tilapia and others groups registered an increase of 46 and 59 per cent. This may be due to monsoon failure in the region causing the river more exposed for fishing for a longer period. However, Invasion of Tilapia in river Yamuna Daraganj landings did not reflect much change over the preceding year. At uppermost zone the fishery was dominated by *Schizothorax* sp. and *T.pititora,* although the catches were of low order. In Delhi- Etawah stretch the fishery was dominated by Tilapia (84-95%). While in Hamirpur-Allahabad stretch fishery was mainly composed of minor carps and Tilapia was around 13 per cent.

SONE

The river Sone originates from the mountain called Amarkantak in the Maikal Ranges and flows north past Manpur and then turns northeast. The river cuts through the Kaimur Range and joins the Ganges above Patna, after a 784-km course.

Fig. 6.11: The Sone River at Koilwar, above Patna

Over the period, CIFRI has generated information on water flow, abundance of biotic communities, production potential and fisheries of the river system. Recent study (2009) on river stretch from Indrapuri barrage to the Koilwar showed that the water quality of river indicated rich oxygen (7.2 mgl^{-1}), alkaline pH (7.6), and moderate alkalinity (68 mgl^{-1}), conductance (190 imhos), dissolved solids (98 mgl·l), hardness (62 mg^{-1}) and very little intra stretch variations indicating pollution free status of the river. Sediment showed complete domination of sand (88-99%) with poor nutrients. The biotic setup revealed poor abundance of macrobenthic organisms during monsoon, which significantly improved (50 nm^{-2} at Koilwar to 592 nm^{-2} at Dehri-on-Sone) during winter when the river became almost stagnant. Mollusc was the dominant group throughout the stretch mainly represented by *Spharium* sp., *Comploma* sp., *Goniobasis* sp., *Lymanea* sp. followed by insect which mainly comprised of dragonfly nymphs. The average commercial catch around the barrage was 45-50 kg day^{-1} at Dehri-on-Sone, followed by 15-20 kg day^{-1} at Tilathu and 20-25 kg day^{-1} at Koilwar.

Fig. 6.12: *Ailia coilia*

Fig. 6.13: Catfishes

The fish catch showed considerable seasonality with dominance of small trash fishes like *Gagata cenia* during post-monsoon period. During winter fingerlings of *Aorichthys* sp. and young ones of *Ailia coilia, Rita rita, E. vacha, C. garua, M armatus, M aculeatus, B. bagarius* etc. formed the main catch. Major carp and minor carps were poor. Gill nets of various mesh sizes and hook and line were the major gears used. A total of 37 fish species belonging to different genera were recorded in commercial fishing and various fish markets. In sixties and seventies an average of 4787 hundis (earthen pots with red soil) of spawn were collected from Koilwar stretch of the river which has drastically reduced to 10 to 12 batis only (150 ml aluminum cup) at the present time. As such, the spawn trade has totally collapsed from the Sone river.

REASONS FOR BIODIVERSITY DECLINE

There are long-standing reasons this decline in biodiversity. All aquatic ecosystems are highly sensitive to a reduction in the water flow. Since the 1850s, the Ganga has been diverted for irrigation as soon as it enters the plains. In most barrages leading to irrigation canals, the diversion is about 50 per cent of the flow. In most stretches, the river ecosystem has acclimatised to such diversions. However, in some places the river has dried up. This happened between Bijnor and Narora when there was no water coming in from the Kalagarh canal. This obviously leads to increased stress on the ecosystem, especially on species like dolphin that need deep pools fast moving water, according to Sandeep Behera, associate director of the River Basin and Biodiversity Programme in WWF-India. Scientists have identified reduced river flow as one of the primary threats to the populations of dolphin, mahseer, crocodiles, turtles and fish in this stretch.For millennia, the Ganga basin has been one of the most intensively farmed regions in the world. Despite that, until the nineteenth century, it had thick forest cover along the Himalayan foothills, the area known as the Terai. But that was systematically deforested, mainly in the first half of the twentieth century, to build South Asia's rail network and for the British Army during I World War.

About 80 per cent of the original forest cover in the Gangabasin has been lost, according to a joint study carried out in 2003 by IUCN, International Water Management Institute, World Resources Institute and the Ramsar secretariat. This means loss of habitat for terrestrial species, plus the freshwater species dependent on them. It also means a higher sediment load in the rivers, as the tree roots that used to hold the soil together are no longer there. The water becomes even more turbid, and many species are unable to cope.Another problem is that in the upper stretches of the river, only about 10 per cent of the original floodplains of the Ganga remain, the rest having been taken over for farming, factories or houses. That is a serious loss of habitat. With 532 people per square kilometre, this is already one of the most densely populated river basins in the world, and that figure is projected to rise.For decades, the level of pollutants in the Ganga has been well above the permissible value. Basic indicators of the state of the water, such as biological oxygen demand and dissolved oxygen, also show water quality is nowhere near what it should be.

While impacts of climate change on the aquatic ecosystem are expected to vary over the long term, global climate model data show an increased run-off with longer dry periods for all the sub-basins of Ganga. The impact of this on aquatic ecosystems would vary depending on individual species preference and these need to be investigated now. The increased dry weather flows predicted by most models can affect nesting sites of turtles and the seasonal habitats of the dolphin. This is an area where more information is required to ensure that the results of current conservation efforts are not destroyed.

ISSUES OF THE INDO-GANGETIC RIVER SYSTEMS WITH REFERENCE TO FISHERIES

There are various critical issues such as aquatic pollution including industry, domestic and agricultural runoff, anthropogenic activities and use of destructive fishing gears that kills the juveniles and fish seeds. In addition to the climate change the major issues in the riverine ecosystem is alteration hydrological regimes by construction of dams and barrages. Some extent this issue has become a treat for sustenance of river ecosystem by declining fish catch and native fish species, resulting loss of riverine fish germplam.

The causes for loss of riverine biota are also attributed to changes in the hydrological regimes along with many other natural and human influences viz., changing pattern of water discharge, variations in sediment load, non judicious-irrational fishing, increased water abstraction, river course modifications, population growth, deforestation, agricultural activities, urbanization, fertilizer and fossil fuel consumption etc. Presence of heavy metals and organochlorine pesticide residues in water and sediments derived from the industrial and agricultural effluents are also found to affect the fishery. All these have inconceivable adverse impact on the health and natural regeneration capacity of the river basin.

The presence of micropollutants in water and sediments of this river turn the system unsustainable to the biota. These are the major challenges for the river researcher to address to save the ecology and fisheries of the major river systems in Indo-Gangetic basin. The indo-Gangetic basin is currently witnessing an unstoppable boom in groundwater pumping in its northwestern region. At the same time a large region in the eastern part of the basin (eastern India, Nepal and Bangladesh in Ganga basin) is unable to make good use of the available resource due to economic scarcity and policy inadequacy. Potential impacts of climate change on the Himalayan ecosystem and the changes in severity and frequency of floods shall further heighten the management challenges.

Fig. 6.14: Structure of a Barrage on River Sone at Indrapuri

AERIAL THREAT TO GANGA BASIN

It was the thought that depletion of stratospheric ozone layer happens only over the polar regions, it's time you relocated your view tropically. For, scientists have found the ozone layer over the Indo- Gangetic (IG) basin is getting seriously compromised, due to, among other things, the increasing load of atmospheric pollution. Carried out jointly by researchers from the Indian Institute of Technology (IIT) in Kanpur and the George Mason University in the US, the study found the decadal variation in the ozone column over the densely populated basin is almost three times the predicted trend for the decade ending 2003. The scientists measured the total ozone column (TOC) over 14 cities across the country using data provided by two US satellites Nimbus 7 (for 1979- 1993) and Earth Probe (1997-2003). Ozone layer thickness is expressed in terms of Dobson Units (DU). The normal range for the thickness of the ozone layer is 300-500 DU.

For cities in the IG plain viz. Kanpur, Kolkata, Patna and Varanasi; the values for ozone depletion predicted were 12.6, 10.8, 13.5 and 11.3 DU respectively, while the corresponding actual figures were found to be 37.3, 32.3, 36.2 and 33.8 DU. On the other hand, they found TOC values to be more or less stable over other cities such as Guwahati, Chennai, Bangalore,

Thiruvananthapuram and Nagpur. The depletion of ozone is a potential health threat especially to the 440 million people who live in the basin," Singh said, adding that the factors responsible for the ozone depletion need further investigation. One possible factor could be the sulphate aerosols and dust particles transported from Africa's Sahara desert before and during the summer monsoon.

MANAGEMENT MEASURES

1. **Water resource management:** River basin level has undergone several shifts in paradigms over the last several decades, from largely ignoring the hydrological aspects of a river basin and resorting to interbasin transfers on the one hand, to emphasizing the interconnectedness of unique ecological systems and encouraging an integrated approach to planning, on the other. The shift in paradigm was accompanied by an increased orientation from supply-side solutions to demand-side management and to recognizing the need to preserve ecological services and address issues related to equity in water use (ADB, 2007). River basin organisations support the integrated physical and technical management of water resources and, if developed adequately, can respond to the growing competition for water among agricultural, industrial, urban and in-stream uses within basins. However, Indian and the neighboring countries geographic and geopolitical challenges generally do not favor integrated hydrologic perspective.

   The reasons include a short but intense monsoon season of water availability followed by a long rainless period (instead of steady river flows), and significant decentralized rainwater harvesting in many parts of the basin unrelated to the holistic basin perspective. The basin is also unique in its large-scale dependence on groundwater usage, which is equally seen as seemingly unrelated to the basin perspective. Water resource legislations in the basin countries are also not very effective and conducive to integrated basin management. Water is chiefly a state subject and the union generally does not interfere except for the subjects related to inter-states water sharing and disputes and water/river treaties with the neighboring riparian countries such as India-Pakistan (Indus treaty); India-Nepal and India-Bangladesh (Farakka Treaty). Water administration at the national levels do not treat water as a scarce resource and the states that do not use economic instruments or regulations to increase the efficiency of water use are not worse off and continue to receive national support (ADB, 2007). Water resource management is still developing, is functional and top-down. River basin management organisations are established only for the purpose of constructing large interstate multipurpose projects and water sharing or conflict resolution and have been successful in this respect. The more demanding and complex functions related to conservation of water and improvement of water productivity, allocation of water among the competing sectors, integrating environmental and social concerns related to the resources, ensuring equity to access and compensating for losing access or relocating are inadequately addressed.

The water management thus chiefly focuses on supply augmentation. One such mega recent initiative on supply augmentation is the National River Linking Project of India, wherein a number of river links are proposed to divert potentially surplus water from the east and north-east rivers to the water scarce basins in the south and western region. The discussions on the project have become highly polarized between the proponents and opponents of the concept and the need for undertaking such a mega irrigation infrastructure investment aimed at creating surface irrigation schemes for certain selected regions (Sharma and Upali, 2008). Apart from several issues related to environment, displacement, water and food needs for the future populations; the inadequacies of the existing policies for sharing and transferring of water between riparian and non-riparian states appears to be a major institutional issue.

However, there have been several direct and indirect policies in the past which helped in the spread of Green revolution technologies in certain parts of the basin and helped India to achieve food self-sufficiency and security. These included massive investments in surface irrigation infrastructure, spread of high yielding varieties, subsidies on fertilizers and energy supply for agriculture, minimum support prices for agricultural commodities, farm-credit policies and support for farm extension programmes. Focus of the efforts remained confined to certain well endowed pockets and several states in the east, including Nepal and Bangladesh have not much benefited from these policies and remain poverty hotspots. A new and innovative set of policies which are more equitable and inclusive (small and marginal farmers), away from infrastructure construction to emphasis on management; proper mechanisms for water sharing and transfer, conducive energy policies, proper targeting of subsidies and creation of responsive institutions at different levels shall be required to ensure higher productivity and support to the livelihoods.

2. **Regulatory management:** In past, some clean-up efforts have been made, including the very expensive and much critiqued Ganga Action Plan. It started in 1983, and the pollution levels in the river have only gone up since then. The plan is now in its second phase under a new name, and results are awaited. Designating protected areas on and around the river or its tributaries has had better results. The 2,073 square-kilometre Hastinapur Wildlife Sanctuary abuts the Ganga, close to the Bijnor barrage. Though the forest in the area has been degraded, the

establishment of the sanctuary in 1986 has provided protection to the two-toed Barasingha (swamp deer), Sambhar, Cheetal, blue-bull, wolf, leopard, hyena and wild-cat.

The area has a number of bird colonies, including migratory birds from north Asia and those on the IUCN red list Greater Spotted Eagle, Swamp Francolin, Sarus crane and Finn's Weaver. In November 2005, the stretch of the Gangain the upper plains – between Narora and Brijghat was declared a Ramsar Site, which means it is a "wetland of international importance." The declaration came largely thanks to WWF India's dolphin conservation programme. This 85-kilometre stretch is habitat for several species of turtles and infrequently, game fish like the Tor tor as well as the Ganga dolphin. The most important protected area of the mid- and lower-Gangetic plains is the Vikramshila Dolphin Sanctuary. But even in the sanctuary, the dolphin population continues to decline at around 10 per cent per year, mirroring the overall decline in the basin.

FUTURE PERSPECTIVE

The Indo-Gangetic basin presents both great opportunities and serious challenges for the water and agriculture-centric poverty reduction interventions. One of the main opportunity in the large part of the Ganges basin is that in spite of adequate water and land resources, the productivity levels are exceptionally low and can be potentially enhanced through suitable physical, economic and policy interventions. Multiple water use systems through integration of crops, horticulture, aquaculture, livestock and other water-centric livelihood options offer a great opportunity for improving agriculture and water productivity (both in net and $ terms) and thus improving the livelihoods. Though a large part of the Indus basin has reasonable levels of agricultural productivity, it is largely supported through government subsidies (water, energy, fertilizers) but still does not make great margins for the farmers as the production systems are highly grain dominated with little opportunities for value-addition and diversification.

Moreover, the present production systems are also supported by the over-exploitation of groundwater resources which in the long run are hydrologically and economically unsustainable. A substantial part of the Indus basin in both India and Pakistan also suffers from geogenic and secondary salinity and alkalinity and water-logging problems and require individual and community interventions and supportive policy instruments for implementing sustainable solutions for productivity improvements under such environments. Rainfed agriculture regions, especially in the upper catchments have also received inadequate attention in the past, and have good opportunities for value-added agriculture. The basin as a whole and Indian region in particular is witnessing a good expansion in economy and income levels which shall have substantial implications for future water and food requirements. Land use, cropping and water use patterns are changing, partly as responses to changing demographic and consumption patterns, and partly as responses to changing investment scenarios and economic growth.

CONCLUSION

Rapid urbanization, above said threats and changes in food consumption patterns are so significant that they have considerable impact on the needs of future food and water demand. Parts of this basin lying in the different countries have traditionally served as food bowls for the remaining parts and this exerts a tremendous pressure for improving the uncontrolled fisheries and agricultural activities. Potential future interventions must take cognizance of the existing opportunities and challenges for development to meet the ever-increasing water and food demands of a vast population of the Indo-Gangetic basin.

REFERENCES

Annual Report 2009-2010., CIFRI, pp. 84.

Asian Development Bank. 2007. Institutional Options for Improving Water Management in India: The potential Role of River Basin Organisations. Asian Development Bank, Chanakyapuri, New Delhi, India (Publication No. 110507), 127 pp.

Collonsoj, N.D. 1986. Alluvial Sediments. In: *Sedimentary Environments and Facies,* 2nd edn (Ed. by H.G. Reading), pp. 20-62. Blackwell Scientific Publications, Oxford.

Guttikunda, S. K., Carmichael, G. R., Calori, G., Eck, C., and Woo, J.H. 2003: The Contribution of Mega Cities to Regional Sulfur Pollution in Asia, Atmos. Environ., 37(1), 11-22.

Jethva, H., Satheesh, S.K., and Srinivasan, J. 2005. Seasonal Variability of Aerosols Over the Indo-Gangetic Basin, J. Geophys. Res., 110, D21204.

Massie, S.T., Torres, O., and Smith, S. J. 2004. Total Ozone Mapping Spectrometer (TOMS) Observations of Increases in Asian Aerosol in Winter from 1979 to 2000, J. Geophys. Res., 109, D18211.

Mishra, S.K., Dey, S., and Tripathi, S. N. 2008. Implications of Particle Composition and Shape to Dust Radiative Effect: A Case Study from the Great Indian Desert, Geophys. Res. Lett., 35, L23814.

Monkkonen, P., Uma, R., Srinivasan, D., Koponen, I. K., Lehtinen, K. E. J., Hameri, K., Suresh, R., Sharma, V.P., and Kulmala,M. 2004: Relationship and Variations of Aerosol Number and PM10 mass Concentrations in a Highly Polluted Urban Environment. New Delhi, India, Atmos. Environ., 38, 425-433.

Moza Usha and Mishra D. N. 2003. Ecodynamics and Fishery Status of Upper Stretch of River Yamuna and Associated Canals, *CIFRI bull. No.* 123. pp 51.

Moza Usha and Mishra D. N. 2009. River Beas Ecology and Fishery., *CIFRI bull. No.* 159 pp 59.

Pakkas, H. B., and Kumar, S. 1991 The Indo-Gangetic Basin. In: *Sedimentary Basins of India, Tectonic Context* (Ed. By S.K. Tandon, C.C. Pant and S.M. Casshypa), pp. 147-170. Gyanodaya Prakashan, Nainital, India.

Pathak V and Tyagi R. K. 2010 Riverine Ecology and Fisheries *vis-a-vis* Hydrodynamic Alterations Impacts and Remedial Measures. *CIFRI bull. No.* 161, pp. 35.

Sharma, B.R., Upali, A., Amarasinghe, Alok, S. 2008. Indo-Gangetic River Basins: Summary Situation Analysis. Draft Prepared for the IWMI-CPWF Project on "Strategic Analysis of National River Linking Project of India".

Sharma, B.R., Amarasinghe, U.A. 2008. Strategic analysis of India's National River Linking Project: Providing Analytical Rigor to 'Opinions' and 'Assertions'. Proceedings Seminar on Role of Water Sector in India, Indian National Academy of Engineering, Indian Institute of Technology, New Delhi (February 21-22, 2008), pp. 75-82.

Vass, K.K. Samant, S., Suresh, V.R., Katiha, P., and Mandal, S.K. 2008. Current Status of River Ganges, *CIFRI bull. No.* 152. pp. 34.

Vass K.K., Raina H.S. and Sundar, S. 1978. On the Breeding Behaviour of *Schizothorax niger* in Dal lake. *J. Bombay nat. Hist. Soc.* 76: 180-184

Vass, K.K., Mandal, S.K., Samanta, S., Suresh, V.R., and Kathia, P.K. 2010. The Environment and Fishery Status of the River Ganges. *Aqu. Eco. Health Mang.*, 13 (4), 385-394.

CHAPTER – 7

Physico-Chemical Characteristics of Water in the Ponds Fed With Different Level of Protein Diets in Tarai Region of Uttarakhand

B.C. Joshi, *India*; A.K. Upadhyay, *India*; Manjulata Bisht, *India*

ABSTRACT

The effect of different level of protein in the practical diets for *Labeo rohita* was evaluated through the feeding trail of 180 days for adolescent fish. Four experimental diets (D_1, D_2, D_3, and D_4) containing different levels of protein (28%, 31%, 34% and 37%) were formulated using these locally available by-catch ingredients as a protein supplement along with the conventional feed ingredients like mustard oil cake, rice bran and tapioca. The diet D_0 served as control which contained rice bran and mustard oil cake in equal proportion. 1 per cent vitamin & mineral mixture and 1 per cent chromic oxide was added to each diet. 60 adolescent fish (average weight: 16.06 ± 0.03) were stocked in earthen ponds of suitable size. Fish were fed at a rate of 2 per cent body weight in the experiment. There was no significant influence of supplementary diets on water qualities such as pH, dissolved oxygen, total alkalinity, free CO_2 and biological parameters.

Key Words: Feed formulation, Protein level, Physico-chemical parameter, *Labeo rohita*.

INTRODUCTION

The Hydrobiological parameters are important factors in contributing to the growth of carps including rohu in farming operation. Application of artificial feed in intensive farming operations affects water quality criteria more than any other management factors. This is perhaps not surprising since the bulk of the dissolved and suspended inorganic or organic matter, contained within the effluents of intensively managed open aquaculture production system, are derived from feed inputs, either directly in the form of the end-products of feed digestion and metabolism or from uneaten/ waste feed, or indirectly through eutrophication and increased natural productivity.

Poor quality feed may cause severe water quality problems by building up of toxic ammonia, nitrite, hydrogen sulfide, increased biological oxygen demand and chemical oxygen demand, thereby inducing stress in fish (Paulraj, 1995; Tacon and Forster, 2003; Keshavanath, 2005). Therefore, the amount of fish that can be produced in lentic water bodies is dependent upon feeds formulation with increased digestibility and by optimizing the feed distribution strategies and practices, while maintaining proper water quality suitable for fish growth. Also the application of artificial feed in fish culture is the most important and expensive item and therefore, supply of optimum quantity of feed under various environmental factors is necessary.

Deficient feed often leads to diseased fish while excess diet pollutes the ambient water and enhances the cost of fish production. It has been reported that excess diets have led to various abnormalities in fishes (Azad, 1996). It is therefore essential that the optimal balance of feed be maintained to nurture the fish growth without polluting the water quality of culture system.

Water quality is influenced by many other factors, both environmental and biological. Some environmental conditions such as temperature and rainfall are beyond control. Other factors, such as vegetations, soil quality, stocking density and feeding are managed prior to flooding the ponds and during the culture period. Important water quality variables are temperature, dissolved oxygen, pH, free carbon dioxide, total alkalinity etc.

The growth and activity of the fish depends on its body temperature, which is about the same as the water temperature and varies with changes in it. Each fish species is adapted to grow and reproduce within well-defined ranges of water temperatures, but optimum growth and reproduction take place within narrower ranges of temperature. It is important, therefore, to have knowledge of water temperatures of the fish farm in order to select the right species of fish and to plan its management accordingly.

Dissolved oxygen is the most important factor, influencing fish life. Low oxygen concentration may be responsible for the death of fish in ponds. Temperature has a major effect on oxygen levels in ponds. Warm water cannot hold as much oxygen as cold water. Also, rising temperature increase biological activity, so oxygen is consumed at a faster rate.

pH is related to a ratio of the base components to the acid components. If a substance has one acid component for each base component, it is said to be neutral and has a pH value of 7. Water with a pH below 7 is acidic and pH levels above 7 are considered alkaline. pH should normally be between 7.0 and 8.5, but it is probably acceptable to be anywhere between 6.0 and 9.0. The alkalinity of water is related to the actual number of base components and can be thought of as the intensity of the pH. If alkalinity is low, it indicates that even a small amount of acid can cause a large change in the pH. Alkalinity measurement should be around 100 ppm, but readings from 50 to 200 ppm are acceptable.

The biological parameters *viz.*, plankton and benthos which together determine the water quality, govern the aquatic production either individually or synergistically and affect the survival and growth of all kinds of organisms present in the ecosystem including fish (Boyd *et al.*, 2002).

In view of the above, detailed study of the various hydrographical parameters was carried out in relation to different supplementary protein enriched diets in the pond and compared to the control pond The results of the hydro-biological parameters from the different treatments are presented and discussed.

METERIAL AND METHODS

The present investigation was carried out at College of Fisheries Sciences, G. B. Pant University of Agriculture and Technology, Pantnagar. The research trials were conducted during Sept. to Oct. 2005 and March to August 2006.

Geographical Location and Climatic Condition of Experimental Sites

Pantnagar is situated at 29°N latitude, 79°E longitude and altitude of 243.84 m above sea level, in Tarai belt of Shivalik range of Himalayan foot hills. The climate of Pantnagar is humid, sub-tropical and is characterized by very hot and dry summer and extremely cold winter. The fog generally occurs towards the end of December and may continue till February. The monsoon normally commences during the third week of June and ceases by the end of September. The metrological information of rainfall, relative humidity, seasonal atmospheric temperature and insolation period during experiments is given in Table 7.1. (*See Table on next page*)

Formulation of Diets

The feed were formulated using different by–catch fish wastes for protein enrichment mixed with conventional feeds ingredients like, rice bran, oil cake etc. Tapioca was used as binder for preparation of the feed. Test diets having varying levels of protein content (28%, 31%, 34% and 37%) were formulated using Pearson and Square method (Jain, 1998a). These diets were earmarked as D_1, D_2, D_3 and D_4, and the diet D_0 served as control which contained rice bran and mustard oil cake in equal proportions but no ingredients of protein enrichment. The above test diets were prepared separately by mixing all the ingredients in appropriate proportions with adequate quantity of water to get dough (Jayram and Shetty, 1981).

Table 7.1: Fortnightly Fluctuation in Meteorological Condition during the Course of Investigation

Month	Temperature (°C)		Relative Humidity (%)		Rain Fall (mm)	Insolation Period (hrs)	Evaporation (mm)
	Max.	Min.	Max.	Min.			
March. I	27.72	13.55	88.13	45.00	00.47	06.81	03.20
March. II	30.53	14.63	87.00	29.44	00.07	09.48	05.25
April I	35.15	14.95	75.60	23.53	00.00	09.30	07.25
April II	35.20	19.40	59.66	22.73	00.20	09.22	08.08
May I	37.15	23.69	67.53	29.93	01.10	09.31	09.78
May II	33.75	23.57	77.06	49.81	05.97	07.33	07.14
June I	34.72	25.05	74.73	48.40	02.61	07.43	06.06
June II	35.52	25.13	76.60	45.13	01.12	08.43	07.51
July I	33.39	26.73	82.47	61.53	05.05	05.13	05.83
July II	32.06	25.49	88.69	68.69	13.77	04.36	04.03
August I	33.10	25.42	86.33	62.93	2.01	8.56	5.35
August II	32.14	25.07	89.31	69.00	18.62	5.43	1.19

Plate 7.1: Experimental Fish Ponds

Plate 7.2: Estimation of Physiochemical Parameters

Plate 7.3: Plankton Collection by Plankton Net

Vitamin and mineral mixture was added and mixed thoroughly in each of the formulated feeds. The mixture was then passed through a pelletizer (2 mm dia) and then pellets were collected on aluminium tray. The pellets were then kept for drying in the hot air oven at 60°C for 24 hours, till the moisture content was reduced to less than 10 per cent. The dried pellets were then broken into small pieces and packed in air tight plastic containers, labeled and stored in cool and dry place. The proximate composition of feed is given in Table 7.2.

Table 7.2: Proximate Composition of Diets on per cent Dry Weight Basis (± SE)

Diets	Parameter						
	Moisture	Crude Protein	Crude Lipid	Crude Fibre	Ash	NFE	Gross Energy (Kcal/g)
D_0	7.34 ± 0.03	20.19 ± 0.04	8.34 ± 0.02	12.38 ± 0.02	16.54 ± 0.03	35.21 ± 0.17	2.79-
D_1	6.81 ± 0.02	28.60 ± 0.05	7.48 ± 0.04	10.80 ± 0.03	15.87 ± 0.04	30.44 ± 0.12	2.81-
D_2	6.95 ± 0.03	31.24 ± 0.06	7.76 ± 0.02	10.06 ± 0.03	14.98 ± 0.04	29.01 ± 0.07	3.07-
D_3	6.93 ± 0.02	34.08 ± 0.05	7.94 ± 0.04	9.25 ± 0.03	13.41 ± 0.07	28.38 ± 0.13	3.10-
D_4	7.28 ± 0.03	37.10 ± 0.07	8.28 ± 0.04	8.29 ± 0.04	13.12 ± 0.06	25.93 ± 0.22	3.24-

Values given in the table are means (n = 3).

Estimation of Hydrobiological Parameters

The survival, feeding rate, assimilation and growth in fish are governed and influenced by different hydrobiological parameters. Hence the assessment of these parameters while in feeding trials is highly essential. Through out the study period the water sample of both experiments (indoor and outdoor) was analysed for following hydrobiological parameters. All the parameters were recorded at weekly interval.

Temperature

Temperature was measured with the help of a good grade mercury thermometer having range of 0-50°C, with mark up to 0.1°C. The water temperature was determined by dipping the mercury bulb of the thermometer directly into the water at about one foot depth for few minutes. The water temperature for the experimental tubs and ponds was recorded daily in the morning and evening.

Hydrogen ion Activity (pH)

pH of the water sample for weekly duration from the feeding trials were determined electrometrically with the help of pH meter. The pH of the sample was determined immediately after collection. The pH electrode was dipped in a glass beaker having sample and the pH value was read directly from the meter and expressed directly.

Dissolved Oxygen

The dissolved oxygen content of pond water was determined following Winkler titrimetric method (APHA 1985).

Water samples were collected carefully in 100 ml glass stoppered sampling bottles within the water body to exclude air bubbles. 1.0 ml each of manganous sulphate and alkaline iodide reagents were added by means of 1 ml pipette, that was immersed to the bottom of the bottle and the pipette was slowly drawn out after addition. The stopper was replaced and the bottle was inverted 3-4 times for thorough mixing. The resultant flocculent was dissolved by adding 1 ml concentrated H_2SO_4, mixed and dissolved by gentle inversion. 50 ml of this solution was then transferred to an Erlenmeyer flask and 0.025 N $Na_2S_2O_3$ solution was added drop by drop till the colour turned to pale straw. 1 ml starch solution was added and titration continued to reach the end point, i.e. disappearance of the blue colour.

Calculation

$$\text{Dissolved oxygen (mg/l)} = \frac{8 \times 1000 \times N(0.025) \times V'}{V}$$

where,

V = Volume of water sample taken (ml)

V′ = volume of titrant (sodium thiosulphate) used (ml)

N = Normality of the titrant

Free Carbon Dioxide

The free carbon dioxide was estimated by standard titrimetric method using phenolphthalein as an indicator (APHA, 1985).

100 ml of the sample was taken in a Nessler's tube and 5-10 drops of phenolphthalein indicator was added. The appearance of red colour indicated absence of free CO_2 in the sample. Sample, remaining colourless indicated presence of free CO_2. 50 ml of this sample was titrated rapidly into the cylinder with standard alkali solution (N/44 NaOH) until a definite pink colour persisted.

Calculation

Free CO_2 was calculated by using the following expression:

$$\text{Free Carbon dioxide (mg/ l)} = \frac{\text{ml of titrant used}}{\text{ml of sample taken}} \times 100$$

Total Alkalinity

Alkalinity was assessed titrimetrically using phenolphthalein and methyl orange as indicators (APHA, 1985).

(a) Phenolphthalein alkalinity

5-6 drops of phenolphthalein indicator solution were added to 50 ml of the sample. If the sample remained colorless, phenolphthalein alkalinity was absent. The appearance of pink color indicated the presence of phenolphthalein alkalinity. The sample was titrated against 0.02N H_2SO_4 solution to a colorless end point. Phenolphthalein alkalinity was calculated using the following expression.

Calculation

$$\text{Phenolphthalein alkalinity } (C_aCO_3 \text{ mg/ l}) = \frac{A \times 1000}{\text{ml of sample}}$$

where,

A = ml of 0.02N H_2SO_4 used in titration

(b) Methyl orange alkalinity

5-6 drops of methyl orange indicator solution were added to 50 ml of the sample. The sample was titrated against standard 0.02 N sulphuric acid till yellow to faint orange color developed.

Calculation

$$\text{Methyl orange alkalinity } (C_aCO_3 \text{ mg/ l}) = \frac{B \times 1000}{\text{ml of sample}}$$

where,

B = ml of titrant (0.02 N H_2SO_4) used for sample to develop pink colour.

The total alkalinity was calculated using the following expression.

$$\text{Total alkalinity } (C_aCO_3 \text{ mg/ l}) = \frac{(A + B) \times 1000}{\text{ml of sample}}$$

Transparency

The water transparency for weekly duration was measured for each pond by a secchi disc of 20 cm diameter, having the alternate bands of white and black colours. A graduated rope of known length operated the disc. The disc was suspended from a rope till it visually disappeared and then was hauled slowly till it again became visible. The depth (d_1) of disappearance and the depth (d_2) of reappearance of secchi disc were noted and the average of the two taken as secchi disc transparency.

Calculation

$$\text{Transparency} = \frac{di + d2}{2}$$

Plankton Analysis

The plankton samples were collected at weekly intervals. 100 litres of water was filtered using a plankton net made of No. 30 bolting silk cloth (60 μ mesh size).

For expressing the amount of plankton as wet weight, the plankton concentrate was placed on pre weighed filter paper (A) and retained there until the moisture was removed. Then the weight of plankton concentrate along with the filter paper was taken (B). After deducting the weight of filter paper (A) from the final reading (B), the wet weight of plankton was obtained.

For dry weight expression, plankton concentrate was evaporated in a previously weighed filter paper and dried at 60°C for 24 hours and cooled in a desiccator. The heating and cooling process was repeated till a constant weight was achieved. Wet weight and the dry weight of plankton were expressed as mg/100 litre of water.

RESULTS AND DISCUSSION

Water for fish is the medium that must supply or support all their needs, including breathing, eating, reproducing and growing. Numerous investigations have been carried out to understand physical and chemical properties of water suitable for the culture of specific fish species (Tripathi, 1982; Unni, 1982; Jhingran, 1988; Deorari, 1993; Gupta *et al.*, 2004; Tewari and Dwivedi, 2004). The ranges and mean values of different hydrographical parameters from both the experiments are presented in Table 7.3 to 7.10.

Temperature

Temperature plays a vital role on the primary production of an aquatic system. Water temperature is an important factor in controlling the growth of Indian major carps (Singh *et al.*, 1979; Jhingran, 1991) and depends on sunlight, climate, depth and transparency of water (Das *et al.*, 2001).

In the present study the average fortnightly air and water temperature of different treatments are given in the Table 7.3 (*See Table on next page*). The air temperature ranged from 20.63°C to 30.42°C, whereas water temperature varied from 20.11°C to 29.35°C and minor differences existed in the water temperature in different experimental ponds. Water temperature showed a trend more or less similar to that of the air temperature (*See Fig. 7.1 on next page*). Similar results have also been obtained by Vijaykumar (1995). Water temperature ranging between 20°C to 30°C is considered to be most suitable for the growth and survival of fishes (Boyd and Pillai, 1984; Alam *et al.*, 1990). Jhingran (1982) reported a water temperature range of 18°C to 32°C as suitable for carps whereas Bankthavathsalam *et al.* (2003) found the temperature range of 26 and 32°C to be optimum for growth of fish under composite carp culture. Low temperature reduces the metabolic activities of organisms (Khanna, 1993) while the growth rate of Rohu increased when temperature rose above 25°C (Singh and Mishra, 2004). Suitable temperature, for a number of fish species, which promotes maximum growth, has also been explained by many other workers (Ekanem, 1994; Nath, 2001; Das and Chand, 2003; Sarkar and Ray, 2004).

The minimum value of temperature was recorded in the months of March and maximum values were recorded in the months of May in all ponds. The pattern of variation of temperature in all the ponds was similar.

Table 7.3: Average Air and Water Temperature (ºC) during Experimental Period

Days of Culture	Air Temperature	Water Temperature
15	21.92	20.88
30	22.58	21.62
45	25.05	23.74
60	27.30	26.17
75	30.42	28.72
90	28.66	27.30
105	29.88	28.64
120	30.32	29.35
135	30.06	29.00
150	28.77	27.68
165	29.26	28.91
180	28.60	28.40

Values given in the table are means (n = 3).

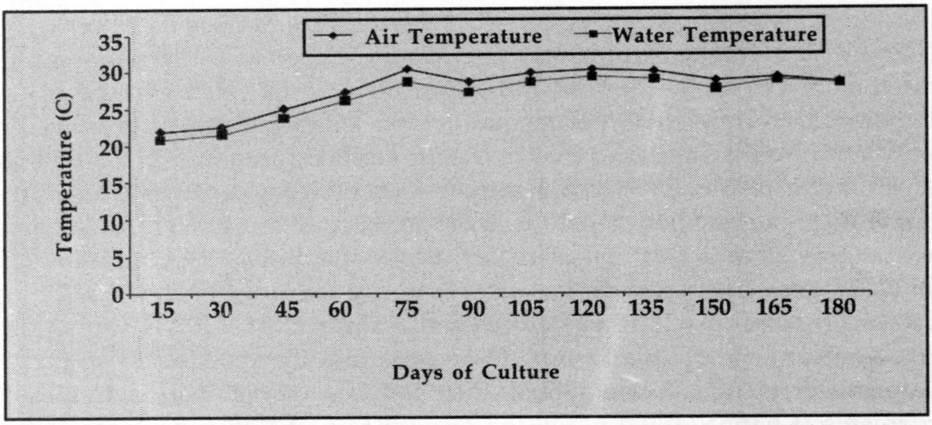

Fig. 7.1: Variation in Air and Water Temperature during the Experimental Period

Water pH

pH is an important factor and determines the solubility and chemical nature of most substances in natural waters. It affects the chemical and biochemical reaction and controls the activities and distribution of aquatic fauna and flora. Better fish production could be possible in pond water with pH value ranging between 6.5 and 9.0 (Boyd and Pillai, 1984; Sharma, 2000). It has direct effect on fish growth (appetite and food conversion ratio) as well as on the growth and survival of fish food organisms (Das *et al.*, 2001).

Acidic pH is the result of accumulation of significant concentration of free CO_2 in water. The relationship between CO_2 and carbonate regulates the pH in pond water (Jhingran, 1991).

The water pH in the all treatments was varying from 7.71 to 8.04, 7.28 to 8.02, 7.57 to 8.25, 7.47 to 8.23 and 7.24 to 8.26 in P_0, P_1, P_2, P_3 and P_4 respectively (Table 7.4).

Table 7.4: Value of pH of Water Recorded from Different Treatments (± SE)

Treatment	Days of Culture						
	0	30	60	90	120	150	180
P_0	$7.71^a \pm 0.19$	$7.50^a \pm 0.23$	$7.59^a \pm 0.14$	$7.48^a \pm 0.10$	$8.02^a \pm 0.14$	$8.04^a \pm 0.92$	$7.61^a \pm 0.03$
P_1	$7.28^a \pm 0.09$	$7.33^a \pm 0.25$	$7.96^a \pm 0.05$	$7.76^a \pm 0.08$	$8.02^a \pm 0.06$	$7.85^a \pm 0.06$	$7.64^a \pm 0.11$
P_2	$7.57^a \pm 0.09$	$7.81^a \pm 0.10$	$7.66^a \pm 0.11$	$7.74^a \pm 0.12$	$8.25^a \pm 0.06$	$7.85^a \pm 0.15$	$7.72^a \pm 0.09$
P_3	$7.47^a \pm 0.17$	$7.75^a \pm 0.08$	$7.83^a \pm 0.06$	$7.87^a \pm 0.24$	$8.23^a \pm 0.13$	$8.07^a \pm 0.10$	$7.43^a \pm 0.10$
P_4	$7.24^a \pm 0.13$	$7.81^a \pm 0.07$	$7.91^a \pm 0.03$	$7.83^a \pm 0.14$	$8.26^a \pm 0.10$	$7.81^a \pm 0.08$	$7.67^a \pm 0.10$
SEM	0.14	0.17	0.10	0.15	0.11	0.11	0.10
CD (5%)	0.47	0.57	0.32	0.50	0.37	0.37	0.32

Figures having different alphabet superscripts in the same column are significantly different.

Values given in the table are means (n = 3).

Among the treatments the average value was highest for the treatment P_3 followed by P_2, P_4, P_0, and P_1. The maximum average value for all the treatments was registered during 120 days of rearing period followed by 150 days, 60 days, 90 days, 30 days 180 days respectively and minimum at the start of the experiment (*See Fig. 7.2 on next page*). The pH values in the present study were on the alkaline side throughout the culture period. The values ranged from 7.24 to 8.26 mg/l in experiment are favorable for fish growth. So, there is no adverse effect of protein concentration in the pH values of the experimental ponds.

Dissolved Oxygen

Pond systems containing free oxygen molecules are aerobic; those without are anaerobic. Anaerobic systems will not support higher life forms. They are characterized by the presence of noxious chemicals such as hydrogen sulfide, which can cause odors; therefore the range of DO may be maintained above 4 mg/l (Singh and Mishra, 2006). The oxygen content in pond water is generally decreased with rise of temperature indicating diurnal as well as seasonal variation (Jhingran, 1991).

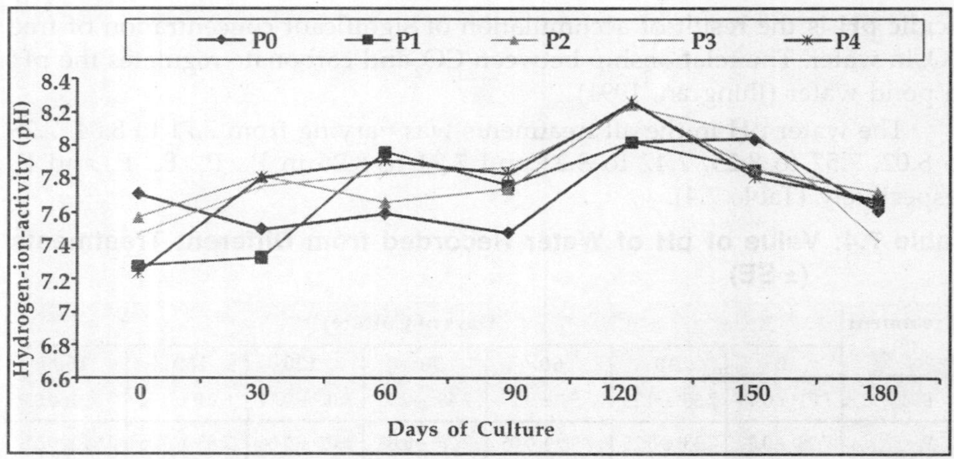

Fig. 7.2: Variation in Hydrogen ion Activity (pH) Different Treatment

The dissolved oxygen values of water recorded from the experiment is presented in Table 7.5. The value of dissolved oxygen ranged from 7.09 to 8.06, 7.11 to 8.10, 7.03 to 8.46, 7.17 to 8.36 and 7.19 to 8.11 in P_0, P_1, P_2, P_3 and P_4 respectively. Among the treatments the average value was highest for the treatment P_3 followed by P_4, P_2, P_0, and P_1 (Fig. 7.3).

Table 7.5: Dissolved Oxygen Levels (mg/l) Recorded from Different Treatments (± SE)

Treatment	Days of Culture						
	0	30	60	90	120	150	180
P_0	$8.06^a \pm 0.38$	$7.95^a \pm 0.03$	$7.68^a \pm 0.03$	$7.27^a \pm 0.19$	$7.49^a \pm 0.10$	$7.09^a \pm 0.16$	$7.22^a \pm 0.13$
P_1	$8.10^a \pm 0.06$	$7.99^a \pm 0.07$	$7.77^a \pm 0.08$	$7.18^a \pm 0.14$	$7.11^a \pm 0.06$	$7.25^a \pm 0.07$	$7.19^a \pm 0.05$
P_2	$8.46^a \pm 0.09$	$8.07^a \pm 0.09$	$7.61^a \pm 0.05$	$7.03^a \pm 0.23$	$7.19^a \pm 0.05$	$7.11^a 0.11$	$7.57^a \pm 0.07$
P_3	$8.36^a \pm 0.07$	$8.04^a \pm 0.08$	$7.59^a \pm 0.15$	$7.33^a \pm 0.12$	$7.17^a \pm 0.33$	$7.38^a \pm 0.22$	$7.61^a \pm 0.15$
P_4	$7.78^a \pm 0.09$	$8.11^a \pm 0.07$	$7.47^a \pm 0.08$	$8.04^a \pm 0.37$	$7.48^a \pm 0.16$	$7.22^a \pm 0.11$	$7.19^a \pm 0.31$
SEM	0.17	0.75	0.08	0.22	0.18	0.12	0.16
CD (5%)	0.56	0.24	0.26	0.74	0.59	0.40	0.54

Figures having different alphabet superscripts in the same column are significantly different.
Values given in the table are means (n = 3).

The maximum average value for all the treatments was registered at the start of experiment followed by 30 days, 60 days, 90 days, 180 days 120 days respectively and minimum during 150 days of the experiment. The dissolved oxygen values recorded in the present investigation were within the recommended levels, ranging from 7.03 to 8.46 mg/l in the experiment.

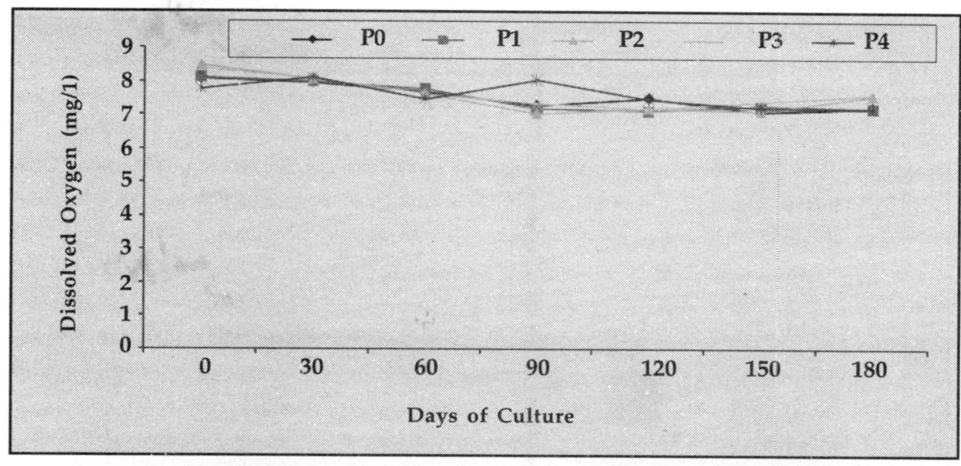

Fig. 7.3: Variation in Dissolved Oxygen in Different Treatments

Free Carbon Dioxide

Presence of free carbon dioxide is essential for photosynthesis but its excess is harmful to the aquatic animals. CO_2 is highly soluble in natural water, regulates biological processes in aquatic communities and can form many compounds (Das, 2000). Baruah *et al.* (1998) registered minimum and maximum value of CO_2 during summer and winter month respectively. According to Jhingran (1988) the decomposition of organic sediments in water bodies is always associated with accumulation of carbon dioxide, decrease in pH and increase in bicarbonate.

Table 7.6: Free Carbon Dioxide Levels (mg/l) Recorded from Different Treatments (± SE)

Treatment	Days of Culture						
	0	30	60	90	120	150	180
P_0	$1.38^a \pm 0.34$	$0.33^a \pm 0.30$	$0.03^a \pm 0.00$	$0.01^a \pm 0.003$	$0.00^a \pm 0.00$	$0.29^a \pm 0.11$	$1.28^a \pm 0.46$
P_1	$1.88^a \pm 0.56$	$0.66^a \pm 0.02$	$0.13^a \pm 0.00004$	$0.00^b \pm 0.00$	$0.003^a \pm 0.0003$	$0.47^a \pm 0.14$	$1.47^a \pm 0.24$
P_2	$1.29^a \pm 0.40$	$0.75^a \pm 0.14$	$0.00^a \pm 0.00$	$0.003^b \pm 0.00$	$0.00^a \pm 0.00$	$0.77^a \pm 0.12$	$1.35^a \pm 0.52$
P_3	$0.61^a \pm 0.09$	$0.36^a \pm 0.25$	$0.20^a \pm 0.04$	$0.00^b \pm 0.00$	$0.03^a \pm 0.04$	$0.65^a \pm 0.03$	$1.46^a \pm 0.15$
P_4	$1.48^a \pm 0.38$	$0.44^a \pm 0.09$	$0.03^a \pm 0.00$	$0.00^b \pm 0.00$	$0.10^b \pm 0.01$	$0.71^a \pm 0.11$	$1.73^a \pm 0.21$
SEM	0.42	0.17	0.06	0.002	0.01	0.12	0.38
CD (5%)	1.40	0.56	0.19	0.007	0.04	0.39	1.26

Figures having different alphabet superscripts in the same column are significantly different.

Values given in the table are means (n = 3).

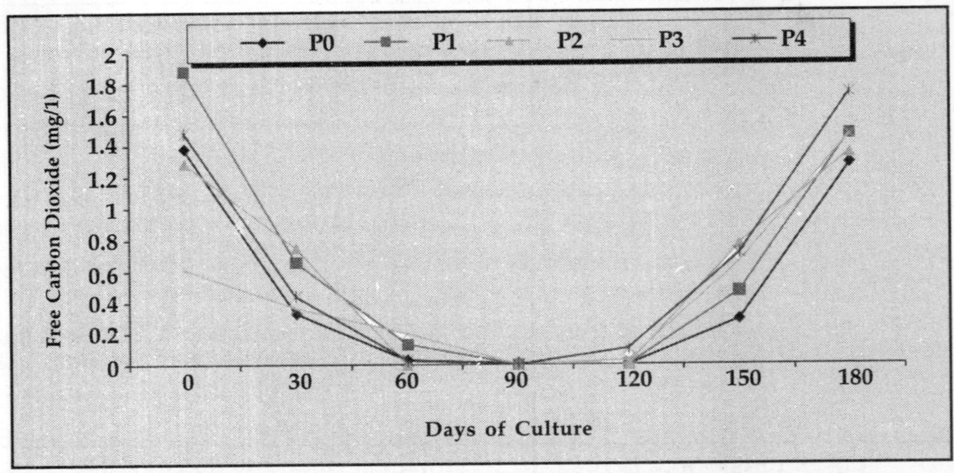

Fig. 7.4: Variation in Free Carbon Dioxide in Different Treatments

The values of free carbon dioxide are given in Table 7.6. It ranged from 0.00 to 1.38, 0.00 to 1.88, 0.00 to 1.35, 0.00 to 1.46 and 0.00 to 1.73 in P_0, P_1, P_2, P_3 and P_4 respectively. Among the treatments the average value was highest for the treatment P_1 followed by P_4, P_2, P_0, and P_3. The maximum average value for all the treatments was registered during 180 days of rearing period followed by 0 days, 150 days, 30 days, 60 days and 120 days respectively and minimum during 90 days of the experiment (Fig. 7.4). Free carbon dioxide in the experiment was either undetectable or very low. The value ranged from 0.00 to 1.88 ppm in the experiment. Thus, it can be said that the free carbon dioxide in the present study did not have any adverse effect on the survival and growth of fish.

Total Alkalinity

Alkalinity is related to amount of dissolved calcium, magnesium and other compounds in the water. Singh *et al.* (1999) reported that the values of alkalinity depend upon the location, season, plankton population, rainfall and nature of bottom deposits.

The total alkalinity ranged from 87.91 to 160.05 mg/l, 91.77 to 140.89 mg/l, 97.54 to 154.47 mg/l, 86.33 to 145.49 mg/l and 101.79 to 149.04 in P_0, P_1, P_2, P_3 and P_4 respectively (Table 7.7).

Among the treatments the average value was highest for the treatment P_0 followed by P_4, P_2, P_1, and P_3 (Fig. 7.5). The maximum average value for all the treatments was registered during 90 days of rearing period followed by 120 days, 180 days, 60 days, 150 days and 30 days respectively and minimum at the start of the experiment. The total alkalinity values in the present study ranged from 86.33 to 160.05 ppm. These levels were sufficient to prevent drastic fluctuations in pH and maintained the water productive.

Table 7.7: Total Alkalinity Values (mg/l) Recorded from Different Treatments (± SE)

Treatment	Days of Culture						
	0	30	60	90	120	150	180
P_0	87.91[a]±5.16	118.60[a]±4.20	141.23[a]±11.97	160.05[a]±7.33	159.92[a]±11.28	127.89[a]±3.74	151.22[a]±2.65
P_1	91.77[a] ±5.78	140.89[a]±14.36	129.18[a]±10.57	124.93[a]±3.38	131.19[a]±11.30	109.44[a]±9.47	135.78[a]±6.81
P_2	97.54[a] ±1.31	119.44[a]±5.57	111.47[a]±6.36	154.47[a]±6.35	144.31[a]±9.41	116.68[a]±8.25	126.59[a]±11.00
P_3	86.33[a] ±0.87	105.25[a]±5.00	142.41[a]±5.02	138.39[a]±4.72	105.64[a]±7.12	128.40[a]±2.37	145.49[a]±9.51
P_4	101.79[a]±4.23	121.83[a]±2.42	149.04[a]±8.11	136.46[a]±13.66	148.68[a]±12.50	135.47[a]±5.80	121.24[a]±6.47
SEM	4.15	7.77	8.92	8.02	11.14	5.38	8.70
CD (5%)	13.53	25.34	29.08	26.14	36.32	17.53	28.36

Figures having different alphabet superscripts in the same column are significantly different.
Values given in the table are means (n = 3).

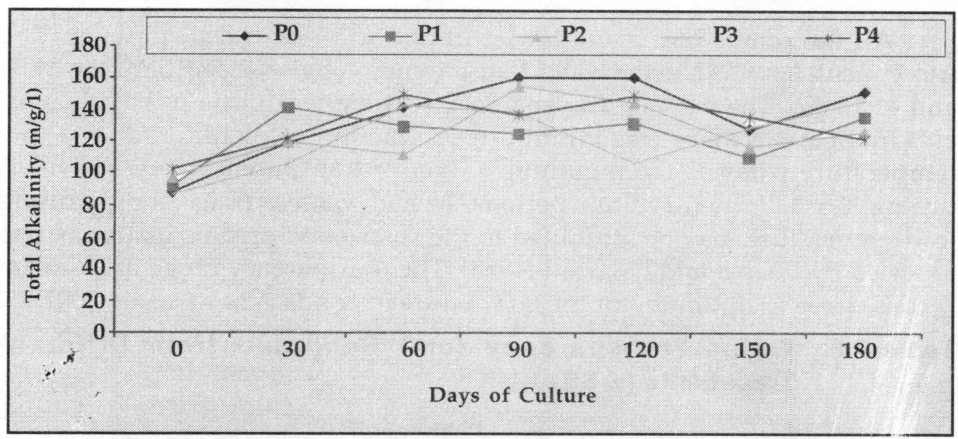

Fig. 7.5: Variation in Total Alkalinity in Different Treatments

Water Transparency

Transparency is also an important factor which influences survival and growth of fishes in the ponds (Das and Chand, 2003). Lower transparency values cause possible threat of low dissolved oxygen during night whereas higher transparency result in higher water temperature and weed growth.

The water transparency ranged from 35.96 to 41.16 cm, 35.76 to 40.80 cm, 35.33 to 40.66 cm, 35.13 to 40.33 and 34.96 to 41.03 cm in P_0, P_1, P_2, P_3 and P_4 in the experimental ponds respectively (Table 7.8). Among the treatments the average value was highest for the treatment P_0 followed by P_2, P_1, P_3 and P_4 (Fig. 7.6). The maximum average value for all the treatments was registered during initial phase of the experiment which is followed by 30 days, 60 days, 90 days, 180 and 150 days respectively and minimum at the 120 days of the experiment.

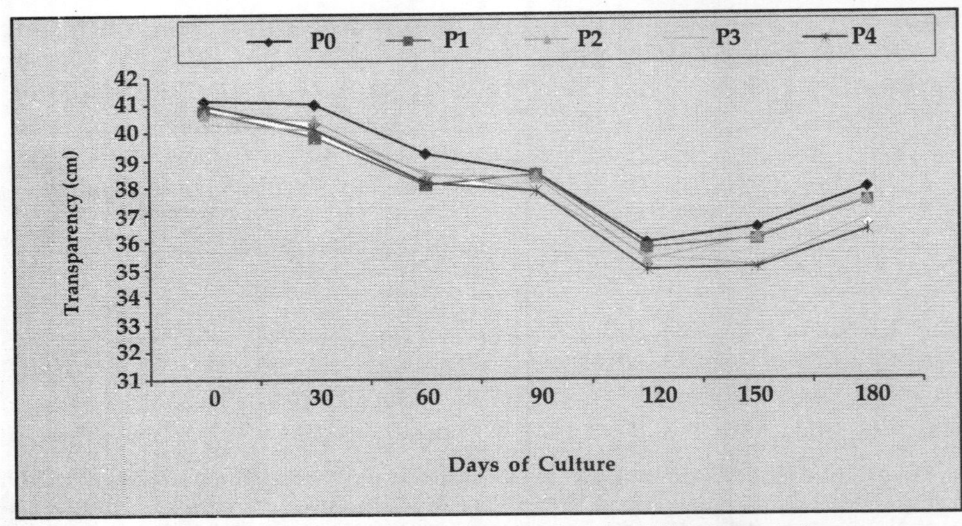

Fig. 7.6: Variation in Transparency in Different Ponds

All the ponds had a similar trend of variation in transparency. The experimental ponds had the water transparency values ranging between 34.96 and 41.16 cm. The value of transparency was higher during initial phase of culture because there was minimum production of plankton due to low temperature whereas the minimum values of transparency were observed during 90 to 120 days of culture period. The high value of transparency during low temperature may be attributed to the suspended organic matter as also reported by Bhagat and Dwivedi (1988). The transparency range of 25-35 cm is considered as optimum for the fish culture in ponds (Vijay Anand, 2005).

Table 7.8: Water Transparency (cm) Recorded from Different Treatments (± SE)

Treatment	Days of Culture						
	0	30	60	90	120	150	180
P_0	$41.16^a \pm 0.28$	$41.03^a \pm 0.23$	$39.23^a \pm 0.55$	$38.50^a \pm 0.32$	$35.96^a \pm 0.34$	$36.50^a \pm 0.36$	$37.96^a \pm 0.23$
P_1	$40.80^a \pm 0.40$	$39.83^a \pm 0.20$	$38.06^a \pm 0.54$	$38.46^a \pm 0.29$	$35.76^a \pm 0.21$	$36.06^a \pm 0.50$	$37.46^a \pm 0.36$
P_2	$40.66^a \pm 0.61$	$40.46^a \pm 0.38$	$38.43^a \pm 0.67$	$38.36^a \pm 0.64$	$35.33^a \pm 0.20$	$36.16^a \pm 0.18$	$37.50^a \pm 0.42$
P_3	$40.33^a \pm 0.37$	$40.10^a \pm 0.61$	$38.56^a \pm 0.61$	$37.83^a \pm 0.72$	$35.43^a \pm 0.35$	$35.13^a \pm 0.28$	$36.83^a \pm 0.39$
P_4	$41.03^a \pm 0.17$	$40.16^a \pm 0.20$	$38.16^a \pm 0.76$	$37.83^a \pm 0.43$	$34.96^a \pm 0.37$	$35.03^a \pm 0.35$	$36.40^a \pm 0.11$
SEM	0.44	0.40	0.70	0.50	0.28	1.30	0.64
CD (5%)	1.44	1.29	2.27	1.62	0.93	4.23	2.08

Figures having different alphabet superscripts in the same column are significantly different.

Values given in the table are means (n = 3).

Plankton Analysis

The wet weight and dry weight of plankton biomass obtained in different ponds during the experimental period are given in Table 7.9 and Table 7.10 respectively. The plankton concentration (wet weight) in the ponds ranged from 70.10 to 91.58, 71.29 to 92.40, 71.82 to 93.71, 72.34 to 93.26 and 70.53 to 94.08 mg/100 litre of water in P_0, P_1, P_2, P_3 and P_4 respectively (Fig. 7.7). Comparatively among treatments the average value was highest for the P-$_3$ followed by P_4, P_1, P_2, and minimum in the treatment P_0. The maximum average value for all the treatments was recorded during 120 days of rearing period followed by 150 days, 180 days, 90 days, 60 days and 30 days respectively with minimum at the start of the experiment.

The plankton biomass in all ponds increased up to 120 days of culture and after that there was a slight decrease in the planktonic biomass. The plankton production on wet basis varied from 70.10 to 94.08 mg/100 litre of water whereas on dry weight basis it varies from 16.43 to 27.73 mg/100 litre of water. The quantitative estimation of plankton did not show any significant variation ($P<0.05$) between the treatments indicating that the different level of protein in the fish diet did not have adverse effect on the concentration of plankton.

Table 7.9: Wet Weight of Plankton (mg/100 litre of water) Recorded from Different Treatments (± SE)

Treatment	Days of Culture						
	0	30	60	90	120	150	180
P_0	70.10^a ± 0.26	72.66^a ± 0.64	79.82^a ± 0.77	83.46^a ± 0.23	91.58^a ± 0.53	89.39^a ± 0.71	85.67^a ± 0.85
P_1	71.29^a ± 0.35	74.89^a ± 0.22	81.24^a ± 0.45	85.12^a ± 0.24	92.40^a ± 0.55	90.20^a ± 0.67	86.93^a ± 0.75
P_2	71.82^a ± 0.64	73.53^a ± 0.37	80.77^a ± 0.79	84.96^a ± 0.24	93.71^a ± 0.26	89.96^a ± 0.69	86.19^a ± 0.72
P_3	72.34^a ± 0.37	74.32^a ± 0.43	80.43^a ± 0.69	85.37^a ± 0.54	93.26^a ± 0.52	91.83^a ± 1.16	87.22^a ± 0.47
P_4	70.53^a ± 0.46	73.94^a ± 0.45	80.97^a ± 0.75	85.56^a ± 0.54	94.08^a ± 0.71	91.54^a ± 0.87	87.94^a ± 0.35
SEM	1.19	1.13	0.76	1.64	2.89	0.59	0.69
CD (5%)	3.88	3.68	2.47	5.33	9.42	1.92	2.24

Figures having different alphabet superscripts in the same column are significantly different.

Values given in the table are means (n = 3).

Ahmed and Siddiqui (2001) suggested 34 per cent protein diet with live food (plankton) could be used to increase the production from the pond. Singh and Sharma (1999) and Srivastava and Roy (2007) revealed that primary productivity and water quality characteristics are very much affected by the type of manure used for fertilization along with supplementary diets. Rahman *et al.* (2006) described that the formulated feed administration increase the zooplankton and benthic macro invertebrate availability in the pond.

Supplementary feeding and accumulation of faecal matter provide favorable conditions for plankton growth (Venugopal, 1980; Murthy, 1989; Milstein *et al.*, 1995).

Table 7.10: Dry Weight of Plankton (mg/100 Litre of Water) Recorded from Different Treatments (± SE)

Treatment	Days of Culture						
	0	30	60	90	120	150	180
P_0	16.43^{a}± 0.37	17.98^{a}± 0.23	20.86^{a}± 0.74	22.68^{a}± 0.3.8	26.11^{a}± 0.77	25.12^{a}± 0.78	23.98^{a}± 1.03
P_1	17.14^{a} ± 0.42	19.10^{a} ± 0.80	21.98^{a} ± 0.89	22.94^{a} ± 0.83	26.48^{a} ± 0.60	25.46^{a} ± 0.41	24.47^{a} ± 0.97
P_2	17.46^{a} ± 0.70	18.24^{a} ± 0.56	21.33^{a} ± 0.56	23.42^{a} ± 0.61	27.40^{a} ± 0.50	25.38^{a} ± 0.51	24.19^{a} ± 0.85
P_3	17.78^{a} ± 0.61	18.84^{a} ± 0.82	21.08^{a} ± 0.81	23.72^{a} ± 0.50	26.97^{a} ± 0.62	25.84^{a} ± 1.16	24.51^{a} ± 0.47
P_4	16.82^{a} ± 0.97	18.58^{a} ± 0.70	21.71^{a} ± 0.90	23.91^{a} ± 0.38	27.73^{a} ± 0.95	26.00^{a} ± 0.73	24.91^{a} ± 0.36
SEM	0.58	0.68	0.84	0.58	0.76	0.49	0.86
CD (5%)	1.91	2.21	2.74	1.89	2.48	1.60	2.82

Figures having different alphabet superscripts in the same column are significantly different.

Values given in the table are means (n = 3).

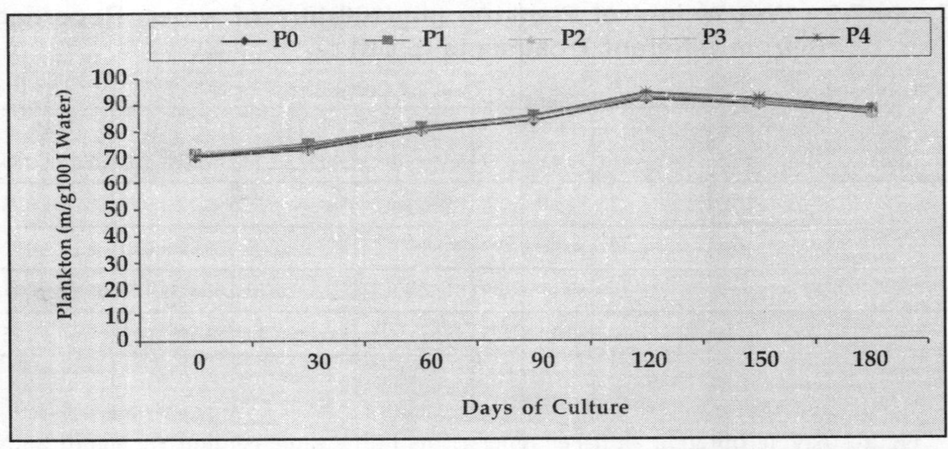

Fig. 7.7: Average Production of Plankton (Wet Weight) in Different Ponds

The dry weight of plankton biomass obtained from the ponds ranged from 16.43 to 26.11, 17.14 to 26.48, 17.46 to 27.40, 17.78 to 26.97 and 16.82 to 27.73 mg/100 litre of water in P_0, P_1, P_2, P_3 and P_4 respectively. The highest average dry weight of plankton was recorded as 22.81 mg/100 litre of water from the treatment P_4 and the lowest was registered as 21.88 mg/100 litre of water from the treatment P_0. Intermediate values of 22.68, 22.51 and 22.49 mg/100 litre of water were found in the treatments P_3, P_1 and P_2 respectively. The maximum average value for all the treatments was recorded during 120 days of rearing period followed by 150 days, 180 days, 90 days, 60 days and 30 days respectively with minimum at the start of the experiment.

Among the parameters studied, the water temperature, pH, total alkalinity, free carbon dioxide, transparency and planktonic concentrations did not show any significant variations ($P < 0.05$) in their values between the different treatments and were with in the optimal range for the growth of carps (Jhingran, 1991). The results of the present study are similar to the findings of Dhawan and Singh (1994), Milstein *et al.* (1995), Basavaraja and Antony (1997) and Singh *et al.* (2004b) who also did not record any adverse effect of the hydrobiological characteristics in their feeding experiments using different supplementary diets.

REFERENCES

Alam, W.; Sheri, A.N. and Afzal, M. 1990. Effect of Poultry Manure on the Growth Performance of *Labeo rohita* Under Polyculture System. *In:* Proc. Pakistan Congress on Zoology. 10: 301-306.

APHA. 1985. Standard Methods for the Examination of Water and Waste Water. 16th ed. American Public Health Association. New York.

Azad, I.S. 1996. Nutrition and Health Management in Aquaculture. *Fishing Chimes.* 16: 31-33.

Bankthavathsalam, R.; Vishnupriya, S.R.; Panimalar, S.; Kavita, S. and Perianayaki, D. 2003. Diurnal and Weekly Variations of some Physico-chemical Factors of a Natural Carp Culture Pond. *Environ & Ecology*. 21 (1): 227-233.

Barauah, B.K.; Talukdar, S. and Borhtakur, C.R. 1998. Limnological Studies of Ponds in Relation to Pisciculture. *Environment and Ecology*. 16: 518-522.

Basavaraja, N. and Antony, J.M. 1997. Rearing of Spawn and Fry of *Cyprinus carpio* on Conventional and Supplementary Feed. *Indian J. Fish.*, 44(2): 165-170.

Bhagat, M.J. and Dwivedi, S.N. 1988. Limnological Studies of a Freshwater Tropical Impoundment-Powai Lake I, Morphometry and Physical Features. *Journal of the Indian Fisheries Association*. 18: 529-536.

Boyd C.E. and Pillai, V.K. 1984. Water Quality Management in Aquaculture, CMFRI. Special publication, pp. 22-97.

Boyd, C.E.; Wood, C.W. and Thunjai, T. 2002. Pond Soil Characteristics and Dynamics of Soil Organic Matter and Nutrients. McElwee, K.; Lewis, K.; Nidiffer, M. and Buitrago, P (eds). Nineteenth Annual Technical Report. Pond Dynamics/Aquaculture RSP, Oregon State University, Corvallis, Oregon. pp. 1-10.

Das, A.K. 2000. Role of Physical and Chemical Features of Soil in Reservoir Productivity. *Fishing Chimes*. 20 (7): 30-32.

Das, S.K. and Chand, B.K. 2003. Limnology and Biodiversity of Ichthyofauna in a Pond of Southern Orissa, India. *J. Ecotoxicol. Environ. Monit.* 13 (2): 97-102.

Das, S.K.; Bhattacharya, B.K. and Goswami, U.C. 2001. Dial Variation of pH in Fish Ponds of Nagaon District, Assam. *J. Inland Fish Soc. India*, 33 (1). 45-48.

Deorari, B.P. 1993. Productivity Potential of a Man Made Reservoir of Tarai of Uttar Pradesh with Particular Reference to Fish Fauna. Ph. D Thesis, Rohilkhand University, Bareilly, U. P. 291 p.

Dhawan, A. and Singh, R. 1994. Efficacy of Different Protein Ingredients Use in Practical Feeds on the Growth and Reproductive Potential of Common Carp. *In*: Proc. of III Indian Fish. Forum. Oct. 11-14: 23-26.

Ekanem S.B. 1994. Water Temperature of Typical Freshwater Ponds and its Effects on *Chryschthys Nigrodigitatus* (Lacepede) culture. J. Aqua. Trop., 9; 141-149.

Gupta, R.K.; Yadava, N.K.; Agarwal, R. and Jain, K.L. 2004. Effect of Physico-chemical and Biological Parameters on Growth Performance of Indian Major Carp Fingerlings in Village Ponds Under Composite Fish Culture System. Abstract, *In: National Workshop on Integrated Aquafarming for Rural Development*. Organized by, G.B.P.U.A.&T., Pantnagar. 15p.

Jain, K.K. 1998a. Aquafeed Formulation and Management. *In*: N.K. Thakur, K.K. Jain and N.P. Sahu (Eds) Training Manual on Modern Approach to Aquafeed Formulation and on Farm Feed Management. CIFÉ, Mumbai publication, 75-82.

Jayram, M.G. and Shetty, H.P.C. 1981. Formulation, Processing and Water Stability of Two New Feeds. *Aquaculture*, 23: 355-359.

Jhingran, A.G. 1988. Reservoir Fisheries in India. *J. Ind. Fish. Assoc.* 18: 261-273.

Jhingran, V.G. 1982. *Fish and Fisheries of India*, 2nd edition. Hindustan Publ. Crop., New Delhi, India.

Jhingran, V.G. 1991. *Fish and Fisheries of India*. Hindustan Publishing Corporation, India. 727 p.

Keshavanath, P. 2005. Present and Future of Fish Nutrition. *Fishing Chimes*, 25 (1): 162-164.

Khanna, S.S. 1993. *An Introduction to Fishes*. Central Book Depot, Allahabad. 530 p.

Milstein, A.; Alkon, A.; Karplus, I.; Kochba, M. and Avnimelech, Y. 1995. Combined Effect of Fertilization Rate, Manuring and Feed Pellet Application on Fish Performance and Water Quality in Polyculture Ponds. *Aqua Res.* 126: 55-65.

Murthy, H.S. 1989. Utility of Three Floating Aquatic Weeds as Feeds for Carps. *M.F.Sc. Thesis. University of Agricultural Sciences*, Bangalore. pp. 191.

Nath, D. 2001. Methods of Evaluating Primary Production in Small Water Bodies. *Summer School on Culture-based Fisheries for Inland Fisheries Development*. CIFRI Barrackpore.

Paulraj, R. 1995. Balance of Nutrients. *In*: R. Paulraj (ed.). *Aquaculture Feed*. MPEDA House, Panampilly Avenue, Kochi. 9-41.

Rahman, M.M.; Verdegem, M.C.J.; Nagelkerke, L.A.J.; Wahab, M.A.; Milstein, A. and Verreth, J.A.J. 2006. Growth, Production and Food Preference of Rohu *Labeo rohita* (H.) in Monoculture and in Polyculture with Common Carp *Cyprinus carpio* (L.) under Fed and Non-fed Ponds. *Aquaculture*, 257(1-4): 359-372.

Sarkar, D. and Ray, N. 2004. Assessment of Fishery Status in Coochbehar District in Relation to Pond Water and Soil Characteristics. *Environment and Ecology*. 22 (2): 382-385.

Sharma, A.P. 2000. *Manual Fishery Limnology*. Department of Fishery Hydrography, College of Fishery Sciences, G. B. Pant. University of Agriculture & Technology, Pantnagar, 115p.

Siddiqui, A.Q.; Howlader, M.S. and Adam, A.A. 1988. Effects of Dietary Protein Levels on Growth, Feed Conversion and Protein Utilization in Fry and Young Nile Tilapia, *Orechromis nilotica*. *Aquaculture*, 70: 63-73.

Singh, B.N. and Mishra, S.K. 2004. Effect of Feed Quality and Temperature on the Growth of Genetically Improved Rohu-Jayanti. Abstract, *National Symposium on Advances in Fish Physiology: Ecological Considerations*, 20-21 March, 2004, Deptt. of Zoology, B. H. U., Varanasi, India, p. 50.

Singh, B.N. and Mishra, S.K. 2006. Farming of Genetically-Improved Rohu (Jayanti Rohu) Using Semi-balanced Feed Supplemented with soybean & Vitamin-Mineral Mix. *Fishing Chimes*. 25(10): 79-83.

Singh, B.N., Sinha V.R.P. and Chakraborty, D.P. 1979. Effect of Protein Quality and Temperature on the Growth of Fingerlings of Rohu, *Labeo rohita* (Hamilton). *In: Proceedings of World Symposium on Finfish-Nutrition and Fish Feed Technology.* Humburg. (20-23, June 1978) Vol. II, pp. 303-311.

Singh, D.; Yadava, N.K. and Saroha, R.P. 2004b. Effect of Livestock Manure and Supplementary Feeds on Growth Performance of Common Carp and Rohu Fingerlings. *Environment & Ecology* 22(3): 494-499.

Singh, H.P.; Mahaver, L.R. and Mishra, J.P. 1999. Limnological Characterization of River Ghaghara in U.P. *J. Inland Fish. Soc. India.* 31 (1): 28-32.

Singh, V.K. and Sharma, A.P. 1999. Hydrological Characteristics and Primary Production in Fish Ponds Manured with Different Organic Manures. *Indian J. fish.*, 46(1): 79-85.

Srivastava, P.K. and Roy, D. 2007. Effect of Certain Organic Manures on Mass Culture of Zooplankton and Physico-chemical Parameter of Water. *Fishing Chimes*. 27(1): 82-84.

Tacon, A.G.J. and Forster, I.P. 2003. Aquafeeds and the Environment: Policy Implications. *Aquaculture* 226(2003), 181-189.

Tewari, N.P. and Dwivedi, A.C. 2004. Studies on the Phytoplankton Biodiversity of User Ponds Created in Alkaline/Sodic Soil for Aquaculture. Abstract, *In: National Workshop on Integrated Aquafarming for Rural Development*. Organized by, G.B.P.U.A. & T., Pantnagar. 2 p.

Tripathi, C.K.M. 1982. Investigation on Ganga River to Determine Biological Indicators of Water Quality. Ph.D. Thesis, Banaras Hindu University, Varanasi.

Unni, K.S. 1982. Limnological Studies on Sampna Reservoir Betul, M.P. *Proc. Nat. Acad. Sci. India* 52(B), (4): 367-372.

Venugopal, M.N. 1980. Studies on the Growth Response of *Catla catla* (Ham.), *Cirrhinus mrigala* (Ham.) and *Cyprinus carpio* (Linn.) to Proteins of Different Sources in the Pelleted Feed. *M. F. Sc. Thesis, Univ. Agric. Sci., Bangalore.* p. 14.

Vijay Anand, P.E. 2005. Considerations for the Use of Floating Feeds for Fish Under Farming. *Fishing Chimes*. 25(9): 45-47

Vijaykumar K. 1995. *Limnology of Freshwater Pond of Gulbarga.* Recent Researches in aquatic environment. 87-97. Daya Publishing House.

CHAPTER – 8

Ecological Assessment of Molluscs and their Relation with Physico-chemical Parameters of River Narmada, Madhya Pradesh, India

Shailendra Sharma, *India*; L.K. Mudgal, *India*
Zahoor Pir, *India*; Imtiyaz Tali, *India*; Anis Siddique, *India*

ABSTRACT

Molluscs comprise an important group of aqua fauna by way of their contribution to ecosystem stability. Besides this, freshwater molluscans have been known to play important role in public and veterinary health and thus need to be scientifically explored more extensively.

The river Narmada is the third holy and fifth largest west flowing river of India and the biggest west flowing river of the state M.P. The Narmada river covers large areas in the states of Madhya Pradesh (86%), Gujarat (12%) and a comparatively smaller area (2%) in Maharashtra.

The present study was carried out for the period of ten months from August 2009 to July 2010. This study attempts to provide an overview of relation between molluscan fauna and Physico chemical variables of river Narmada. Two sampling sites were selected namely the Omkareshwar and Mandleshwar for studying the ecological distribution of molluscans. In the present study about seven species of class Gastropoda and seven species of class Pelecypoda were recorded. Among Gastropoda *Vivipara bengalensis* was dominant through out the season.

The value of Correlation coefficient (r) indicates that there was positive correlation between the molluscan population and transparency, alkanity, DO and there was moderate negative correlation between moluscan fauna and water temperature, BOD.

Our study raise an important point concerning the regular monitoring of physico-chemical as well as biological parameters of the Narmada river which will be useful in maintaining the productivity of the river. This study shows that the diversity of molluscan fauna alters with the change in physico-chemical characteristics and flow of water.

Key words: Molluscs diversity, correlation coefficient, Narmada river, bioindicators, macrobenthos.

INTRODUCTION

Molluscans have parasitological importance due to being hosts to parasitological organisms, which are agricultural pests. Freshwater molluscans have been known to play an important role in public and veterinary health and need to be scientifically explored more extensively. Besides this, different species of molluscans are edible and consumed by people (Chhetry 2011). Thus it need measures because the freshwater molluscs population are declining at an alarming rate through habitat destruction, pollution declines in host fish and the invasion of non native biota (Sharma et al 2010). Besides molluscans have scientific importance as they are used in Biomonitoring and risk assessment (Barbour et al 1999, Salanki et al 2003). Anthropogenic activities, especially involving chemical contaminants that pollute the environment, can also affect molluscan ecological and physiological parameters (Morley 2010).

Environmental conditions have a significant effect on molluscan health, both directly (within the ranges of physiological tolerances) and indirectly (enhancing susceptibility to infections). This is especially important for species grown under conditions which differ significantly from the wild (Muralidharan et al 2010). Important environmental factors for molluscan health include water temperature, salinity, turbidity, fouling and plankton blooms. Extremes and rapid fluctuations in these can seriously compromise molluscan health. Anthropogenic factors include a wide range of biological and chemical pollutants (Palharya and Malviya 1988). In addition, molluscs have low tolerance of some other water uses/abuses (*e.g.*, dynamite and cyanide fishing, dragging, creosote and other anti-fouling chemical compounds, agricultural run-off).

Benthic macro invertebrates (Molluscans) have been attractive targets of biological monitoring efforts because they are diverse group of long lived, sedentary species that react strongly and often, predatory to human influence on aquatic ecosystem (Rosenberg and Resh 1993). Macro invertebrates and water quality are interrelated to each other as macro invertebrates are potential indicators of water quality (Sharma and Rewat 2009). They are most frequently used in bio monitoring studies because the response of macro invertebrates to organic and inorganic pollution have been extensively documented (Thorne and Williams 1997; Kazanci and Dugal 2000). They have sensitive life stages that respond to stress and integrate effects of both short term and long term environment stressors (EPA 1998) and they are important areas for maintaining biodiversity(Meyer et. al. 2007; Richardson and Danely 2007).

Freshwater molluscans are long-lived organisms, often living for decades, and some species can survive over 100 years (Bauer 1992). Typically, *Unio* species live buried in fine substrate in unpolluted streams and rivers with benthic, sedentary, suspension-feeding lifestyle. The Molluscans use their exposed siphons to inhale water and use their gills to filter out fine food particles, such as bacteria, algae, and other small organic particles. The Bivalves play a vital role in the natural ecosystem. They purify water bodies because these are saprophytic animals. They eat algae, zooplankton and organic waste, and provide food for many types of fish, birds and also for human beings. They are passive indicators to environmental degradation. Through their high respiration rate they mineralize a great amount of organic matter and through filtration decrease the concentration of suspended particles. (Burdi et al 2009).

The distribution and diversity of freshwater molluscs depend on their ability of colonization in a habitat and survival. That is regulated by the physico-chemical factors like temperature, hardness and pH.

MATERIAL AND METHODS

Study Area

The river Narmada is the third holy and fifth largest west flowing river of India and biggest west flowing river of the state. The river takes its origin from Maikal hillocks from eastern highlands of Vidhyas ranges near Amarkantak, district Shahdol (M. P.) at an elevation of 1051 meters (Gazetteer of Hoshangabad, 1979). Out of the total length of 1312kms, the river flows for 1077 kms in Madhya Pradesh. The whole river passes through big gorge formed by Vidhyas on one side and Sutpuras on the other side. It has only about 82 meters of fall beyond Madhya Pradesh in Gujarat and Maharashtra before it meets the Arabian Sea. Its blue water cuts on one hand through the marble rocks near Jabalpur and on the other side through the coal deposit of Madhya Pradesh. The Narmada empties itself in the Gulf of Cambay in Gujarat. Nearly 90 per cent of the flow is in M. P. and most of the remaining is in Gujarat. It flows for a very brief stretch through Maharashtra.

The river Narmada receives 41 principal tributaries (Alvares and Ramesh 1988), each with a catchment area exceeding 500 sq. kms. Out of these 22 (21 in M. P. and 1 in Gujarat) join the river from left bank and 19 (18 in MP and 1 in Gujarat) from right bank (Ghosh et al 2004). The total length of these principal tributaries is 3,387 Kms. Besides this, there are other 50 important rivulets joining the river Narmada. Most of the tributaries and some of the rivulets arise from the highlands of Vidhyas and Sutpuras ranges and possess lot of rocks providing immense opportunity for the growth of macro benthos.

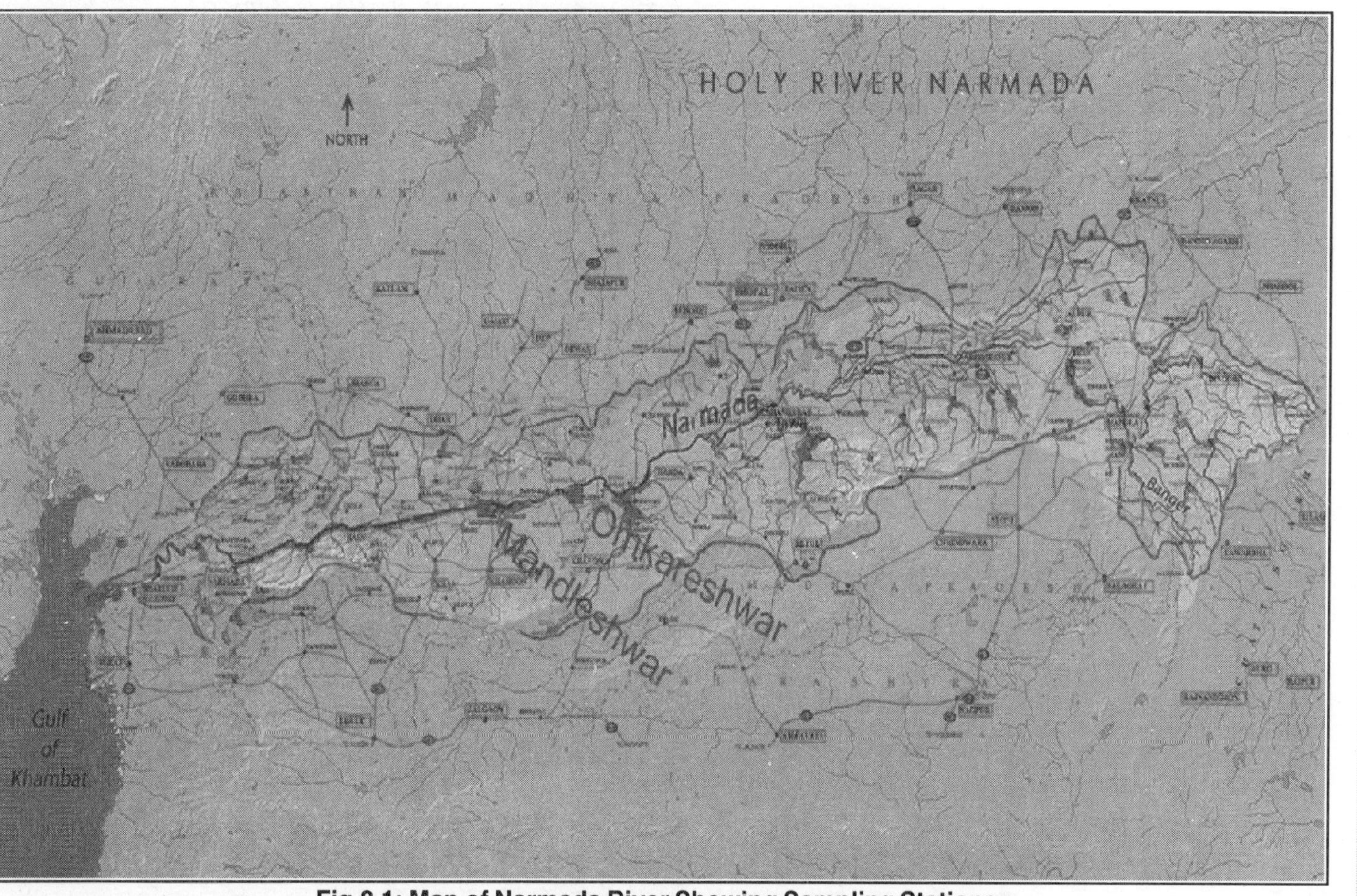

Fig.8.1: Map of Narmada River Showing Sampling Stations

SAMPLING SITES

Omkareshwar

Omkareshwar is a famous place of pilgrimage, situated 77 km from Indore in Khandwa District, Madhya Pradesh. Shaped like the holy Hindu Symbol 'OM' this sacred island, on the conflux of the river Narmada and Kaveri is visited by pilgrims from all over the country to seek blessing at the temple of Shri Omkar Mandhata. Millions of the pilgrims of both local & foreigners visit the place every year.

It's Latitude (DMS) - 22°15, 1 "N and Longitude – (DMS) 76°8', 48"E.

Mandleshwar

Mandleshwar is a town and a Nagar Panchayat in Khargone district in the Indian state of Madhya Pradesh. It is a town of historical and religious importance situated on the banks of Narmada River, 8 km east of Maheshwar, and 99 km south of Indore. Mandleshwar in Central India is on the bank of the Narmada river at a narrow point where in the monsoon the stream often rises 60 feet above its normal level becoming a roaring torrent. It has an average elevation of 153 metres (501 feet).

It's latitude- 22.18, latitude (DMS) 22°10', 60 "N and Longitude -75.67, longitude (DMS) 75°40', 0"E.

Physico-chemical Analysis

In the analysis of the physico-chemical properties of water, standard methods prescribed in limnological literature were used. The Physico-Chemical parameters were determined as per standard methods of APHA (2002) and Welch (1998).

BIOLOGICAL ANALYSIS

Collection of Samples

Different methods were employed to collect molluscs from the target habitat. Samples were collected from the deeper profundal zone by using Ekman grab and at shallow profundal zone by using Surber sampler following Wetzel (2001). Quantitative sampling was done by Kick net and Surber sampler and hand net. Organisms were collected by stirring and disturbing the substrate for about 5 minutes to the depth of several inches to dislodge the borrowing molluscs ahead of the net per square meter (Hoffsten and Malmqvist 2000; Ilmonen and Paasivira, 2005). Samples were obtained from the same location by brushing the organisms from the cobbles and rocks, following standard methods of Borror et al (1976) and APHA (2002).

The Number of molluscans per unit area was calculated as follows:

$$\text{Molluscan No.} / cm^2 = \frac{N \times 104}{A}$$

Where as N = No. of organisms per sample.

A = Area of the sampler (20 × 20 cm).

The samples were preserved in 4 per cent Formalin solution and transported to the laboratory for further investigation. Samples were assigned to a family and genus using taxonomic keys like; APHA (2002); Pennak (2004); Tonapi (1980), Welch (1998) and Needham and Needham (1998).

Statistical Analysis

The relationship between the physico chemical parameters and freshwater molluscs species was calculated by pearson's correlation coefficient (r) by the help of various software's. The graphs were plotted by using software's like Microsoft Excel 2010, SPSS and Minitab-15 (academic addition).

RESULTS AND DISCUSSION

The present study was carried out for a period of ten months from August 2009 to July 2010. Seasonal variations of various physico-chemical parameters are shown in table 1. The water temperature during study period fluctuated from 20°C to 31°C in station I and from 18°C to 38°C in station II, showing a distant seasonal trend of maximum values in summer and Minimum in winter. During the early summer season at Station I, pH showed slightly alkaline 7.8 and during winter season it shows highly alkaline 9.0 attributed by decreased rate of decomposition of organic matter. The mean of total alkalinity ranged from 173 mg/l at station I and 187 mg/l at station II. The average dissolved oxygen was recorded 8.6 mg/l at station I and 8.5 mg/l at station II indicating significant seasonal variability. The BOD was recorded maximum in post monsoon season in both stations which have significant effect on the biodiversity of molluscans.

In the present study about seven species of Class Gastropoda and seven species of Class Pelecypoda were recorded. The *Lymnaea acuminate* was recorded dominant in station I (Fig 8.2) and *Vivipara bengalensis* was recorded most dominant species in station II (Fig. 8.3) through out the study period. Out of seven species of class Gastropoda, the *Vivipara bengalensis* was dominant through out the season and among the class Pelecypoda the species like *Lymnaea acuminate* and *Lymnea auricularia* were recorded dominant.

The value of correlation coefficient (r) indicates that there was positive correlation between the Gastropods and transparency, alkanity and D.O. (Fig. 8.2) while the pelecypods were positively correlated with transparency, total solids, total hardness, alkanity and dissolved oxygen (Fig. 8.3). On the other hand there exists negative correlation between water temperature, B. O. D. and Molluscan fauna. (Table 8.2).

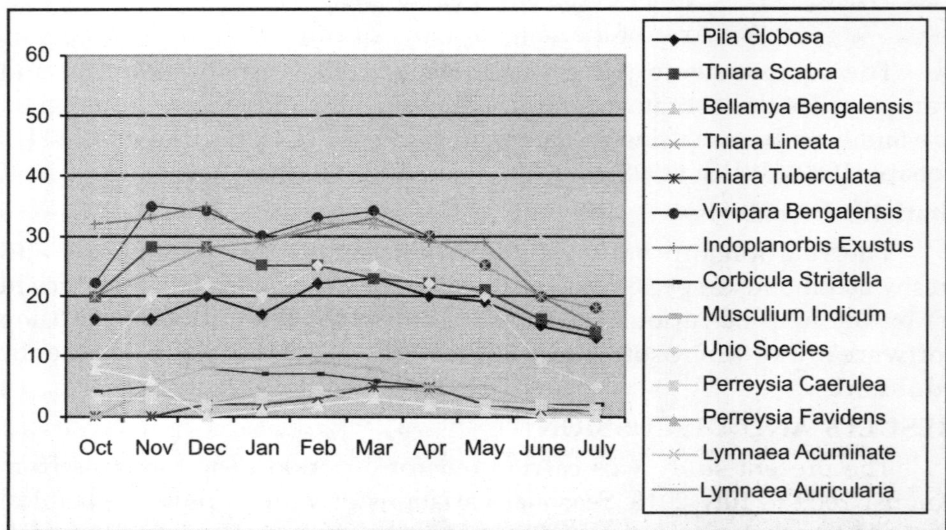

Fig. 8.2: No. of Species seen during Months from August 2009- July 2010 in Omkareshwar

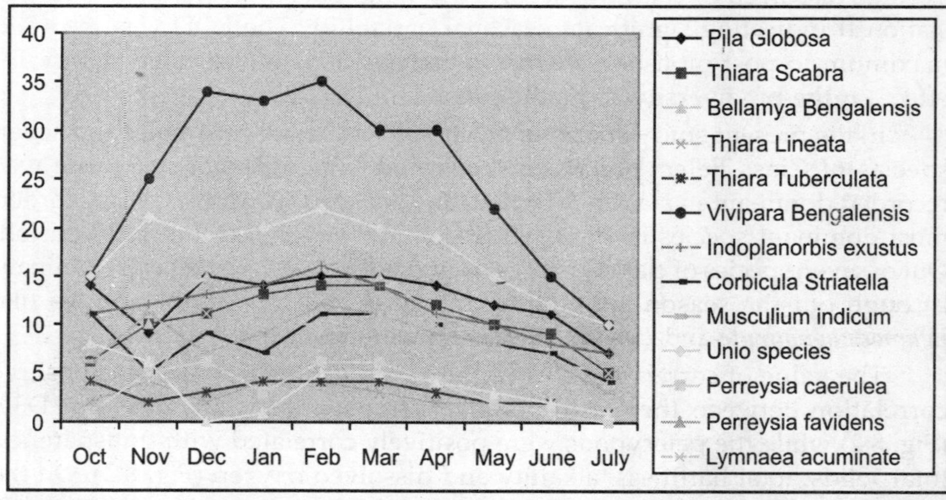

Fig. 8.3: No of Species seen during Months from August 2009- July 2010 in Mandleshwar

Table 8.1: Summary Statistics of Physico-chemical Parameters of Water at Omkareshwar and Mandleshwar Sites of Narmada River (from August 2009- July 2010)

Station	Statistics	Temp.	Transp.	pH	Total Solids	Total Hardness	Alkanity	DO	BOD
Station-IOMKARESHWAR	Average	25.7	29.5	8.46	296	141	173	8.6	2.99
	SD	3.83	9.43	0.37	40.83	28.58	37.97	0.61	0.55
	Maximum	31	48	9	380	210	234	9.3	3.9
	Minimum	20	16	7.8	220	110	110	7.8	2.4
Station-II MANDLESHWAR	Average	28	22.3	8.46	370	166.5	187.5	8.58	2.8
	SD	6.22	4.64	0.39	39.72	16.68	32.35	0.66	0.59
	Maximum	38	29	9	420	200	240	9.4	3.8
	Minimum	18	16	7.8	300	140	135	7.6	2

Table 8.2: Pearson's Correlation Coefficient (r) Between Physico Chemical Parameters and Molluscan Abundance in River Narmada

Sl. No.	Parametres	Gastropoda	Pelecypoda
1.	Temperature	-0.593	-0.354
2.	Transparency	+0.765	+0.490
3.	pH	-0.194	-0.189
4.	Total Solids	-0.219	+0.245
5.	Total Hardness	-0.151	+0.608
6.	Alkanity	+0.379	+0.598
7.	D. O.	+0.288	+0.384
8.	B. O. D.	-0.802	-0.664

The distribution and abundance of freshwater molluscs may be attributed to the availability of food, shelter and oviposition sites. Water bodies rich in organic and silt matter are known to support thriving populations of macro invertebrates because of reduction in water current and as such the substratum tends to make molluscans indistinguishable from their typical lentic habitat (Whitton 1975). The abundance of molluscans might be attributed to the presence of vegetation in the shallow depth, and formed a good feed leading to their multiplication as has also been observed (Manoharan et al., 2006).

The molluscan species like *Lymnaea acuminate* and *Lymnea auricularia* are highly resistant to pollution and were recorded dominant in station I, as the station I was highly influenced by anthropogenic activities. Such abundance was also recorded by Pir Z. et al (2010).

The water temperature ranges from 20-31°C at station I and 18-38 at station II. Water temperature exhibits a moderate negative correlation with molluscan population during the study period. This shows that increase in temperature alters the growth of molluscans. Ricker (1952), Shrivastava (1956) and Vasisht and Bhandal (1979) also recorded negative correlation between temperature and molluscs. However Micheal (1968), Dutta and Malhotra (1986) and Malhotra et al (1996) recorded positive correlation between molluscs and temperature. Burdi et al (2009) concluded that bivalves show positive correlation with temperature and negative correlation with pH.

The pH was recorded alkaline and ranges from 7.8 to 9 in both stations. The molluscans were found independent of the fluctuations with respect to pH. Since a very weak and insignificant correlation was observed between the molluscan population and pH, such weak correlation has also been observed by Garg et. al (2009). Burdi et al (2009) concluded that bivalves show positive correlation with temperature and negative correlation with pH. The molluscans show strong correlation with transparency and alkanity, thus their increase had a significant effect on the growth of molluscans (Garg et. al 2009). Dissolved oxygen was found to be positively correlated with the molluscans but not to the significant extant.

The total hardness has shown a significant positive correlation to the pelecypod population in the Narmada river. The increase in hardness favours the growth of pelecypods, however the gastropod population was negatively correlated with total hardness (Figs. 8.2; 8.3). BOD showed negative correlation with molluscan population. Cheatum (1934) and Sharma (1986) have reported some molluscans can survive in very low oxygen condition and show inverse relation with BOD. Cloherty and Joseph (2011) concluded that Macro invertebrates had significant correlations with physico-chemical and development factors, including ambient temperature, hardness, dissolved oxygen, conductivity, total dissolved solids, pH.

In the present study, the maximum pollution load was observed in rainy months followed by summer and winter months. However, the maximum diversity was observed during April- June due to breeding season of organism, suitability for shelter in low current, wind velocity, the high nutrients and DO concentration. The same maximum diversity was observed by Sreenivasan (1976). The higher diversity was observed in shallow profundal zone when compared to deeper profundal zone which could also be due to impoundments, flow reduction, bottom topography etc. which influenced the flora and fauna in terms of their diversity (Godfrey, 1978).

As the molluscans form an important link in the food chain and serve as an important protein diet of fishes. Besides that some species of molluscans are edible and consumed as food. The result of the present study emphasize the importance of conserving the worlds freshwater molluscan population, which are declining at an alarming rate through habitat destruction, pollution declines in host fish and the invasion of non native biota (Alridge 2004 & 2007). Our results raise an important point concerning the regular monitoring of physico-chemical as well as biological parameters of the Narmada river which will be useful in maintaining the productivity of the river. This study shows that the diversity of molluscs fauna alters with the change in physico-chemical characteristics and flow of water.

REFERENCES

Aldridge D., Fayle T. & Jackson N. (2007) Freshwater Mussel Abundance Predicts Biodiversity in UK Lowland rivers. *Aquatic Conservation: Marine and Freshwater Ecosystems,* 17(6) pp. 554-564.

Alridge, D. C. (2004) Conservation of Freshwater Uninoid Mussels in Bristish. *Journal of Conchology,* Special Publication 3: 81-90.

Alvares C. and R. Billorey (1988) Damming the Narmada. *Third World Network,* Malaysia: pp. 196.

APHA (2002) Standard Method for Examination of Water and Waste Water, American Public Health Association Inc. New York, 22nd Ed.

Barbour M.T., J. Gerritsen., B.D. Snyder and J.B. Stribing (1999) Rapid Bioassessment Protocols for Use in Streams and Wadeable Rivers. 2nd Edn. Periphyton, Benthic Macro Invertebrates and Fish. pp. 127-160.

Bauer. G. (1992) Variation in the Life Span and Size of the Freshwater Pearl Mussel. *Journal of Animal Ecology* 61: 425-436.

Borror D.J., D.M. Delong and C.A. Triplehorn (1976) An Introduction to the Study of Insects. 4th Edn., Holt Reinhert and Winston, USA., pp. 852.

Burdi, G.H., W.A. Baloch., F. Begum., A.N. Soomro., M.Y. Khuhawar (2009) Ecological Studies on Freshwater Bivalve Mussels (Pelecypoda) of Indus River and its Canals at Kotri. *Sindh University Research* 41(1): 31-36.

Chhetry D.T. (2011) Studies on Molluscs of Betna Wetlands and its Surroundings, Nepal. *BIBECHANA* 7, 30-32.

Cheatum E. P. (1934) Limnological Investigation on Respiration, Annual Migratory Cycle and Other Related Phenomena in Freshwater Pulmonate Snails. *Tans. Am. Microscope Soc.* 53: 348.

Cloherty T.M. and W.R. Joseph (2011) Physico Chemical and Shoreline Development Factors Affecting Lake Littoral Benthic Macro Invertebrates. *Journal of Freshwater Ecology*, 26 (4) pp 517-525.

Dutta S.P.S, Y.R Malhotra (1986) Seasonal Variations in the Macrobenthic Fauna of Gadigarh Stream (Miran Sahib), Jammu. *Indian J. Ecol.* 13: 138-145.

EPA (1998) Lake and Reservoir Bioassessment and Biocriteria, Technical Guidance Document. US Environmental Protection Agency, Washington, D.C., USA.

Garg R.K., R.J. Rao and D.N. Saksena (2009) Correlation of Molluscans Diversity with Physicochemical Characteristics of Water of Ramsagar Reservoir, India. *International Journal of Biodiversity and Conservation* 1(6) pp. 202-207.

Gazetteer of Hoshangabad (1979) Govt. of India, Madhya Pradesh.

Ghosh T.K., B. Shakila and S.N. Kaul (2004) Protection of Ecologicaliy Sensitive Areas: Origin of Rivers and Upper Catchment Areas, *J. of Indian Association for Enviro. Management*, 31, 59-64.

Godfrey P.J. (1978) Diversity as a Measure Benthic Macroinvertebrate Community Response to Water Pollution. *Hydrobiologia* 57: 111-122.

Hoffsten P.O. and B. Malmqvist (2000) The Macroinvertebrate Fauna and Hydrogeology of Springs in Central Sweden. *Hydrobiologia*, 436: 91-104.

Kazanci N. and M. Dugel (2000) Ordination and Classification of Macroinvertebrates and Environmental Data of Stream in Turkey. *Water Sci. Technol* 47, 7-8.

Ilmonen J. and L. Passivirta (2005) Benthic Macrocrustacean and Insect Assemblages in Relation to Spring Habitat Characteristic: Patterns in Abundance and Diversity. *Hydorbiologia* 533: 99-113.

Manoharan S., V.K. Murugesan and R. Palaniswamy (2006) Numerical Abundance of Benthic Macroinvertebrates in Selected Reservoirs of Tamil Nadu. *J. Inland Fish. Soc. India.* 38(1): 54-59.

Malhotra Y.R., K.K. Sharma., M.R. Thakial (1996) Ecology of Macroinvertebrates from a Fish Pond. *Pro. Nat. Acad. Sci.* India 66: 53-59.

Morley N.J. (2010) Aquatic Molluscs as Auxiliary Hosts for Terrestrial Nematode Parasite: Implication for Pathogen Transmission in a Changing Climate. *Paristology*; 137(7): 1051-1056.

Meyers N., R. Mittermeier., C. Mittermeier., G. Fonesca, and J. Kent (2000) Biodiversity Hotspots for Conservation Priorities. *Nature*, 403(6772), 853-858.

Muralidharan M., C. Selvakumar., S. Sundar and M. Raja (2010) Macroinvertebrates as Potential Indicators of Environmental Quality. *IJBT*, pp. 23-28.

Needham J.C. & P.R. Needham (1998) A Guide to the Study of Fresh Water Biology. Reiter's Scientific and Professional books. Washinton, D.C.

Palharya J.P. and Malviya (1988) Pollution of Narmada River at Hoshangabad in Madhya Pradesh and Suggested Measures for Control. In: Ecology and Pollution of Indian Rivers, R.K. Trivedi (eds.) Daya Publishing House, New Delhi.

Pennak R. W. (2004) Fresh Water Invertebrates of United States: Protozoa to Mollusca , 4rd Ed. John Wiley and sons, New York, U.S.A.

Pir Z., I Tali., L.K. Mudgal, Siddique A. (2010) Distribution of Molluscans in Narmada River, India. *Researcher*. 2(10):41-46.

Ricker W.E. (1952) The Benthos of Cultus Lake. *J. Fish. Res.* Canada 9: 204-212.

Richardson J.S. and R.J. Danehy (2007) A Synthesis of the Ecology of Headwater Streams and Their Riparian Zones in Temperate Forests. *For. Sci.* 53, 131-147.

Rosenberg D.M. and V.H. Resh, (1993) Fresh Water Bio Monitoring and Benthic Macro Invertebrates. Chapman & Hall, New York. 488 p.

Salanki J., A. Farkas., T. Kamardina and S.R. Katalin (2003) Molluscans in Biological Monitoring of Water Quality. *Toxicol. Lett.*, 140-141.

Sharma K. K., C. Samita and A. Sharma (2010) Malacofauna Diversity of River Chenab Fed Stream (Gho Manshan). *The Bioscan* 6(2): pp. 267-269.

Sharma R.C. (1986) Effect of Physico-chemical Factors on Benthic Fauna of Bhagirathi River, Garhwal Himalayas. *Ind. J. Ecol.* 13: 133-137.

Sharma R.C. and J.S. Rawat (2009) Monitoring of Aquatic Macro Invertebrates as Bio Indicator for Assessing the Health of Wetlands: A Case Study in the Central Himalayas, India. *Ecological Indicators*. 9: 118-128.

Sreenivasan A. (1976) Limnological Studies and Primary Production in Temple Pond Ecosystems. *Hydrobiologia*, 48: 117-123.

Srivastava V.K. (1956) Studies on the Freshwater Bottom Fauna of North India. Quantitative Fluctuations and Qualitative Composition of Benthic Fauna in Lake in Lucknow. *Proc. Nat. Acad. Sci.* 25: 406-416.

Thorne, R.J., and W.P. Williams. (1997) The Response of Benthic Invertebrates to Pollution in Developing Countries: A Multimetric System of Bioassessment. *Freshwater Biol.* 37: 671-686.

Tonapi, G.T. And Mohan H. N. (1980) A biometrical analysis of growth in the larvae of Dineustes indicus Aube (Cryrinidae: Coleoptera). *Indian J. Ent.* 32 (1) 39-50.

Vasisht H.S. and Bhandal R. S. (1979) Seasonal Variations of Benthic Fauna of Some North Indian Lakes and Ponds. *Ind. J. Ecol.* 6: 77-83.

Welch P.S. (1935) Limnology, Mc Graw Hill Book Co. New York, 539 pp.

Wetzel R.G. (1975) Limnology, W.B. Saunderts Co. Philadelphia, 743 pp.

Whitton, B.A. (1975) Zooplanktons and Macroinvertebrates. pp. 87-118. In: Whitton. B.A. (Ed.). Studies in River Ecology. 2: Baker Publisher Limited London.

CHAPTER – 9

Recovery of Proteins from Fish Processing Industrial Waste and Waste Management

D.K. Meena, *India*; G.G. Phadke, *India*; Keerti Meena, *India*

INTRODUCTION

The increasing demand for fish protein throughout the world has to be met with available resources in the form of underutilized fish and fish by products, as the marine fish production is almost saturated. In recent years, researchers have made the significant progress in the development of technology to attain the maximum recovery of protein and their utilization for the development of value added products from such sources. The technologies available for protein recovery from fish processing industrial waste includes enzymatic hydrolysis, pH shifting process, ultrafiltration, chemical hydrolysis, nanofiltration, ohmic heating as options.

GENERATION OF WASTE FROM FISH PROCESSING PPERATIONS

Similar to most food industries, fish processing operations produce waste in a solid (fish carcasses, viscera, skin, heads) or liquid form (washing and cleaning water discharge, bloodwater from drained fish storage tanks, brine). This waste must be stored so as to prevent the contamination to the processing environment, and should be disposed of in a manner that is not detrimental to the receiving environment. The magnitude of the problem of waste management in the fish industry depends on the waste volume, its polluting charge, rate of discharge and the assimilatory capacity of the receiving medium. On average, only 30-40 per cent of the global fishery production is consumed fresh and the rest 60-70 per cent is processed for human consumption and other purposes. Although the proportion of the total fishery production that are processed remained relatively stable over the last decade, the total bulk of processed fishery commodity increased due to the steady increase in the total fishery production.

Processing of large bulk of fish, shrimp and other aquatic organisms produces a corresponding large bulk of byproducts and wastes. Although recent trend shows that much of these wastes are made into various value added products, considerable quantities are discharged as the processing effluents with large volume of waters used in processing. Reports suggest that fish and shrimp processing effluents are very high in biological oxygen demand (BOD), chemical oxygen demand (COD), total suspended solids (TSS), fat-oil-grease (FOG), pathogenic and other microflora, organic matters and nutrients, etc. Fish and shrimp processing effluents are, therefore, highly likely to produce adverse effects on the receiving coastal and marine environments. Although substantial reduction of the waste loads is possible by applying available simple techniques, this is not in practice in most part of the world due to lack of proper managerial and regulatory approach.

The present chapter reviews the characteristics of fish and shrimp processing effluents as a potential source of coastal and marine pollution and, using the existing data, analyzes the global production and discharge of waste loads from the rocessing plants and discusses available options for waste treatment and management. About 117.8 mt of the estimated world fish production in the year 2009 was used for direct human consumption, whereas, the remaining 27.3 mt was destined for other non- food uses (FAO, 2010). Fish is one of the major commodities from which a large domestic and export revenue is earned. Fish processing activities generate potentially large quantities of organic waste and by-products from inedible fish parts and endoskeleton shell parts from the crustacean peeling process which are generally discarded.

Fish industry by-products can account for up to 75 per cent of the catch depending on postharvest or industrial preparation processes. Different terms such as 'fish waste', 'by-product' and 'rest raw materials' have been used. The review gives an overview of value-added processes that provide an alternative to low-profit uses such as silage, fish meal and mince. The preparation of different by-product fractions such as fish blood, marine lipids, omega-3 fatty acids, fish protein fractions and bioactive components with nutraceuticals potential, i.e. antioxidants and bioactive peptides, is considered. There are several future opportunities for the preparation of high-value by-products such as enzymes, minerals and other bioactive substances including hydroxyapatite, phosphorus, taurine and creatine. Both regulatory status and future market potential need to be considered. In addition, there is a need for technologies that maintain good quality by-products and 'simple' processes to produce bulk products for further refining. By-products provide an inexpensive raw material that increases the total utilization, profitability and allows better management of fisheries resources (Davenport and Kristinsson, 2011, Rustad, et al., 2011).

However, a large amount of waste materials, which generally amount to 50 per cent of the weight of the fish materials, were generated accompanying fishery processing. These fishery wastes can cause serious environmental problems if disposed improperly. On the contrary, these fishery wastes can be valuable bio-resources because they contain an abundant supply of valuable bio-materials, such as proteins, lipids, enzymes, and chitins (Wang and Hwang, 2001). Presently, fishery wastes are reprocessed into fish or shrimp powders and fish or shrimp solubles. These recovered products are low in market values, making the recovery process uneconomical. Therefore, there is necessity of converting these wastes into higher value products (Wang and Chang, 1997). The solid waste consist of the head, viscera, meat, frames generated from seafood processing industry ranges from 30 to 85 per cent of the landed fish depending upon the fishery (Chandra and Shamasundar, 2011) that are land-filled or ground-and-discarded. This solid waste has approximately the same protein content as fish flesh. In order to recover these proteins of high nutritive value for human consumption different approaches have been described.

The actual proportion depends on the edible fraction of each species being processed. Fish waste is a rich source of essential amino acids, and all inedible fish waste should be converted into by-products (e.g. fishmeal or silage).The increasing demand for fish protein throughout the world has to be met with available resources in the form of underutilized fish and fish by products, as the marine fish production is almost saturated. In recent years, researchers have made the significant progress in the development of technology to attain the maximum recovery of protein and their utilization for the development of value added products from such sources.

Waste Output and Loading in Fish and Shrimp Processing

The main inputs in a processing plant are whole fresh or iced fish and shrimp, water, ice, calcium hypochlorite and other chemicals, packaging materials and electricity plus liquid soap used during cleaning. The outputs are the fresh chilled fillet exported or consumed; swim bladders, removed from fish carcasses and processed separately into valuable product; skins of fishes like sharks and rays are processed into leather; remaining fats, red meat carcasses (with swim bladders removed) and fillets rejected on quality grounds that are either used for human consumption or made into fish meal or silage; wastewater of varying strengths, especially from the filleting and trimming processes, contains fat, oil and grease (FOG) with blood, small pieces of fish and protein;waste heat from ice manufacture, chilling, and the cold room (to atmosphere). The outputs of the processing industries usually contain a large bulk of waste products.

Generally, the head, shell and tail portions of shrimp are removed during processing and these account for approximately 50 per cent of the volume of raw materials. Increasing production of inedible parts of shrimp, such as heads, shells and tails, is causing environmental problems as a result of uncontrolled dumping. The wastewater from seafood processing plants contains large amounts of organic matter, small particles of flesh, breading, soluble proteins, and carbohydrates. Mauldin and Szabo (1974) reported that as much as 65 per cent of the tuna is wasted in the canning process.

WASTE DISPOSAL

In many countries, solid waste is recycled into fish meal plants or treated along with the municipal waste, whereas liquid waste is disposed of through the municipal sewage system or directly into a waterbody. In the latter case, care must be exercised to ensure that the receiving waterbody can degrade the biological and chemical constituents of the waste in a manner that is not detrimental to the aquatic fauna and flora.Designing appropriate measures to dispose of liquid waste from fish processing operations requires assessment. This is done through the evaluation of various physicochemical and biological parameters of which the most important ones are: solid content, pH, temperature, odor, organic matter, biochemical oxygen demand or BOD, chemical oxygen demand or COD, oil and grease content, nitrogen and phosphorous content

WASTE CHARACTERISTICS

Physico-chemical Characters

Although the volume and characteristics of shrimp and fish processing effluents often exhibit extreme variability, waste production in seafood processing industries are usually high in volume .The BOD may be as low as 100 mg/l to as high as 200,000 mg /l.Suspended solids may be found in concentration as high as 120,000 mg/l. The waste may be highly alkaline (pH 11.0) or highly acidic (pH 3.5). Nutrients such as nitrogen and phosphorous may be absent or they may be present in quantities in excess of those necessary to promote suitable environmental conditions for biological treatment.

Carawan et al. (1986) reported a BOD of 200–1000 mg/l, COD of 400–2000 mg/l, TSS of 100-800 mg/l and FOG of 40-300 mg/l from seafood processing plant wastes. Fish meal plants were reported to have a BOD of 100-24,000 mg/l, COD of 150-42,000 mg/l, TSS of 70-20,000 mg/l, and FOG of 20-5000 mg/l, COD of 150-42,000 mg/l, TSS of 70-20,000 mg/l, and FOG of 20-5,000 mg/l. Effluents from shrimp canning have been reported to have concentrations of BOD, COD, Oil and Fat, TN, and NH3– N of 1081, 2296, 258, 196, and 802 mg/l respectively with corresponding net waste loads of 46, 109, 11, 7.6,and 37.7 g/kg respectively. Seafood processing wastewater was noted to sometimes contain high concentrations of chlorides from processing water and brine solutions, and organic nitrogen (0-300 mg/l) from processing water.

Microbiological Characters

Bagge-Ravn et al. (2003) demonstrated that the processing equipment of food industries harbors a microbial ecosystem both during production and after cleaning and disinfection. The microflora is partly a reflection of the raw material used (fish and shrimp) and partly a reflection of the preservation parameters used in the products (e.g., NaCl and acid). Pseudomonas spp. and yeasts were identified after cleaning and disinfection in all of the four production environments investigated. In some of the products, these organisms may negatively influence quality. Yeasts have been identified as spoilage organisms of semi-preserved herring and pseudomonads may spoil aerobically stored cold-smoked salmon.

Therefore these organisms must be specifically targeted when developing cleaning and disinfecting procedures for these industries. Karunasagar and Karunasagar (2000) reported the occurrence of food-borne human pathogens such as Listeria spp. in fresh fish as well as processed fishery products. Rashid et al. (2000) in an investigation to identify the critical control points (CCPs) and the quality of exportable frozen shrimps from Bangladesh reported that the raw material bacterial load increased along the different steps of processing and it varied from 5.88 per cent to 35.46 per cent.

GLOBAL PRODUCTION OF SEAFOOD PROCESSING WASTES

Any literature is hardly available regarding the magnitude of regional and global loads of effluents produced by the seafood processing industries and related impacts on ecosystem. Given the absence of any reliable estimate of the global production of seafood processing wastes and the waste characteristics, an attempt was made to analyze the approximate waste loads from the reported values of waste characteristics (e.g., quantities of different parameters per quantity of seafood processed) and the reported quantities of seafood processed. Fishery production (mainly fish and shrimp) showed a steady increase over the last decade; however, the amount of fish and shrimp processed remained relatively stable indicating that the amount of fresh consumption increased. On average, 60-70 per cent of the total fishery production was processed from 1992 to 2001 corresponding to 78,466-71,727 thousand tons. The water flow and waste loads were calculated from the amount processed and the average concentration of different waste parameters as reported by Carawan (1991) and Park et al. (2001).

On average, 64 per cent of the total fishery production were processed which corresponded to 75,412 thousand tons of raw materials, producing surprisingly high amounts of different waste parameters. As high as 1,110,522 million liters of water was used by the processing plants and the effluents contained 159.12 thousand tons of BOD, 749.09 thousand tons of suspended solids, 426.07 thousand tons of dissolved solids, 493.19 thousand tons of organic solids, 459.69 thousand tons of fats-oils-grease (FOG) and 293.35

thousand tons of ash (Table 9.1). According to the daily production of the volume of effluents (27,000 l/ton of fish) and the average waste loads (500-1550 mg/l BOD; 1300-3250 mg/l,COD; 17,000 mg/l TSS) reported by Mauldin and Szabo (1974) in tuna processing industry, the total daily waste discharge would be as high as 1.35-41.85 kg BOD, 35.1-87.75 kg COD, and 459 kg TSS (*See Table 9.1 on next page*). Clearly, processing plants produce heavy loads of wastes that are complex mixtures of a good many substances including fish and shrimp muscles, scales and shells, soluble proteins, fats and oils, partially decomposed organic matters, different chemical substances, pathogenic bacteria, virus and other microflora, inorganic nutrients particularly nitrogen and phosphorus and many others.

Most of the wastes generated are discharged into the nearby coastal waters through discharge channels and are potentially hazardous to the receiving environments. In most instances, the pollutants exceed the assimilative capacities of nearby coastal waters. Moreover, too many processing plants in one area will eventually overwhelm natural ecosystems nearby, frequently causing unwanted fertilization and eutrophication of coastal waters.

POTENTIAL IMPACTS

Processing wastes are primarily organic in nature and therefore subject to bacterial decay. As a result, the oxygen concentration in the water is reduced with an increase in BOD. This can starve aquatic life of the oxygen it needs and anaerobic decomposition of organic matters lead to the breakdown of proteins and other nitrogenous compounds, releasing hydrogen sulphide, ammonia and methane, all of which are potentially hazardous to the ecosystem and toxic to marine organisms in low concentrations. Nutrients resulting from decaying organic matter enhance plant growth and excessive plant growth together with oxygen depletion can lead to alterations in ecosystem structure and these are both features of eutrophication. Partially decomposed processing effluents entering coastal waters contain a variety of harmful substances and pathogens and a variety of other organic and inorganic wastes.

Around the point of discharge, there is a short-term increase in nutrients and, hence, prey items for the fish and, on occasions an increase in habitat complexity, which may cause an initial population rise in fish species. Yet, as nutrient levels increase so does the chance of algal bloom development, toxin production and a corresponding decrease in dissolved oxygen. Long-term effects include phytoplankton biomass increases and large scale decreases in species diversity with benthic and fish communities (Bonsdorff et al., 1997). Fish species feeding in water contaminated by algal toxins will absorb these toxins and are subject to mass mortality. Eutrophication has been shown to cause major changes in species composition, structure and function of marine communities over large areas.

Table 9.1: Relative Proportion of the Amount of Fishery Production, the Amount Consumed Fresh and the Amount Processed (Thousand Tons) and Corresponding Waste Loads Produced (Water Flow is in Million Litres and the Other Parameters are in Thousand Tons)

Year	Utilization		Corresponding Amount of Water Flow and Waste Produced						
	Fresh (%)	Processed (%)	Flow	BOD	TSS	TDS	OS	FOG	Ash
1992	29,488 (29.1)	71,727 (70.9)	961,141	151.34	755.28	405.25	469.09	817.68	279.01
1993	33,115 (31.8)	71,665 (68.2)	960,311	151.21	754.63	404.90	468.68	816.98	278.77
1994	35,774 (31.7)	77,073 (68.3)	1,032,778	162.62	811.57	435.46	504.05	878.63	299.81
1995	40,821 (35.0)	75,856 (65.0)	1,016,470	160.067	798.76	428.58	496.09	864.75	295.07
1996	43,764 (36.3)	76,680 (63.7)	1,027,512	161.79	807.44	433.24	501.48	874.15	298.28
1997	47,154 (38.4)	75,698 (61.6)	1,014,353	159.72	797.09	427.69	495.06	862.95	294.46
1998	48,470 (41.0)	69,643 (59.0)	933,216	146.95	733.34	393.48	455.46	793.93	270.91
1999	50,033 (39.4)	77,065 (60.6)	1,032,671	162.61	811.49	435.41	504.00	878.54	299.78
2000	50,679 (38.7)	80,248 (61.3)	1,075,323	169.32	845.01	453.40	524.82	914.82	312.16
2001	51,741 (39.7)	78,466 (60.3)	1,051,444	165.56	826.24	443.33	513.16	894.51	305.23
Average	43104 (36.1)	75412 (63.9)	1,010,522	159.12	794.09	426.07	493.19	859.69	293.35

The general response of phytoplankton communities to eutrophication involves an increase in biomass and productivity (Riegman, 1995). A general shift from diatoms to dinoflagellates, and also down shift in size in phytoplankton towards a dominance of small size nanoplankton generally observed (Kimor, 1992). A similar response is observed in zooplankton communities, with herbivorous copepods being replaced by small-size and gelatinous zooplankton (Zaitsev, 1992). Eutrophication also promotes proliferation of macroalgae and filamentous algae. This often becomes a nuisance, and may affect benthic fauna, nursery and feeding of fish, amenity, recreational uses and tourism (Riegman, 1995). Eutrophication-induced hypoxia alters the structure, diversity as well as trophic structure and food web of benthic and fish ommunities (Riegman, 1995). Other potential problems caused by the mass release of processing wastes and associated debris are the loss of amenities affecting the recreational use of water. The spatial and temporal scale of the impacts of seafood processing wastes may vary depending on the amount and nature of the waste output. However, local impacts are particularly obvious because wastes from processing industries are generally produced throughout a year giving no chance for the environment to recover. Impacts are more likely to be detrimental when the same ecosystem receives wastes from cluster of processing industries

IMPORTANCE OF WASTEWATER TREATMENT AND PROTEIN RECOVERY FROM FISH WASTE

Fish processing requires large amounts of water, primarily for washing and cleaning purposes, but also as media for storage and refrigeration of fish products before and during processing. In addition, water is an important lubricant and transport medium in the various handling and processing steps of bulk fish processing.

Environmental issues in fish processing primarily include the following:

1. Solid waste and by-products
2. Wastewater
3. Water consumption and management
4. Emissions to air and energy consumption

Surimi is water washed minced meat added with cryoprotectants and frozen stored. For a two-step industrial washing process, more than 70 per cent of protein losses occurred during the first washing operation in surimi manufacture as per the available estimated values. This washing water represents 60 per cent of the total effluent volume.

Fish by-products contain both valuable lipid and protein fractions as well as other interesting and valuable compounds. The protein fraction is easily digestible and can be used for the production of hydrolysates, surimi, thermostable protein dispersions, different peptides and amino acids, gelatin and collagen as well as protamine. By-products are a very complex group of fractions, and the composition as well as the stability may therefore vary over a wide range. (Falch et al., 2006; Kerry & Murphy, 2007; Rustad, 2007). Different types of protein fractions can be produced from fish rest raw material. Flesh from backbones and cut-offs can be used for the production of fish mince, surimi or products based on surimi. The flesh is removed by mechanical separation where the raw material is pressed through perforations that are small enough to retain the bones without reducing the size of the flesh particles so much that the fibrous structure is destroyed.

To use mince for readymade products, there is a need for a high and stable raw material quality that is difficult to achieve (Taylor and Himonides, 2007; Morrissey and Sylvia, 2004). Surimi is fish mince that has been repeatedly washed to remove sarcoplasmic proteins and other components that may promote protein denaturation during frozen storage (Kim and Park, 2007). It is often mixed with cryoprotectants and has good functional properties (gelling, emulsifying and water-holding properties). However, production of surimi requires high amounts of process water, about twenty times the amount of deboned meat (Gehring et al., 2011). This water has a high biological oxygen demand and therefore needs to be treated before it can be released to the environment.

In recent years, researchers have made the significant progress in the development of technology to attain the maximum recovery of protein and their utilization for the development of value added products from such sources. Fish is a well known food commodity as the source of high quality protein consists of all the essential amino acids in recommended proportion. Fish processing by products contain considerable quantity of protein which is similar to the raw material in quality. This protein can be recovered from the frame waste and added back to increase the yield of mince. Developing methods to recover the protein from byproducts with minimum changes in the nutritional and functional properties is one of the active areas in protein research. Techniques such as chemical hydrolysis and enzymatic hydrolysis, pH shifting method, ultrafiltration, ohmic heating and super critical fluid hydrolysis are some of the methods employed in the recovery of proteins. There is an increasing interest in the recovery of proteins from fish processing waste for their utilization as food ingredients as they may possess good functional and nutritional properties (Sanmartin *et al.*, 2009). The proteins could be recovered and used subsequently in the development of value added products, human food products, dietary supplements, etc.

The by-products can be reduced to animal feed, but are often disposed of in land fills. The fish by-products can not be fully utilized by the rendering industry due to the fishy odor caused by the auto-oxidation of the fish oil they contain. The odor is transferred to the meat of the animals fed excessive amounts of fishmeal, resulting in lower meat quality, and thus, limited consumer acceptance. Better profits can be obtained by making products for industrial use and human consumption such as biopolymers for the pharmaceutical and biotechnological industries, extraction and purification of enzymes and bioactive peptides. Stick-water and fish by-products may also serve as a good source of desirable peptide and amino acids that can be extracted and used as food and/or feed ingredients to impart desirable technological properties (colour, antioxidant activity, solubility, fat absorption, emulsification stability, etc.). Fish processing wastewater has a high organic content, and subsequently a high biochemical oxygen demand (BOD), because of the presence of blood, tissue, and dissolved protein.

It also typically has a high content of nitrogen (especially if blood is present) and phosphorus. Detergents and disinfectants may also be present in the wastewater stream after application during facility cleaning activities. A range of chemicals is typically used for cleaning, including acid, alkaline, and neutral detergents, as well as disinfectants. The disinfectants commonly used include chlorine compounds, hydrogen peroxide, and formaldehyde. Other compounds also may be used for select activities (e.g. disinfection of fishmeal processing equipment). Waste from fish-filleting units is used in the production of fish meal or directly used in animal feeds but more frequently is simply discarded (Batista, 1999).

A common feature of these raw materials like underutilized fish and fish by-products is a complex bone structure makes rendering/physical separation of the muscle challenging. The complexity also applies to the composition, since there is often an abundance of blood, fat, and pigments which makes stability of the separated muscle a challenge. Mechanical deboning, water washing, cryoprotectants, etc. are the few available solutions (Nolsoe and Undeland, 2009). Again, wastewater treatment is one of the problems in surimi production due to the high volume and high biological oxygen demand (BOD) of the water. Traditional water treatment using biological methods requires long period of time and large digesting volume to hold the wastewater until it is treated to an acceptable level of BOD. This might limit the production capacity if land resources are limited. Thus, finding alternative methods of wastewater treatment that offers shorter process time and require less area is considered useful (Kanjanapongkul *et al.*, 2009).

TREATMENT OPTIONS

The basic options for minimization of seafood processing wastes are to 'reduce', 'reuse' and 'recycle' of the wastes. Reuse and recycling of waste materials are particularly difficult to apply in food industries (McDonald et al., 1999) and, therefore, reduction of wastes is considered the best option in dealing with the processing wastes. Reduction in waste production can be achieved through a number of ways such as conservation of water, improved housekeeping, control of raw material quality,adoption of technological modification and improved general management practices. Conserving water use, although an integral part of waste management, can be hard in industries where hygiene must be the overriding priority. Water use should, therefore, be as low as is feasible while still maintaining hygienic conditions.

Howard (1997) defined three categories of water use per ton of fillets produced: good (<6 m^3); average (6-15 m^3) and poor (>15 m^3). On this scale, the global consumption of water calculated from the figures (total mass of seafood processed and total volume of water used) becomes more than 16 m^3 ton_1 of seafood processed would be considered poor, providing a real opportunity for reduced waste production. Good housekeeping practices that cover prevention of accidental spillages (chemicals, fuel, fish materials) and good management of raw materials and products to avoid contamination and rejection from the main fillet product A majority of the pollutants of concern in the aquatic products processing industry are organic, and compatible with most biological treatment methodologies as well as land disposal. However, the use of chemicals such as chlorine for sanitation and cleaning or sodium chloride for pickling operations causes unique disposal problems. As regulations become more restrictive and analysis techniques more sensitive, a number of wastewaters such as those with highly alkaline or acidic wastes, copper, zinc, chrome, laboratory wastes, and sanitizing solutions containing chlorine, will adversely affect the food processing industry-including aquatic products processors.

PRIMARY AND SECONDARY WASTE TREATMENTS

Depending on the effluent polluting capacity and nature, one or several treatments can be considered. These treatments are classified into primary and secondary treatments.

Fig. 9.1: FAO/18775/I.Balderi (Fish Waste has been Used to Produce these Piles of Compost)

Primary treatments include operations designed to remove floatable and settling solids. They include screening, sedimentation, and flotation to remove oil and grease and other suspended solids. Secondary treatments comprise biological and physicochemical treatments. In biological treatments, the organic polluting matter is degraded by micro-organisms, which metabolise it into energy and biomass. These microorganisms can be aerobic or anaerobic. The most used aerobic processes are activated sludge system, aerated lagoons, trickling filters or bacterial beds and the rotating biological contractors. In anaerobic processes, the anaerobic microorganisms digest the organic matter in tanks to produce gases (mainly methane and CO_2) and biomass. Anaerobic digesters are sometimes heated, using part of the methane produced, to maintain a temperature of 30 to 35°C.

In the physicochemical treatments, also called coagulation-flocculation, a chemical substance is added to the effluent to reduce the surface charges responsible for particle repulsions in a colloidal suspension, thus reducing the forces that keep its particles apart. This reduction in charge causes flocculation (agglomeration) and particles of larger sizes are settled and clarified effluent is obtained. The sludge produced by primary and secondary treatments is further processed in digesting tanks through anaerobic processes or sprayed over land as a fertilizer. In the latter case, care must be exercised to ensure that the sludge is freed of its pathogen.

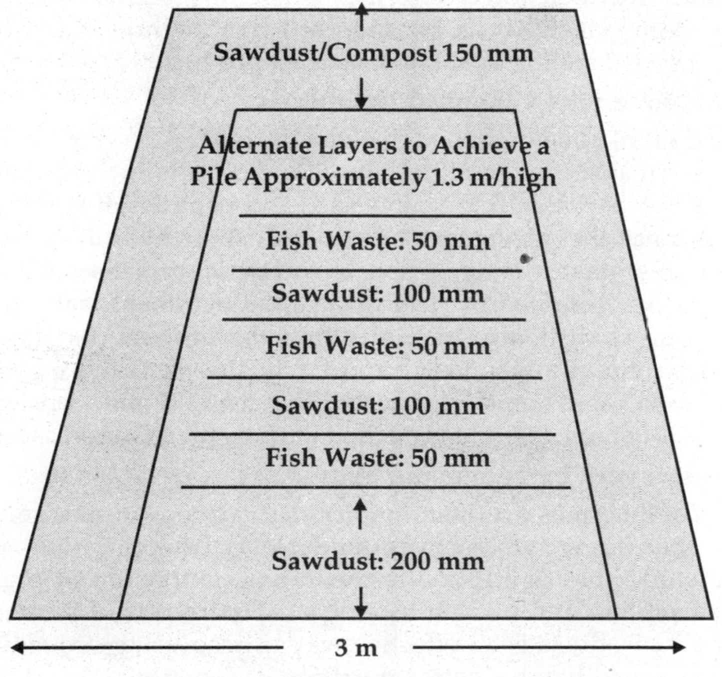

Fig 9.2: Schematic of Compost Structure

COMPOST WINDROW MANAGEMENT

Compost windrows should be left uncovered to maintain aeration and suitable moisture levels within the pile. Depending on the structure of the pile and the type of materials used, unturned compost will sufficiently mature to spread over pasture or gardens in about one year.

Turning the compost windrow three to four times will help maintain an even temperature throughout and will hasten the decomposition process. To reduce the spread of odours downwind from the composting site, avoid turning windrows on windy days. A temperature greater than 55O should be maintained throughout the windrow for at least three consecutive days to prevent proliferation of pathogens (EPA, 1996; Australian Standard 4454-2003).If you intend to sell your compost you, should ensure you address all the issues identified in EPA Publication 508 (EPA, 1996).

TECHNIQUES FOR PROTEIN RECOVERY FROM FISH PROCESSING WASTE

There are various methods which can be employed to recover proteins from fish waste which include chemical hydrolysis using acid and alkali where proteins are broken down into peptides by addition of acid and alkali. This method results into higher yield, quick recovery and it is inexpensive process but it is difficult to control where protein functionality decreases along with imparting bitterness. In enzymatic hydrolysis, proteins are broken down to smaller peptides due to action of enzymes where high recovery yields, low salt product, high selectivity is possible but this method is costly, time consuming process resulting into bitter taste of product.

1. Protein recovery by Chemical hydrolysis

High acid or alkaline treatment is given for fish processing byproducts leading to the breakage of peptide bonds and results into formation of hydrolysate, which is rich in free amino acids and peptides of varying sizes. Acid-hydrolysis has the advantages of low-cost, short hydrolysis time and simple operation so that it is applicable to industrial processes (Gao et al., 2006). Hydrolysates obtained by acid or alkaline treatment lack the better functionality due to difficulty in controlling the process (Batista, 1999). Although this technique was very popular in the past, there are many limitations to food ingredients when using this method and, consequently, the final products obtained with this method are now mainly used as fertilizer.

2. Protein recovery by enzymatic hydrolysis

Proteolytic Enzymes are macromolecules, protein in nature, highly catalytic and specific. Enzymes have found plenty of applications in food processing include selective tissue fermentation, extraction of pigments, coagulation of protein and protein hydrolysis. Hydrolysis of protein from the processing byproducts is an effective way of recovering proteins in the form of hydrolysates having better nutritional, functional and bioactive properties, in turn fetches high value in the market. The properties of hydrolysates depend on the degree of hydrolysis, nature of enzyme used, suitable enzyme/substrate ratios and reaction times.

Hydrolysis of processing by products by exogenous enzymes from other sources like plant, animal, fungal or Hydrolysis of byproducts by endogenous enzymes from the byproducts of same fish species or Hydrolysis of byproducts by enzymes from the byproducts of other species and by Allowing the byproducts to get autolysed or Simultaneous hydrolysis of byproducts by different enzymes. Endogenous proteolytic enzymes are used to produce hydrolyzed products, specifically designed for sauces, silage, and fish feed. To demonstrate the action of these endogenous enzymes, Pastoriza et al (2004) compared the solubility improvement by using commercial enzymes (papain and pepsin) to that of enzymes from fish waste or underutilized species. The results showed that both ways could be considered as important alternatives for protein hydrolysis.

Fish by-products, resulting in a number of products with a wide range of applications in the food and pharmaceutical industries (Kristinsson and Rasco, 2000; Gildberg et al., 2002; Dauksas et al., 2005; Slizyte et al., 2005, Slizyte et al., 2009). Compared with autolysis, accelerated hydrolysis using a commercial protease allows better possibilities for controlling the properties of the product (Yoshioka et al., 2004): choice of enzyme, reaction conditions and time of hydrolysis allow good control of the hydrolysis and production of products with defined and desirable properties. In addition, hydrolysates have high nutritional properties (Shahidi et al., 1995; Slizyte et al., 2005) and exhibit bioactive properties such as antioxidative, antihypertensive, antithrombotic and immunomodulatory activities (Kim and Mendis, 2006).

3. pH shifting process

Type of concentrated fish protein product isnfish protein isolates (FPI). This is fish protein that has been purified to have a protein content of at least 90 per cent of the dry material. Surimi can therefore be regarded as one type of FPI. However, the term FPI is most often used for fish muscle proteins that have been produced by the pH shift process, which is seen as a more efficient process for raw materials such as whole fish or fish rest raw materials (Kristinsson and Hultin, 2003; Kristinsson and Liang, 2006; Thorkelsson et al., 2008). FPI have good functional properties, and this is probably due to increased surface hydrophobicity and reactive SHgroups. The protein recovery is highest with the acid procedure while the functional properties of the FPI have been found to be best for the alkaline process. The yield of recovered proteins in the production of FPI ranges between 42 per cent and 90 per cent (Gehring et al., 2011).

These protein fractions contain less ash, have an amino acid profile meeting the recommendations for adults, can produce a surimi gel of medium strength, and can be used as a functional food protein. However, in general, gutted fish or fish fillet is used as a starting material. The pH shift techniques could be used for dissolving and obtaining the valuable fish proteins from fish by-products or from sediment fractions after oil extraction. Recently, several authors reported the use of isoelectric processing on fish by-products or low-value fish (Chen and Jaczynski, 2007; Chen et al., 2007). The addition of flocculants could improve the separation of precipitated fish muscle proteins from the process water and would facilitate process scale-up (Taskaya and Jaczynski, 2009).

A new technology, called pH-shift processing or acid/alkaline solubilization and precipitation or isoelectric processing yielded the possibility to isolate protein from complex muscle materials. The effort was designed to better utilize low value raw materials from fish processing. A water molecule is composed of hydrogen and oxygen. In meat systems, water provides a reaction medium in which macro and micromolecules are in solvated or suspended state. A molecule of water is commonly called a dipole due to its slight electro-negative and electro-positive charges of oxygen and hydrogen atoms, respectively. It occurs because the larger oxygen atom is powerful enough to attract the electrons from the two hydrogens causing a slight shift of electrons towards oxygen, which consequently makes hydrogen a little more positively charged.

Water molecules have electrostatic charges on their surface. These charges allow interaction between water dipoles and other charged molecules such as proteins which is an important property in food technology, because many major compounds in meats such as proteins may also be charged; and therefore, have an ability to interact with water dipoles via these interactions. The general mechanism for base addition is similar to that with the acid; however, the final protein charge will be negative due to the base instead of positive that is imposed by an acid. As a protein assumes more overall positive or negative charge, it gradually starts electrostatic interaction with water dipoles (i.e., protein-water intearctions). As protein-water interactions increase, the protein-protein hyrdrophobic interactions decrease. Therefore, as the protein molecules become more polar (charged), their water solubility increases and they become water soluble.

However, it is possible to adjust pH of a protein solution at which the number of negative charges on a protein's surface is equal to the number of positive charges; and therefore, the protein molecule assumes an overall neutral electrostatic charge. The pH at which the overall electrostatic charge of a protein is equal to zero is called isoelectric point (pI). The pI is very specific for different proteins. It is very important from a food technologist/ scientist standpoint to know the pI of proteins, because as the charges on protein's surface diminish, so do the protein-water interactions; and hence, water solubility.

In general, there are five steps in the protein recovery based on acid/ alkaline solubilization process.

The first step is to homogenize (i.e. grind) the fish or by-products with water at 1:6 (wt/wt) ratio in order to provide reaction medium and increase surface area for the subsequent protein solubilization reaction.

In the second step, the fish muscle proteins are solubilized at either acidic or basic conditions. As the pH moves further away from the pI, the fish muscle proteins assume more uniform either negative or positive surface electrostatic charge for basic or acidic conditions, respectively. This charge shift results in weaker protein-protein hydrophobic interactions, while the protein-protein electrostatic repulsion becomes more predominant, resulting in protein-water interaction (i.e., water solubility).

While the muscle proteins are in full interaction with water (i.e., solubilized), the third step i.e. centrifugation is applied which separates the light, medium, and heavy fractions containing fish oil, solubilized muscle proteins, and impurities (bones, skin, scale, skin, insoluble proteins, and etc.), respectively. It is desirable to remove as much lipids as possible during the separation step to avoid development of rancidity. The third step results in separation of crude fish oil that is rich in w-3 PUFA and can be further processed for numerous food and non-food application. The heavy fraction is rich in minerals such as Ca, Mg, and P and therefore, can be a main ingredient in the development of animal feeds as well as most likely more profitable pet foods. In the fourth step, the medium fraction, containing water-soluble fish muscle proteins is recovered and subjected to the second pH adjustment.

The pH is adjusted to the pI of the fish muscle proteins (pH ~ 5.5). At the pH ~ 5.5, fish muscle proteins precipitate due to increased protein-protein hydrophobic interactions and decreased protein-water interactions as well as decreased protein-protein electrostatic repulsion. The precipitated fish muscle proteins are separated from the process water typically by centrifugation. The muscle proteins retain their gel forming capability and therefore, can be used as a functional and main ingredient in human foods applications such as for example surimi seafood (commonly referred to as imitation crab meat). The process water is typically as clear as the water added in the first step; and therefore, can be re-used if a continuous system is used. However, the purity of process water greatly depends on processing parameters. The temperature during all of the processing steps is typically controlled at 1-8°C in order to reduce protein and lipid degradation.

4. Membrane processes

Surimi processing wash waters generally show low protein concentration that makes classical processes of protein recovery economically not feasible. Ultrafiltration and nanofiltration offer considerable potential to be an integral part of a clean technology process. However, processing of the wastewater by ultrafiltration or nanofiltration without pre-treatment is not practicable. The aim of the present work was to determine the potential use of nanofiltration membrane (polyamide membrane of 500 Da) in treating the wastewater, generated from fish and surimi industry, as well as to examine the possibility of recovering the proteins from the wastewater effectively. During the washing process, 20-30 per cent of the fish muscle proteins especially sarcoplasmic proteins are solubilized and generally not recovered from the wash water.

Increasing concerns over the negative impact of direct wastewater discharge, have led to research in protein recovery from surimi wash-water. Recovering fish proteins from surimi wash-water would not only reduce the negative environmental impact and the cost of waste disposal, but also generate potential profits (Bourtoom *et al.*, 2009). An alternative to methods like evaporation or spray-drying is membrane separation by means of ultrafiltration. One of its most important advantages is that it can recover proteins while concentrating soluble proteins. The good quality of permeate is also notably important as it can be recycled into the fish processing plant, as well as the simultaneous recovery and concentration of soluble proteins. Numerous studies have demonstrated that in vitro controlled enzymatic hydrolysis of fish and shellfish proteins leads to bioactive peptides. Ultrafiltration (UF) and/or nanofiltration (NF) can be used to refine hydrolysates and also to fractionate them in order to obtain a peptide population. Fractionation of an FPH using membrane separation, with a molecular weight cut-off adapted to the peptide composition, may provide an effective means to concentrate CGRP-like peptides and peptides enriched in selected amino acids enriched in selected sizes (Picot et al., 2010).

Ultrafiltration is a membrane separation process, driven by a pressure gradient, in which the membrane fractionates components of a liquid as a function of their solvated size and structure.The membrane configuration is usually cross-flow and proteins larger than the pore size rating are retained by the filter and can be concentrated. The ultrafiltration of water-soluble fish proteins is significantly influenced by the type of membrane, operating pressure, temperature, and liquid pretreatment (Paredes and Borquez, 2001).The recovery of fish proteins from effluents by membrane separation processes showed highly functional properties in the recovered proteins and a reduction of the organic load. However, further investigations are needed to achieve complete recovery of the proteins contained in these effluents. The use of ultrafiltration to recover proteins from oyster wash water was found to increase the protein concentration by 18 folds. The concentrations of total suspended solids and chemical oxygen demand in the permeate were reduced by 98 and 47 per cent, respectively.

Fermentation was a good method to improve the flavor of the retentate from ultrafiltration. The increase in concentrations of extractive-N, free amino acids and small peptides supported the idea that the fermentation process with Koji (cultured with *Aspergillus oryzae*) could accelerate the hydrolysis of the recovered protein. The Koji fermented juice was made into oyster sauce, which was accepted by the panel as being equivalent in quality to commercial oyster sauces. Recovery of proteins present in oyster wash water could be economically feasible in terms of their potential utilization, as well as the eventual reduction of organic matter in effluent disposal (Shiau and Chai, 1999).

There have been several studies on recovering proteins from surimi processing wash waters. Ultrafiltration has been used to produce protein concentrates with good functional properties via myofibrillar proteins recovered from surimi wash water (Morr, 1976; Chang-Lee et al., 1989; Lin et al., 1995; Morrissey et al., 2000)

5. Subcritical water hydrolysis

The production of hydrolysates by applying water above its boiling temperature (100° C), but below its critical temperature (374°C), which is in a "liquid state" due to the application of pressure is the basis for this technique. Using this mechanism, it is possible to obtain acid-hydrolyzed cleavages of peptide bonds with no use of catalysts. Optimization of parameters, such as temperature and time, is critical for the reaction control to achieve acceptable yields in amino acid content, but preventing its degradation from extreme conditions (Kang et al 2001).

6. Ohmic treatment

This thermal treatment is based on the passage of an electric current through a food product that acts as an electrical resistance. Protein is then coagulated under heating and subsequently separated from the rest of the material. This is an alternative method to reduce biological oxygen demand of surimi wastewater having high protein concentration (Kanjanapongkul et al., 2009)

CONCLUSION

Production of fish and shrimp processing wastes and their discharge into the coastal and nearshore environment have not been quantified in details. Little is known about the probable role of fish and shrimp processing industries in polluting the coastal and marine environment. General impacts of processing wastes are believed to be the same as other sources of pollution that cause eutrophication of the environment. The hypothetical global values of the volume of water used by the seafood processing plants and the associated waste loading parameters reported in this paper show that the processing plants posses high potential for polluting coastal and nearshore environments.

However, application of simple treatment options such as screening can substantially reduce the waste loads. For greater interest and sustainability of the fishery industry, processing plants should establish effective effluent treatment and monitoring facilities to reduce waste loads and pressure on the ecosystem. The design and operation of fish processing plants can significantly impact the quality and quantity of recovered byproducts, especially if they are rendered into fish meal. Most fish processing plants are designed to maximize the recovery and quality of their food products with less consideration for the recovery and transport of non-food waste or processing byproducts. These plants generate a sizable percentage of waste as dissolved solids and very fine particles in wastewater, thereby reducing waste recovery. The recoverable fine particles that are sent to rendering will likely not be recovered as fish meal and will increase the pollutant load in the rendering operation wastewater.

A detailed inspection of a fish processing facility can reveal areas where waste solids can degrade because of inappropriate temperatures and times, and also areas where they can become contaminated. The degradation of the recovered solids has the potential to affect the protein quality of the rendered meal and oil product properly designed waste conveyance systems that recover waste solids before they reach floor drains or sumps are preferable. A Fluming waste solid with water increase the breakdown of solids and decreases the amount of solids that can be recovered. Additionally, if saltwater is used for fluming it can increase the salt and ash content of the waste solids.

If the solids are then rendered the resulting fish meal will be of a lower quality. Hence, dry conveyance of waste solids is preferred. For waste solids that circumvent the waste conveyance system, the design and operation of wastewater floor drains, sumps, and pumps can affect the quality and quantity of recovered waste solids. The same is true for the wastewater treatment equipment used for recovering waste solids. And finally, the methods by which potentially food-grade products are rejected, and unacceptable fish are added to the waste stream, can be of concern. Recovery of protein from liquid part of the waste is the beneficial avenue for processors.

REFERENCES

Bagge-Ravn, D., Ng, Y., Hjelm, M., Christiansen, J.N., Johansen, C., Gram, L., 2003. The Microbial Ecology of Processing Equipment in Different Fish Industries-analysis of the Microflora during Processing and Following Cleaning and Disinfection. International Journal of Food Microbiology 87 (3), 239-250.

Batista I 1999. Recovery of Proteins from Fish Waste Products by Alkaline Extraction. Eur Food Res Technol 210(2), 84-93.

Batista, I., 1999. Recovery of Proteins from Fish Waste Products by Alkaline Extraction. *Eur. Food Res. Technol.*, 210: 84-89.

Bonsdorff, E., Blomqvist, E.M., Mattila, J., Norkko, A., 1997. Coastal Eutrophication: Causes, Consequences and Perspectives in the Archipelago Areas of the Northern Baltic Sea. Estuarine, Coastal and Shelf Science 44 (Suppl A), 63-72.

Bourtoom, T., Chinnan, M. S. Jantawat, P. and Sanguandeekul, P., 2009. Recovery and Characterization of Proteins Precipitated from Surimi Wash-water. LWT - Food Science and Technology 42: 599-605.

Carawan, R.E., 1991. Processing Plant Waste Management Guidelines for Aquatic Fishery Products. Food and the Environment, Available online at http://www.p2pays.org/ref/02/01796.pdf>.

Carawan, R.E., Green, D.P., Thomas, F.B., Thomas, S.D., 1986. Reduction in Waste Load from a Seafood Processing Plant. The North Carolina Agricultural Extension Service. North Carolina.

Chandra, M.V. and Shamasundar, B.A., 2011. Fish Processing Waste Management. *In*: Food Processing Waste Management – Treatment and Utilization Technology, Edt. Joshi, V.K. and Sharma, S. K. edn. 1st, New India Publishing Agency, New Delhi. pp. 161-194.

Chang-Lee, M.V., Pacheco-Aguilar, R., Crawford, D. L. and Lampila, L.E., 1989. Proteolytic Activity of Surimi from Pacific Whiting (*Merluccius productus*) and Heat-set Gel Texture. J food sci., 54(5): 1116-1119, 1124.

Chen, Y.C. & Jaczynski, J. (2007). Protein Recovery from Rainbow Trout (*Oncorhynchus mykiss*) Processing Byproducts via Isoelectric Solubilization D Precipitation and its Gelation Properties as Affected by Functional Additives. Journal of Agricultural and Food Chemistry, 55, 9079-9088.

Chen, Y.C., Tou, J.C. & Jaczynski, J. (2007). Amino Acid, Fatty Acid, and Mineral Profiles of Materials Recovered from Rainbow Trout (*Oncorhynchus mykiss*) Processing by-products Using Isoelectric Solubilization D precipitation. J. Food Science, 72, C527– C535.

Dauksas, E., Falch, E., Slizyte, R. & Rustad, T. (2005). Composition of Fatty Acids and Lipid Classes in Bulk Products Generated during Enzymic Hydrolysis of Cod (Gadus morhua) by-products. Process Biochemistry, 40, 2659-2670.

Davenport, M.P. and Kristinsson, H.G., 2011. Channel Catfish (*Ictalurus punctatus*) Muscle Protein Isolate Performance Processed Under Different Acid and Alkali pH Values. *J. of food sci.*, 76(3): E240-E247.

EPA. 1996. *Environmental Guidelines for Composting and Other Organic Recycling Facilities.* Recycling Organic Material to Benefit the Environment. Publication 508.

Falch, E., Rustad, T., and Jonsdottir, R., 2006. Geographical and Seasonal Differences in Lipid Composition and Relative Weight of Byproducts from Gadiform Species. J. of Food Composition and Analysis, 19: 727-736.

FAO, 2010. *The State of World Fisheries and Aquaculture 2008*, Food and Agriculture Organisation, Rome.

Gao, M.T., Hirata, M., Toorisaka, E. and Hano, T., 2006. Acid-hydrolysis of Fish Wastes for Lactic Acid Fermentation. Bioresource Technol., 97: 2414-2420.

Garcia-Sifuentes, R., Pacheco-Aguilar, M., Lugo-Sánchez, G., Garcia-Sánchez, J.C., Ramirez, S., Garcia-Carreño, F., 2009. Properties of Recovered Solids from Stick-water Treated by Centrifugation and pH Shift. Food Chem., 114: 197-203.

Gehring, C.K., Davenport, M.P. and Jaczynski, J., 2009. Functional and Nutritional Quality of Protein and Lipid Recovered from Fish processing By-products and Underutilized Aquatic Species Using Isoelectric Solubilization/precipitation. *Curr. Nutrition & Food Sci.*, 5: 17-39.

Gehring, C.K., Gigliotti, J.C., Moritz, J.S., Tou, J.C. & Jaczynski, J. (2011). Functional and Nutritional Characteristics of Proteins and Lipids Recovered by Isoelectric Processing of Fish by-products and Low-value Fish: A Review. Food Chemistry, 124, 422-431.

Gehring, C.K., Gigliotti, J.C., Moritz, J.S., Tou, J.C. and Jaczynski, J., 2011. Functional and Nutritional Characteristics of Proteins and Lipids Recovered by Isoelectric Processing of Fish By-products and Low-value Fish: A Review. *Food Chem.*, 124: 422-431.

Gildberg, A., Arnesen, J.A. & Carlehog, M. (2002). Utilisation of Cod Backbone by Biochemical Fractionation. Process Biochemistry, 38, 475-480.

Howard, G., 1997. Water Usage and Minimization in Fish Processing (paper 5). In: Proceedings of the Humber Waste Seminar, Seafish Report SR505, Seafish Industry Authority, Hull, 1997.

Hultin HO, Kelleher SD 2000. High Efficiency Alkaline Protein Extraction. US Patent 6136, 959.

Hultin HO, Kelleher SD, Feng Y, Mark PR, Kristinsson H, Shuming K, Undeland I, Inventors; 2007. High-efficiency Protein Extraction. H.K. patent 1,070, 790.

Hultin, H.O., Kristinsson, H.G., Lanier, T.C. and Park, J.W., 2005. Process for Recovery of Functional Proteins by pH Shifts. In: Surimi and Surimi Seafood. Edn. 2nd, Edt. Park, J. W., CRC Press, Boca Raton, FL, pp. 107-139.

In: Food Chemistry Research Developments ISBN 978-1-60456-262-0 Editor: Konstantinos N. Papadopoulos, pp. © 2008 Nova Science Publishers, Inc. Protein and Lipid Recovery from Food Processing By-Products Using Isoelectric Solubilization/Precipitation *Jacek Jaczynski.*

In: Food Chemistry Research Developments ISBN 978-1-60456-262-0 Editor: Konstantinos N. Papadopoulos, pp. © 2008 Nova Science Publishers, Inc.

Jaczynski, J., 2008. Protein and Lipid Recovery from Food Processing By-products Using Isoelectric Solubilization/precipitation. *In: Food Chemistry Research Developments*, (Edt.) Papadopoulos, K.N.

Kang K, Quitain AT, Daimon H, Noda R, Goto N, Hu HY, Fujie K 2001. Optimization of Amino Acid Production from Waste Fish Entrails by Hydrolysis in Sub- and Supercritical Water. Can J Chem Engr 79(1), 65-70.

Kanjanapongkul K, Tia S, Wongsa-Ngasri P, Yoovidhya T 2009. Coagulation of Protein in Surimi Wastewater Using a Continuous Ohmic Heater. J Food Engr 91(2), 341-346.

Kanjanapongkul, S., Tia, P., Wongsa-Ngasri, T., Yoovidhya, K., 2009. Coagulation of Protein in Surimi Wastewater Using a Continuous Ohmic Heater. J. of Food Engg. 91: 341-346.

Karunasagar, I., Karunasagar, I., 2000. Listeria in Tropical Fish and Fishery Products. International Journal of Food Microbiology 62, 177-181.

Kerry, J.P. and Murphy, S.C., 2007. Physical and Chemical Properties of Lipid By-products from Seafood Waste. In: Maximising the Value of Marine By-Products (Edited by F. Shahidi). pp. 22-46. Cambridge: Woodhead Publishing Limited.

Kim, J.S. & Park, J.W. (2007). Mince from Seafood Processing Byproduct and Surimi as Food Ingredient. In: Maximising the Value of Marine By-Products (Edited by F. Shahidi). pp. 196-228. Cambridge: Woodhead publishing Limited.

Kim, S.K. & Mendis, E. (2006). Bioactive Compounds from Marine Processing Byproducts – A Review. Food Research International, 39, 383-393.

Kimor, B., 1992. Impact of Eutrophication on Phytoplankton Composition. In: Vollenweider, R.A., Marchetti, R., Vicviani, R. (Eds.), Marine Coastal Eutrophication. Elsevier, Amsterdam, pp. 871-878.

Kristinsson, H.G. & Hultin, H.O. (2003). Effect of Low and High pH Treatment on the Functional Properties of Cod Muscle Proteins. Journal of Agricultural and Food Chemistry, 51, 5103-5110.

Kristinsson, H.G. & Liang, Y. (2006). Effect of pH-shift Processing and Surimi Processing on Atlantic Croaker (*Micropogonias undulates*) Muscle Proteins. Journal of Food Science, 71, C304-C312.

Kristinsson, H.G. & Rasco, B.A. (2000). Fish Protein Hydrolysates: Production, Biochemical, and Functional Properties. Critical Reviews in Food Science and Nutrition, 40, 43-81.

Lin, T.M., Park, J.W. and Morrissey, M. T., 1995. Recovered Protein and Reconditioned Water from Surimi Processing Waste. J. Food Sci., 60: 4-9.

Marmon, S.K. and Undeland, I., 2010. Protein Isolation from Gutted Herring (*Clupea harengus*) Using pH-shift Processes. *J. Agric. Food Chem.*, 58: 10480-10486.

Mauldin, A.F., Szabo, A.J., 1974. Shrimp Canning Waste Treatment St.Project No. S 800904. Office of Research and Development, US EPA, Washington, DC.

McDonald, C., Ince, M.E., Smith, M.D., Dillon, M., 1999. Fish Processing in Uganda: Waste Minimization. In: 25th WEDC Conference on Integrated Development for Water Supply and medium. Appl Environ Microb 1997; 66: 380-386.

Morr, C.V., 1976. Whey Protein Concentrates. An Update. Food Technol., 30(3): 18-19, 22, 42.

Morrissey, M.T., Park, J.W. and Huang, L., 2000. Surimi Processing Waste. Its Control and Utilization. Ch. 6. In: Surimi and Surimi Seafood (J. W. Park, Ed.), pp. 127-165, Marcel Dekker, New York, NY.

Morrissey, M.T. & Sylvia, G. (2004). Intrinsic and Extrinsic Factors Affecting Efficient Utilization of Marine Resources. In: More Efficient Utilization of Fish and Fisheries Products (Edited by M. Sakaguchi). pp. 37-43. Amsterdam: Elsevier.

Nolsoe, H. and Undeland, I., 2009. The Acid and Alkaline Solubilization Process for the Isolation of Muscle Proteins: State of the Art. *Food Bioprocess Technol.*, 2: 1-27.

Nolsoe, H., Marmon, S.K. and Undeland, I., 2011. Application of Filtration to Recover Solubilized Proteins during pH-shift Processing of Blue Whiting (*Micromesistius poutasson*): Effects on Protein Yield and Qualities of Protein Isolates. *The Open Food sci. j.*, 5: 1-9.

Paredes HM, Borquez R 2001. Development of an Alternative Treatment System for Fishing Industry Waste Waters Using Ultrafiltration. Latin Am Appl Res 31(4), 359-365.

Park, E., Enander, R., Barnett, M.S., Lee, C., 2001. Pollution Prevention and Biochemical Oxygen Demand Reduction in a Squid Processing Facility. Journal of Cleaner Production 9, 341-349.

Pastoriza L, Sampedro G, Cabo ML, Herrera JJR, Bernardez M 2004. Solubilisation of Proteins from Rayfish Residues by Endogenous and Commercial Enzymes. J Sci Food Agric 84(1), 83-88.

Picot, L., Ravallec, R., Fouchereau-Péron, M., Vandanjon, L., Jaouen, P., Chaplain-Derouiniot, M., Guérard, F., Chabeaud, A., LeGal, Y., Martinez O., Bergé, J., Piot J., Batista, I., Pires, C., Thorkelsson, G., Delannoy, C., Jakobsen, G., Johansson, I. and Bourseau, P., 2010. Impact of Ultrafiltration and Nanofiltration of an Industrial Fish Protein Hydrolysate on its Bioactive Properties. J of the Sci. of Food and Agricult., 90(11): 1819-1826.

Rashid, M.A., Ahmed, M.K., Khan, Y.S.A., 2000. Critical Control Points in the Shrimp Processing Plant of Bangladesh for Quality Control of Frozen Shrimp. Bangladesh Journal of Zoology 28 (1), 55-61.

Riegman, R., 1995. Nutrient-related Selection Mechanisms in Marine Plankton Communities and the Impact of Eutrophication on the Plankton Food Web. Water Science Technology 32, 63-75.

Rustad, T., 2007. Physical and Chemical Properties of Protein Seafood By-products. In: Maximising the Value of Marine By-Products (Edited by F. Shahidi). pp. 3-21. Cambridge: Woodhead publishing Limited.

Rustad, T., Storrø, I. and Slizyte, R., 2011. Possibilities for the Utilisation of Marine By-products. Intl. J of Food Sci. and Technol., 46: 2001-2014.

Sanitation.

Sanmartin, E., Arboleya, J.C., Villamiel, M. and Moreno, F.J., 2009. Recent Advances in the Recovery and Improvement of Functional Proteins from Fish Processing By-products: Use of Protein Glycation as an Alternative Method. *Comprehensive Rev. in Food Sci. and Food Safety*, 8: 332-344.

Shahidi, F., Han, X.Q. & Synowiecki, J. (1995). Production and Characteristics of Protein Hydrolysates from Capelin (*Mallotus villosus*). Food Chemistry, 53, 285-293.

Shiau, C. and Chai, T., 1999. Protein Recovered from Oyster Wash Water by Ultrafiltration and their Utilization as Oyster Sauce Through Fermentation. J. of Marine Sci and Technol, 7(2): 110-116.

Slizyte, R., Dauksas, E., Falch, E., Storro, I. & Rustad, T. (2005a). Characteristics of Protein Fractions Generated from Hydrolysed Cod (*Gadus morhua*) By-products. Process Biochemistry, 40, 2021-2033.

Slizyte, R., Mozuraityte, R., Martinez-Alvarez, O., Falch, E., Fouchereau- Peron, M. & Rustad, T. (2009). Functional, Bioactive and Antioxidative Properties of Hydrolysates Obtained from Cod (*Gadus morhua*) Backbones. Process Biochemistry, 44, 668-677.

Slizyte, R., Rustad, T. & Storro, I. (2005b). Enzymatic Hydrolysis of Cod (*Gadus morhua*) By-products: Optimization of Yield and Properties of Lipid and Protein Fractions. Process Biochemistry, 40, 3680-3692.

State University, Raleigh, NC 27695. 89 pp.

Taskaya, L. & Jaczynski, J. (2009). Flocculation-enhanced Protein Recovery from Fish Processing By-products by Isoelectric Solubilization D precipitation. Lwt-Food Science and Technology, 42, 570-575.

Taylor, K.D.A. & Himonides, A. (2007). Increased Processed Flesh Yield by Recovery from Marine By-products. In: Maximising the Value of Marine By-Products (Edited by F. Shahidi). pp. 91-106. Cambridge: Woodhead Publishing Limited.

Thorkelsson, G., Sigurgisladottir, S., Geirsdottir, M. et al. (2008). Mild Processing Techniques and Development of Functional Marine Protein and Peptide Ingredients. In: Improving Seafood Products for the Consumer (edited by T. Børresen). pp. 363-398. Cambridge: Woodhead Publishing Limited.

Wang SL, Chang WT. Purification and Characterization of Two Bifunctional Chitinase/ Lysozymes Extracellularly Produced by *Pseudomonas aeruginosa* K-187 in a Shrimp and Crab Shell Powder.

Wang SL, Hwang JR., 2001. Microbial Reclamation of Shellfish Wastes for the Production of Chitinase. Enzyme Microb Technol; 28: 376-82.

Wu, T.Y., Mohammad, A.W., Anuar, N. and Rahman, R.A. Potential Use of Nanofiltration Membrane in Treatment of Wastewater from Fish and Surimi Industries Songklanakarin J. Sci. Technol., 2002, 24(Suppl.) : 977-987

Yoshioka, K., Seki, A., Yamada, A. et al. (2004). Bone and Lipid Metabolism in the Bone Modelling of Rats Administered with the Bonito Docosahexaenoic Acid, the Viscera Vitamin D abd the Cuttlefish Calcium. In: More Efficient Utilization of Fish and Fisherie Products (Edited by M. Sakaguchi). pp. 107-113. Amsterdam: Elsevier.

Zaitsev, Y.P., 1992. Recent Changes in the Tropic Structure of the Black Sea. Fisheries Oceanography 1, 180-189.

Index